REMEMBERING WOMEN MURDERED BY MEN

Lest We Forget,
sculpture by Teresa Posyniak
in the Law Building, University of Calgary

REMEMBERING

WOMEN

MURDERED BY MEN

MEMORIALS ACROSS CANADA

To Lynette and Peter, with admiration — & thanks for everything! Christine & Ric

THE CULTURAL MEMORY GROUP*

* Christine Bold, Sly Castaldi,
Ric Knowles, Jodie McConnell
& Lisa Schincariol

SUMACH PRESS

WOMEN'S ISSUES PUBLISHING PROGRAM

SERIES EDITOR BETH MCAULEY

LIBRARY AND ARCHIVES CANADA CATALOGUING IN PUBLICATION

Remembering women murdered by men: memorials across Canada /
the Cultural Memory Group.

Includes bibliographical references.
ISBN-13: 978-1-894549-53-0
ISBN-10: 1-894549-53-8

1. Murder victims — Canada. 2. Women — Crimes against — Canada.
3. Memorials — Canada. I. Cultural Memory Group

HV6535.C3R44 2006   362.88'082'0971   C2006-900272-X

Edited by Beth McAuley
Designed by Liz Martin

Cover photos: Moira Simpson
Back Cover: Peace Symbol and Marker of Change, Moira Simpson

All proceeds from the sale of this book
will go to Guelph-Wellington Women in Crisis.

*Sumach Press acknowledges the support of the Canada Council
for the Arts and the Ontario Arts Council for our publishing program.
We acknowledge the financial support of the Government of Canada through
the Book Publishing Industry Development Program (BPIDP)
for our publishing activities.*

ONTARIO ARTS COUNCIL
CONSEIL DES ARTS DE L'ONTARIO

Printed and bound in Canada

Published by

SUMACH PRESS
1415 Bathurst Street #202
Toronto ON Canada M5R 3H8

sumachpress@on.aibn.com
www.sumachpress.com

Contents

ACKNOWLEDGEMENTS

WE HAVE LEARNED FROM MEMORIAL-MAKERS THAT IT TAKES VERY MANY PEOPLE — with all their resources, energies, contacts and good will — to build a monument. It turns out that it takes at least as many people to create a book about memorials. We're heavily indebted to a vast range of individuals and organizations, many of whom we name below.

Some key figures kept the project going throughout its most challenging stages. Belinda Leach, our partner in the bigger Marianne's Park project from which our group developed, has been steadfast in her encouragement, support and engagement. Sherry Kinsella, as secretary to the Centre for Cultural Studies, created a welcoming and efficient working environment that made all the difference. Chris McDowell made contact late but at a crucial moment in our project, and she has been a fountain of generosity (with her images, her contacts and her insights) and capacious enthusiasm.

Many, many individuals generously provided information, stories, insights and images of their hard-won monuments. Our heartfelt thanks go to T. Aboulnasar, Gilda Kempton Abriel, Beth Alber, Judy Allen, Jan Andrews, Barb Anello, Susan Atkinson, Joanne Benoit, Sandy Bentley, Charlotte Boerkamp, Carol Brooks, Trevor Buckle, Margaret Buist, Kim Bruce, Elizabeth Cannon, Elaine Carr, Jacquie Carr, Kourch Chan, Lori Clermont, Valerie Collicott, Barb Colter, Mike Crooning, Valerie Davidson, Sheila Davis, Eileen Dempster, Priscilla de Villiers, Donelle de Vlaming, Pat de Vries, Judith Dorst Storey, Riel Dupuis-Rossi, Holda El Maraghy, Carolyn Emerson, Mary Faught, Beverly Faryna, Heather Field, c.j. fleury, Constance Forest, Melissa Fortin, Marlene Gareau, Barb Garon, Lin Gibson, Chantal Gloor, the Goulden family, Rose-Marie Goulet, Lorraine Greaves, Theresa Greer, Nancy Hartling, Eloise Harvey, Glen Herman, Regina Homeniuk, Elizabeth Hopkins, Justine Howarth, Gail Hutchinson, Joanne Ings, Patrick Jacob, William James, Donna Johnson, Louise Karch, Joan Kotarski, Mike Kroening, Diane Kroll, Natalie Lambert, Don Larson, Douglas Lauvstad, Melissa Laveaux, Valerie LeBlanc, Alex Leikermoser, Wayne Leng, Roxanne Lepine, Gisèle Levesque, Janet Lewis,

Alyssa Lindsay, Francine Lord, Jane McBee, Brent McKnight, Patty McLean, Barb MacQuarrie, Joanne Magazine, Pauline Maheux, Renate Manthei, Dell Marlow, Sheila Martin, Melanie Miller, Michèle Mitchell, Shadikan Mohamed, Janet Money, Eileen Morrow, Lisa Oegema, Janice Olbina, Michelle Oliver, Joanne Page, Helen Partridge, Lianne Payne, Hugh Peacock, Christine Pilard, Christine Porson, Teresa Posyniak, Norma Jean Profitt, Kate Quinn, Heidi Rankin, Leigh Raney, Leslie Reaume, Linda Reith, Maurray Sample, Liana Sauve, Ellen Schoeck, Michelle Schryer, Edie Schultz, Cara Scott-McCron, Lindsey Setzer, Maureen Shebib, Janice Shoveller, Moira Simpson, Shelly Siskind, Valerie Smallman, Janet Smith, Laura Starr, Allison Stevenson, John Tarasuck, Kirk Thurbide, Arthur Thurston, the Vince family, Lori Wagner, Libby Walters, Nicole Webb, Karen Wells, Judy Wheaton, Jeff Wilkinson, Dini Williams, Esther Wright, Doris Young, Kim Young.

Many organizations — many of them critically under-resourced — responded generously to our endless questions. We particularly thank Guelph-Wellington Women in Crisis — all of the staff, volunteers and board members — for all their work in ending violence against women and children. The Ontario Association of Interval and Transition Houses, the Ontario Coalition of Rape Crisis Centre and all of their members gave us invaluable help in finding the memorials and telling the stories. Other organizations and groups on whose generous responses we greatly depended include Agents of Gaia; Canadian Engineering Memorial Foundation; Canadian Federation of University Women, Guelph Chapter; Chatham-Kent Sexual Assault Crisis Centre; Circle Centre, Brescia College; City of Edmonton Parks and Recreation, Community and Family Services; City of Moncton December 6th Art Project Committee; City of Montreal, Service de la Culture; Conestoga College; CRAB Water for Life Society; DAWN Ontario; Elizabeth Fry Society; Faculty of Engineering, Memorial University; Faculty of Engineering, University of New Brunswick, Fredericton; Haldimand-Norfolk Women's Centre; Haven House; Janet Rosenberg & Associates; Keewatin Community College; Manitoba Women's Directorate; Marker of Change Committee; McMaster University; Monument Sub-Committee, Sexual Assault Committee of Edmonton; Native Friendship Centre, Montreal; OPSEU Women's Committee; Prostitution Awareness and Action Foundation of Edmonton; Riverview Regional Women's Committee; Ryerson December 6th Memorial Committee; School of Engineering, University of Guelph; Services des communications — l'École Polytechnique de Montréal; Sheridan College; Status of Women; Sudbury Coalition to End Violence Against Women; Sudbury Women's Centre; Trafalgar Campus Design; University of Alberta; University of Calgary; University of Ottawa; University of Saskatchewan; University of Western Ontario; West Prince Family Violence Prevention Committee; Women Won't Forget; Women's Events Network; Women's Urgent Action; and YWCA Cambridge.

Our research assistants at the University of Guelph also deserve great thanks for their invaluable work: Cawo Abdi, Sabina Chatterjee, Sonnet l'Abbé, Christine Lenze, Wendy Milne and Mary Newberry.

Over the years, other kinds of important support — professional and personal —came from Sylvia Bowerbank, Susan Callan, Linda Georges, Tracy Kulba, Mary Elizabeth Leighton, Kevin McIntosh, Roxanne Rimstead, Sharon Rosenberg, Vilma Rossi, Lisa Stefaniak, Carole Stewart and Cheryl Suzack.

Our collaboration could not have happened without generous grants from the Social Sciences and Humanities Research Council of Canada, who awarded us a Partnership Development Grant and a Strategic Research Grant. Generous financial and in-kind assistance came from the Dean of Arts Research Fund, the College of Arts Visiting Speakers Fund, and the Vice-President Research at the University of Guelph and from Guelph-Wellington Women in Crisis. For the opportunity to present our work publicly, we thank W.I.S.E., University of Guelph; Violence Action Group, University of Guelph; the Human Rights Centre, McMaster University; Women's Studies, McMaster University; Victoria College, University of Toronto; English Department, University of Victoria; Hamilton Art Gallery; and the Canadian Association of Cultural Studies. A version of chapter four was published in *Topia: Canadian Journal of Cultural Studies*.

We could not have been blessed with a more wonderful publisher than Sumach Press. We thank Lois Pike, Liz Martin and especially Beth McAuley — the finest editor in existence — for unstinting professionalism, rigour and sheer dedication to this work.

Our friends and families have given hospitality, enthusiasm and endless support, and on this note we would like to give thanks in our separate voices. Christine: to my son, Lewis Bold Wark, for his good-humoured participation in MPiCC meals, including all the ribbing about him not having cable tv. Sly: to my partner Jane Ellenton — your encouragement, support and love are beyond words. Ric: to my son Christopher for his help and support on the project. Jodie: to all in my life, whose instinct, deep values and heart brought and keep us together. Lisa: to J.J. McMurtry, for all his insight and understanding.

While the errors and omissions are all ours, we could not have written this book without all these people. And we thank each other for committing to and staying with the project. It has been an amazing journey with amazing companions.

Enclave,
monument vigil in Ottawa

"MURDERED BY MEN"

In memory and in grief for all women who have been murdered by men.
— Marker of Change/À l'aube du changement, Vancouver

In memory of all women abused,
raped and killed by men in Edmonton, Alberta and Canada.
— Vision of Hope, Edmonton

À LA MÉMOIRE DE

TOUTES LES FEMMES

QUI ONT SUBI JUSQU'À LA MORT

LA VIOLENCE DES HOMMES

— Enclave, Ottawa

Across Canada, the landscape is dotted with memorials to women murdered. Pink and grey granite stones hug the ground in Vancouver's poorest area. Conceptual sculpture crumbles down in Calgary while bronze figures reach up in Edmonton. A healing memorial plaque in a field near The Pas connects with an embracing memorial garden in Winnipeg. Ontario is dotted with parks, gardens, stones, sculptures — at city halls, on university and college campuses, in botanical gardens, by churches and malls.

Montreal houses the most intricately designed of memorials at the bottom of its mountain and the most silent at the top. Moncton's sculpture speaks across the Petitcodiac River to Riverview's monument. And in rural Bear River, Nova Scotia, the aged town cemetery holds three memorials to a woman murdered. Yet, astonishingly often, these monuments are simply not seen. City councils tuck them into marginal locations, funding bodies shunt them to the bottom of their agendas, plaque-writers dedicate them in codes that wedge words between silences. Memorials protesting a central scandal of our society occupy the most tentative positions in our public space. We wrote this book to make these memorials newly visible on a national scale, to celebrate the efforts of the women who created them against all odds and to explore their contribution to the struggle against violence against women.

Women are murdered by men in Canada every day, in horrific numbers: from the approximately 500 Aboriginal women missing and murdered in Canada over the past twenty years, to the sixty-nine or more so-called missing women from Vancouver's Downtown Eastside, to the fourteen women murdered at l'École Polytechnique in Montreal on December 6, 1989, to the uncountable acts of femicide, so commonplace and often so casual that they barely make the news.[1] Feminist memorializing of women victims of violence is a key part in preventing those murders from becoming mere numbers or being denied. Yet the commemorative process is fraught indeed. Those who pursue the imperative to "First Mourn then Work for Change / Souvenir pour agir" too often come up against scarce resources and public outcry. The struggle increases when memorial-makers confront the systemic nature of violence against women and publicly name victim and perpetrator. Often women spend years of their lives and run huge personal risks making these monuments happen. In this book, we record, analyze and support these acts of courage.

Setting the record straight involves listening to first-hand voices. In 1993, a group of Vancouver feminists encountered a storm of protest when they decided to build a monument to the fourteen women murdered at l'École Polytechnique. Controversy particularly erupted over one phrase in the planned inscription, which stands as the title to this introduction: "murdered by men." "That's when we all learned that you're not allowed to say who's murdering women," said Christine McDowell, member of the Vancouver Women's Monument Committee (Simpson 1998). Wherever possible, this book features the voices of memorial makers and the truths they tell about bringing public attention to femicide, by including their stories, artistic statements, negotiated inscriptions, sometimes even disagreements and compromises.

Our access to these voices is shaped by the same patterns of violence that the memorials protest. Violence threatens social groups to different degrees. Women are more vulnerable than men, women in poverty more than middle-class women, women of colour more than white women. The very groups most subject to attack are those with least access to the resources needed for public memory-making, least likely to make memorial forms available to us for analysis, most likely to protect their private memorial cultures from outsiders. While we of the Cultural Memory Group are diverse in gender, sexuality and profession, we do not pretend to represent, nor to have won access to, all communities — by region, race, class, generation — living with femicide. In an effort to reach beyond our own cultural perspectives while respecting the limits set by communities with whom we have made contact, we have invited First Nations women — members of a community particularly subject to systemic violence — to voice their own memorials directly in this volume (see chapter 13).[2] This is more than an act of respect to a cultural group decimated by genocide. It is an acknowledgement that the feminist perspective that drives our analysis does not necessarily translate across cultural difference.

Monique Mojica, Kuna/Rappahannock playwright whose voice is heard in chapter 13, has written of the difficulty of making "feminist shoes … fit these wide, square, brown feet" (Mojica 1991, 58). Myra Laramee, a First Nations Elder who blessed the Women's Grove Memorial discussed in chapter 3, has said of her own journey to becoming principal of Niji Mahkwa School in Winnipeg's inner city: "One of the things I had to do when I went to the traditional lodge was get over my feminism" ("Tradition" 2002). While this book does explicitly favour feminist memorializing as a powerful act of resistance, we wish to make space for voices whose differences we respect.

We have organized these monuments and their makers' stories into a journey of memorialization across Canada, exposing a countrywide seam of violence and resistance. The book travels west to east, probing the process of creation, the design and the use of memorials to women murdered in selected communities. That selection also cuts a chronological swathe, from

the impromptu memorials at the Port Coquitlam farm in British Columbia
— one of the most recent commemorative activities protesting femicide
on record — through the monuments in cities, towns and rural locations
across Canada that were built throughout the 1990s, ending with the oldest example of a public memorial to a woman murdered that we found,
this one honouring a young girl killed in Nova Scotia in 1896. We have
taken literally the memorial-makers' emphasis on visibility: in the words of
Jan Andrews, a member of Women's Urgent Action in Ottawa, "The more
public this issue becomes, the more visibility it has, the less men can ignore
it" (Abraham 1992, 1).

Trying to enable that visibility has involved considerable research. On
several occasions, members of a university community — even the most
politically active — would be unaware of the memorial plaque on campus;
on one occasion, a city hall employee did not know of the memorial boulder practically outside her window. Acutely conscious that our own search
is bound to be incomplete, we hope that the geographical presentation of
the memorials that we have discovered will contribute to making their locations and existence more visible. We offer them not as examples of abstract
principles or theoretical concepts but as concrete acts of remembrance and
calls to action by very particular communities working against very specific
odds and making very distinct impressions.

We also explore the marks made on memorials by the organizations
and processes that bring them about. Society's priorities display themselves graphically in the contrast between the modest boulders dedicated
to the women of Vancouver's Downtown Eastside and the aesthetically sophisticated monuments — backed by major fundraising efforts and public art competitions — to the women murdered at l'École Polytechnique.
Reluctance to support the public remembrance of women murdered redou-
bles in the case of societally marginalized women compared with women
who, by class and race, are more securely positioned within the dominant
culture. Institutional sponsorship brings with it pressure to fit memorial designs and inscriptions to suit the organization's imperatives — whether they
be feminist advocacy, civic imprimatur or educational mission. Different
compromises accompany efforts by groups organized for the purpose or
by committed individuals. Often the support of the lesbian community or
well-positioned female administrators is key to a memorial's production,
especially when the larger community is hostile to naming femicide. Some

memorials we have studied were mounted quickly and efficiently on the initiative of men — as at the Universities of Guelph and Western Ontario — for whom feminist or activist intent was not paramount. The wording of these plaques, however progressive within their professional context, nevertheless retains the assumptions of dominant ideology. Collectives such as the women's committees in Vancouver and Toronto have used more laborious and time-consuming feminist processes that result in more explicitly political wording on monuments and that use more interactive designs. Some memorial sites — as in the case of Ottawa's Enclave — grow out of memorial activity driven by the urgent needs of an activist community, as opposed to those sites that are first created and then serve as setting and opportunity for such activity. How do all those differences affect the memorials' visibility and use?

Furthermore, what political and pedagogical work is done by the inscriptions which accompany memorials, potentially their most explicitly consciousness-raising feature? We have seen everything from the most unadorned citation of a woman's name — no date of birth nor death, no acknowledgement of her murder — to euphemistic allusions to virginity and honour to full-blown analysis of society's systemic violence against women. And when and how does a memorial run the risk of serving as a palliative instead of a provocation, inadvertently letting a community off the hook of having to take action on violence against women, on femicide in its midst? What is the relative effectiveness of a memorial that takes the form of an event (a vigil, service, procession or pilgrimage), with its possibility for direct intervention, compared with that of an object (a monument, boulder, park or piece of public art), with the potential to serve as a "permanent memorial," in the words of the Vancouver organizers of the Marker of Change/À l'aube du changement? Does a memorial have stronger resonance or influence if it is located at the site of the murder that it remembers, as in the Theresa Vince memorial service in Chatham, Ontario, or if it visits the site as in the Valentine's Day march in Vancouver? What are the relative advantages of boulders, benches, plaques and parks as opposed to works of art such as those designed for Vancouver, London, Ottawa and Moncton? How can the most interactive of memorials, like the one in Montreal, simultaneously increase visitor participation and the risk of invisibility?

The political significance of remembrance, especially for marginalized groups, has been proven yet again by recent campaigns and reports protesting violence against women. When Sisters in Spirit launched their campaign to end violence against Aboriginal women in March 2004, one of their most moving strategies was naming hundreds of Aboriginal women murdered, under the banner "Remembering Our Missing & Murdered Aboriginal Sisters ... Always in Our Hearts."[3] When Amnesty International produced the report *Stolen Sisters: A Human Rights Response to Discrimination and Violence Against Indigenous Women in Canada* in October 2004, it devoted over a third of the report to remembering, in detail, the stories of nine missing and murdered Indigenous women. A hefty report on workplace violence and harassment released in the same month opened with one of the author's agonizing memory of the harassment and murder of her mother, Theresa Vince.

The bottom line of our analysis is support for feminist memorial-makers, who work with scarce resources, even less time and little official support, but who are driven by the conviction that acknowledging violence against women in a visible and permanent form is a significant step towards social change. Their ingenuity and thriftiness are striking. It is impossible to compute the real costs of memorial creation — the highest fundraising figure we have seen cited is $300,000, the smallest is $500, with most being between $5,000 and $10,000. Set these amounts against the $1.5 million allotted by the Government of Ontario for a new war monument or, indeed, the $9 million (U.S.) raised for the Vietnam Veterans Memorial in Washington, DC ("New War Memorial" 2003). This country is getting its feminist memory-making cheap, though the cost is borne on the lives and bodies of its women. Each memorial tells at least two stories: the terrible one of unremitting violence against women and the triumphant one of women joining against all odds to make these monuments happen.

By bringing together geographically distant and often isolated acts of memory-making, we hope to contribute to a support and information-sharing network for those involved in acts of oppositional or resistant memorializing.[4] Also, by situating the local within the national, we aim to illuminate patterns of discourse, challenges and strategies that emerge at various levels of community and government and at various points on the spectrum of attention, from often overlooked everyday abuse to nationally noticed trauma. Above all, whatever questions we might raise about omissions, compromises or silences in the design and language of feminist memorials, we want to acknowledge and celebrate the achievement of those who have brought about such memorials and inscribed such words into public space against consistently daunting odds.

CLASSIFYING MEMORY

The critical and theoretical literature on cultural memory-making would classify these memorials as "counter-monuments" or "anti-monumental monuments," which challenge dominant social memory and its celebration of the status quo through glorious war monuments, dignified statuary and masterpieces of triumphal architecture.[5] Lynda E. Boose and Maureen Moynagh, among other scholars, have discussed the crucial work of cultural counter-memory in keeping alive "suppressed stories" that nations and societies would prefer to forget: the mass violation of Muslim and Hindu women during the Partition of India, the extermination of European Jews by the Nazi regime, the histories of slavery in Canada and the United States, the Bosnian rape camps powered by Serbian nationalist mythology and the myriad other atrocities against human life and social justice which can too easily succumb to "national amnesia" (Boose 2002, 73; Moynagh 2002, 103). In Paul Connerton's analysis, "control of a society's memory largely conditions the hierarchy of power" and "the struggle of citizens against state power is the struggle of their memory against forced forgetting" (1989, 1, 15). Creating such counter-memorials presents major challenges that run the gamut from the personal danger faced by memorial-makers to the risk of a memorial's design inadvertently facilitating catharsis rather than provoking change.

James E. Young has discussed ways in which monuments can enable societal forgetting: "Instead of searing memory into public consciousness … conventional memorials seal memory off from awareness altogether," reducing the public to "passive spectators" (Young 1992, 272, 274). He has traced how some German artists have faced the ethical challenge of memorializing the Holocaust without invoking glory, authoritarianism, compensation, consolation or redemption. The counter-monuments they created are "self-abnegating" in their attempt "to challenge the very premises of their being" (268). In some ways the epitome of the counter-monument, which Young discusses at length, is the Monument Against Fascism designed by Jochen Gerz and Esther Shalev-Gerz and erected in the suburb of Harburg – Hamburg in 1986. In his book *At Memory's Edge* (2000), Young describes how the sculpture was gradually lowered into an underground chamber:

> a forty-foot-high lead-covered column was sunk into the ground as people inscribed their names (and much else) onto its surface; on its complete disappearance in 1993, the artists hoped that it would return the burden of memory to those who came looking for it. With audacious simplicity, their "counter-monument" thus flouted a number of memorial conventions: its aim was not to console but to provoke; not to remain fixed but to change; not to be everlasting but to disappear; not to be ignored by its passersby but to demand interaction; not to remain pristine but to invite its own violation; not to accept graciously the burden of memory but to throw it back at the town's feet. How better to remember a now-absent people than by a vanishing monument? (7 – 8)

Subsequently, Noam Lupu (2003) has argued ways in which Harburg's residents reacted to the monument limited its effects to that of more traditional memorials. Roger Simon has looked more closely into the theoretical and ethical complexities of "remembering otherwise" as a process of deep human connection and social transformation (2005, 9).

Only recently have memory studies begun to consider the "distinctly feminist strategies of cultural memory work" that are necessary for women to become "agent[s] of memorial transmission" (Hirsch and Smith 2002, 12, 2). Maurice Halbwachs was the first to argue that "memory is a collective function" that works symbiotically: groups stitch together collective memories and vice versa (1992, 83). Paul Connerton brought attention to how habitual bodily practices "make remembering in common possible" (1989, 39). And Iwona Irwin-Zarecka, among others, has expressed how socially shared "frames of remembrance" can create cross-generational "communities of memory" (1994, 9, 48). When the solidarity-in-the-making is feminist, the forging of individual memories into collective memorializing involves overturning the weight of patriarchal social and power relations. Women have created distinctive methods of seizing space in order to force public remembering — for example, in the camps set up next to nuclear military bases by the women of Greenham Common in England and the demonstrations against "the disappeared" by the Madres de Plaza de Mayo in Argentina (Schirmer 1994, 185). Women have forged chains of testimony across generation and national location, giving witness to the sexualized torture practised by Pinochet's regime in 1970s Chile (Kaplan 2002). And women have sustained annual rituals of oppositional performance. On December 6, women across Canada organize vigils to remember the fourteen women murdered in Montreal on that day in 1989 and all women murdered (Bold, Knowles and Leach 2002). Every Valentine's Day, First Nations women of Downtown Eastside Vancouver lead a performance of respect, remembrance and protest at the sites where women from the community have died violently. In Caffyn Kelley's analysis, this "different kind" of memorializing opens a "dialogical space" for remembering across differences of race, ethnicity, class, sexuality, ability while never forgetting how deeply that power differential "runs through the structures of culture and memory, nature and history" (1995, 8, 11).

Distinctly women-centred strategies are also visible in the artistic dimensions of some memorials. Many of the pieces we study in this book did not go through formal artistic processes of creation, often because of limited resources. They are created from inexpensive, readily available materials and take the form of conventional memorializing practice: plaques, boulders, benches and gardens, all of which have the advantages of recognizable and populist appeal while inserting themselves economically and without fanfare into the common space of everyday life. Even these choices are marked by gender, since the binary traditions of memorializing remember men with museums and granite obelisks and women with gardens, trees and "nature." Other memorials that we study, however, are self-consciously artistic, emerging from what Christine McDowell of the Vancouver Marker of Change/À l'aube du changement memorial calls "a conceptual approach to changing society," "a gamble on the powers of art" (Simpson 1998), and what James E. Young calls "art's traditional redemptory function in the face of catastrophe" (2000, 2).

The conventions of public art have shifted considerably over time, increasingly being dedicated to ordinary people rather than to political leaders or military heroes and increasingly claiming as their purview what art critic Rosalind Krauss calls "the public, conventional nature of what might be called cultural space" (qtd. in Dault 1998, 20). Some feminist memorials claim the cultural space of public art for women by reworking vertical or figurative statuary in ways that directly challenge the heroic, masculinist tradition of "men on horses with thrusting swords" (Kimmelman 2002). Take, for example, the three female allegorical figures of A Vision of Hope in Edmonton. The artist, Michèle Mitchell, sculpted them as symbols of "concrete change," each weighing in at 498 kg (1,100 pounds) in order to figuratively represent women's triumph (Ringma 2000). The first figure, Despair, is bowed down with suffering; the second, Grief, rises to the kneeling position; and the third, Hope, reaches upward, fully vertical.

More common among the public art works we examine, however, are those that employ the minimalist designs that, according to Michael Kimmelman, have "become the unofficial language of memorial art" (2002, A1). Like "the heroic, self-aggrandizing figurative icons of the late nineteenth century" (Young 2000, 93), minimalism in the art world has most often been the preserve of the masculine, as muscular modernism has asserted abstract form on a human or natural world it constructs as feminine. And, of course, in rejecting representational realist statuary, the minimalist memorial may bump up against the high-culture exclusions of abstraction, arousing suspicions of aestheticism, stylization and self-referential elitism. Nevertheless, as a memorial form, "minimalism has gradually ... made its way into the public's heart," as "those bare walls [serve as] blank slates onto which we project our deepest commonly held feelings" (Kimmelman 2002, A1).

Perhaps the best known of such minimalist counter-monuments is the Vietnam Veterans Memorial in Washington, DC, designed by Asian American Maya Ying Lin, and which has influenced most memorials built since. Not surprisingly, many of the public art memorials that we examine in this book, all designed by women, avoid the ironies and exclusions of an elitist modernism, inappropriate to feminist memorializing, and share with Maya Lin's design the use of horizontal rather than vertical lines, an organic relationship to the landscape, an interactive or reflective form and, most notably, the insistent use of names. The memorials we examine here focus less on the heroic stories of individual modernist artists struggling with the limitations of the memorial form of public art than on the women that they remember and the cultural work of memory-making in producing social change.

Memorializing violence against women, then, involves a huge range of challenges. The great weight of public discourse denies the systemic nature of femicide. When yet another woman's murder is reported, most often it is treated as an aberrant event, the deed of a pathological individual. How can memorial forms mark the everyday nature of violence without losing any sense of the horror of each individual act and without themselves, as cultural forms, disappearing into the everyday landscape? How can memorializing be participatory, dynamic and respectful of diversity without either becoming ephemeral or collapsing under the weight of community tensions? How can it garner the necessary material resources and public space without becoming entirely contained by the powers of patriarchy? How can it remain identifiably women centred without being trivialized with stereotypes of sentimentalism? How can it enact public political protest without betraying the privacy of the woman murdered or her friends' and family's private grief? How can it take advantage of the aesthetic power of public art without prettifying the memory of violence? In other words, how can feminist memorializing promote active, resistant remembering that encourages communities to take responsibility for the systemic nature of gendered violence while respecting individual trauma and individual accountability?

REMEMBERING RESPONSIBLY

The responsibilities shouldered in the process of making counter-monuments do not end with the memorial-makers. In writing about the hinge between memorializing and activism, we feel equally bound by principles of active and activist remembering, respect and trust. In our approach, we aim to keep the memory of women murdered and the challenges facing their memorializers firmly in view and to remain sensitive to difference and differential power across race, ethnicity, class, sexuality and ability. Cultural memory-making is a social process hemmed in by complex conditions, restrictions and possibilities and, therefore, the meanings and ramifications of memorial sites are always in flux. As activist researchers, we enter into that process analytically and appreciate the complexities of the process in understanding the memorial outcomes. We intend to be true to those who have given us access to those processes, not betraying their trust by an unrealistically purist, overly critical or unrelentingly interrogative analysis.

As a writing collective, we try to realize these aims in both our composition and our methods.[6] We come to this project from very different places, both professionally and personally, and have forged an approach that combines the politics, analysis and knowledges of those different locations. Some of the collective are social justice workers who have made various contributions over the years to the struggle against violence against women. Sly Castaldi works at Guelph-Wellington Women in Crisis (WIC) and has long-standing links to and working relations with sexual assault workers and feminist activists here and elsewhere in Canada. Jodie McConnell has spent her career working in the area of human rights and the advancement of women's equality. She, too, belongs to a network of social justice and feminist advocates. Christine Bold and Ric Knowles are academics from different humanities disciplines working in cultural studies with access to the resources needed to support the research and writing process. Lisa Schincariol has crossed over from academic to activist employment in the social justice field and back again, bringing insight from both perspectives to the deliberations of the group. When we conduct our research and write up our analysis, we work across our differences, including gender and sexuality. We are committed to a kind of thinking that supports the link between remembering the past and changing the future, that takes into account the relationship between process and product and that attempts to discriminate among different memorializing effects without betraying the trust of those who have given us access to the "inside story."

Our cultural memory group emerged originally from the wish of some members of the Centre for Cultural Studies at the University of Guelph to engage in research that might make a political difference. That meant exploring cultural memory across various kinds of difference, including disciplinary difference within the academy and the divide between politicized research and activist practice. The principles that have guided us are that it must be collaborative, feminist, activist, localist and site specific. The initial "object" of our research was Marianne's Park (discussed in chapter 6), a site in downtown Guelph dedicated to the memory of a woman who had been one of the earliest clients, subsequently a volunteer and finally an employee at WIC, who was murdered by her male partner. A partnership development grant from the Social Sciences and Humanities Research Council of Canada allowed academics at the Centre for Cultural Studies and members of WIC, who had been involved in the founding of Marianne's Park and retained an informal guardianship over it, to launch a long-term relationship that was rooted in finding useful ways to support one another's work. WIC became a formal "community partner," providing human resources in the form of memories, experience, contacts and documents. The academics found resources to support such WIC-organized activities as the annual Take Back the Night marches and December 6th vigils for the fourteen women murdered at l'École Polytechnique and all women murdered each year in Ontario, events which were regularly held at Marianne's Park.[7] We hired student researchers to engage in the organization and analysis of these events. One of those researchers, Lisa Schincariol, became a full member of the Cultural Memory Project and co-author of this book.

The five of us gradually and through a process of self-selection came to constitute the team that would research and write this book. We began to meet regularly to negotiate goals and working principles and plan research activities, drawing upon our very different knowledges, epistemologies and personal contacts. We agreed that our work should attempt both to analyze and to support the work of the often beleaguered women across the country who managed to construct counter-memorials, often in the face of considerable opposition from hostile local politicians, journalists and others. Tracing continuities between the processes by which memorials were established, their design and their eventual use, we attempted to identify goals, concerns, problems, compromises, successes, decisions and results that were common among those engaged in counter-memorializing. We documented unrealized and under-realized memorial efforts, but we also attempted to account for and provide accounts of work that has been especially successful in activating memory and in reconciling memorializing with activism: in using the past to change the future.

We agreed, too, that our own work should try to serve a memorializing and consciousness-raising function comparable to those of the memorials about which we were writing — that we should participate *in* rather than simply study the political project of the memorializers and activists. We saw participation and analysis as equally important parts of a continuum rather than opposite or mutually exclusive poles of a binary. This meant that we could neither pretend to apply the detached objectivity of traditional academic scholarship nor engage in activism without analysis. The tensions between remembering the past and changing the future that were regularly addressed by the activists involved in counter-memorializing, often through negotiation and compromise, were the tensions that we ourselves had to face and resolve.

Working within a feminist research collective is slower, more arduous, more challenging, more companionable and, ultimately, more rewarding than working alone, as every unspoken assumption is interrogated, each procedure, practice and phrase is subject to scrutiny, and each observation raises the stakes and the level of the discourse. As members of the Cultural Memory Group, we grew to respect and allow for one another's areas of expertise around strategic naming, language use, research practices and sensitivities. Sly's experience in the field was such that the group gave her virtual veto power over what information might or might not be included that might be sensitive to the families of femicide victims or their local communities. Jodie became the group's expert adviser on the strategic use of terminology, with her acute ear for inappropriate, unproductive or politically risky constructions of social position. Lisa exercised considerable social and diplomatic skill in making contacts and following up leads. Christine and Ric contributed their training in writing up and editing textual and performance analysis. But perhaps our most productive (and enjoyable) practices that evolved involved some or all members of our group working together. Chief among these activities were "road trips," as we attempted to visit as a group sites that were accessible to all of us, in order to interview the prime movers behind their creation, to photograph and otherwise document their design and use, and to engage as a group in making observations and preliminary analysis.[8]

As we visited memorial sites, attended memorial events and talked with memorial-makers, our multiple roles began to interact and merge. Sly, Jodie and Lisa had all been involved in feminist memorial-making, had organized memorial events themselves and expect to do so again. As researchers on this project, they began to notice more details and dwell longer on their significance, but they continued to carry with them the organizer's pragmatic appreciation of the labour and limits involved in memorial production. Christine and Ric learned to temper some of their theoretical positions with the nuance of activists' analysis and the charged, visceral reactions provoked by memorial work. We all agreed that participation as members of the research team provided both mutual support and some analytical distance from events that can be traumatic for individuals.

Although at times tensions emerged among those multiple roles, together they immersed us more deeply, made us more moved by and engaged in the memorial acts which we were analyzing. With the comparative context of our accumulating research and the experience of activists, we were buoyed up by one memorializing group's triumphs — appreciating, for example, the magnitude in the achievement of feminist community and the victim's family co-operating around a memorial event, or cast down by another's defeat by depressingly familiar attacks on naming gendered violence and its perpetrators. The sense of injustice, outrage and unutterable pain and sadness was, if anything, heightened for us because of this project, because of the inseparability of research and participation, analyzing and caring. We all agreed that, because of what we went through, it was a different kind of process than any of us had engaged in before, moving through theory, beyond theory, into practical application.

Clearly, too, we were not regarded as a typical research team by those with whom we met and corresponded — organizers, community activists, family members, friends. The relationships established over the years by the women's and human rights advocates in the group inspired responsiveness and trust in those we approached. We believe that a differently situated research team without this history of community service, however careful in its methods, would not have been granted access to so much and such private detail. But with the opportunities that such welcome and trust bring are, of course, pressures and responsibilities. The obligation goes further than accurately representing information; the question becomes whose interests does our analysis serve? Knowing that we had taken on the responsibility of engaging in analysis of families' and communities' memorializing practices, we were always conscious, throughout the visits and conversations, that we might feel the need to critique practices that were genuinely well intentioned and that perhaps represented the best possible outcome within the local circumstances. The observation that began to haunt our deliberations came after our participation in a particularly moving memorial event, led by family members and activists who had been astonishingly generous in their responses to our questions. On that occasion, Sly voiced her anxiety: "In the back of my head I was always conscious of the fact that we were going to be critiquing this memorial, and there was a possibility that we would betray their memory."

How, then, has the nature of our collaborative research group, with its evolved principles and practices, shaped the results of our research? What we have felt able to say and not say has been shaped by the constitution of our research team, our processes of collaboration, the attempt to address a more general public concerned with issues of violence against women and the decision to reach beyond the academy for participants that were informed, theoretically and practically, by a wide range of experience and ways of knowing. We are not striving for ideological purity but for politically supportive — and *therefore* accurate — analysis. Perhaps the most significant results of our collaborative working processes have had to do with learning to position ourselves simultaneously as participants and researchers. When we visited sites, attended events and mixed with the family and friends of women murdered, it was incumbent upon us to do so as *both* researchers and supporters, neither to masquerade as friends while honing our keen analytical skills nor to position ourselves as outsiders. Similarly, when we met to share our analyses and to write the story of these memorials, it was incumbent upon us neither to detach ourselves from the experience we had lived through at these sites and events nor simply to relive those emotions in support and solidarity. To engage in this work as both participants and researchers is to attempt to sustain a double identity without duplicity, one which "betrays" neither the research nor the activism. It is to follow through on what happens when memorializing meets activism, research meets participation, theory meets praxis. And, always, it is to position our work as one part of a larger, collaborative and mutually supportive project.

Marita Sturken characterizes cultural collectivity as "the memory landscape that we inhabit" (1999, 234). We are acutely aware that we would not have been able to negotiate our way around this landscape nor appreciate its contours without the generosity of so many people (thanked by name in our acknowledgements) who made our work possible — all the memorial-makers, feminist activists, women's shelter workers, family members, friends, survivors, advocates, artists, administrators who took time out of hectic schedules, dug exhaustively and painfully into their archives of personal memory and shared the immediate vividness of their loss, their struggles, their insights and their accomplishments. We have found that the five years spent in conversation with these witnesses have transformed this project into a series of personal pilgrimages, moving each of us into a renewed and enhanced understanding of men's violence against women, particularly in terms of the political dynamics and socio-economic factors that work to minimize the reality of this violence and keep women at risk. We hope that this work keeps the trust of those to whom we owe so much. We offer it in memory and in solidarity.

Chapter 1

VANCOUVER:
MISSING, MURDERED
AND COUNTING

A place of violence and horror does not appeal to me as a memorial site. If I had to go somewhere ... it would be a place of peace. I'm more interested in seeing violence against women stopped.
— PAT DE VRIES (QTD. IN TRACEY 2002)

IN SPRING 2002, ALMOST AS SOON AS THE REMAINS OF VANCOUVER'S "missing women" began to be recovered from the Pickton site in Port Coquitlam, BC, the need to memorialize them made itself felt both powerfully and painfully. On the partly excavated site a healing tent was set up, which represented each of the women with a candle and a tag bearing her name (M. de Vries 2003, 254) and a First Nations healing ceremony was held, "a cleansing ceremony to free the spirits of the women trapped in the ground, to honour the women whose lives may have been lost there," according to Terri Brown, then president of the Native Women's Association of Canada (Fournier 2002a). A makeshift memorial also took shape at the farm gate:

> a shrine to the missing women of Vancouver's skid row has sprung from the gravel. There are photographs, candles, stuffed animals and poems, all dedicated to the missing and presumed dead. With the arrival of spring, someone has dug a proper flower bed and planted primroses. Families of the

missing are often seen at the gate reading inscriptions, laying flowers and lighting candles. (Armstrong 2002, F4)

Longer-term memorial plans proved more controversial. The quotation above was the reaction of the mother of Sarah deVries, identified as one of the murder victims when her DNA was found on the farm, to the debate about whether to convert the property into a memorial site. The reaction of Andrea Joesbury, mother of Karin Joesbury, another of the women Robert Pickton stands accused of murdering, was different. In April 2002, she filed a civil lawsuit seeking "forfeiture of the Pickton farm for use as a memorial site for the plaintiff's daughter and ultimately all the women who may have died there" ("Two Suits" 2002).[1] Other tributes have also emerged that are not site specific. Vancouver artist Wyckham Porteous developed the Buried Heart Project with the support of some eighty Canadian musicians. This musical tribute was recorded "as a permanent memorial to the missing women," with the proceeds going to a residential treatment and recovery home in Downtown Eastside, the heavily deprived area of the city in which most of the sixty-nine or more women worked (Fournier 2002b). Some members of the Missing Women Trust Fund, led by family members, resented the musicians' initiative: "The missing women are us, and the families who have been at this for years, looking for our loved ones," said Val Hughes, sister of Kerry Koski, who disappeared in 1998.

The Missing Women Trust Fund also linked their memorializing to fundraising and education efforts. In addition to working towards a rapid opiate detox centre in the Downtown Eastside and establishing other support systems, they respond in a positive way to young people's expressions of interest: "'We had four teenagers come to the pig farm and light candles in honour of our missing women, and we were so touched we offered to come to the Archbishop Carney School in Port Coquitlam, talk about how our loved ones came to be on the Downtown Eastside and the dangers of alcohol abuse and drug addiction,' said Hughes" (Fournier 2002c). More recently, Carol Martin and Marlene Trick — who work with women on the Downtown Eastside — announced plans for a lasting memorial to honour all women from the Downtown Eastside who died. They hope to involve the local community in the creation of the memorial, slated at a cost of $100,000 and to be unveiled in the summer of 2007 (Burrows 2005).

The stakes in these efforts and disagreements are raw and immediate: how to honour women's lives while marking the violence of their deaths; how to specify individual victims while including all abused women — across lines of race, ethnicity, class, economic situation —in the remembrance; how to acknowledge that these social and cultural conditions put marginalized women at much higher risk; how to make a memorial publicly acceptable without compromising on naming murder; and how to make memorializing politically effective, not deflecting from but contributing to the struggle against violence against women. Vancouver has a particularly powerful history to draw on in response to these questions. The city has a range of memorials, clustered around a dozen blocks of a deprived neighbourhood, that protest violence against women. These range from granite stones brought all the way from Quebec to a permanent installation in a city park to annual performances of mourning and outrage by the city's First Nations community. The stories of the making of these memorials, their design and their use say much about the complexity and sheer hard work of memory-making, the different kinds of protest embodied in different physical forms, and their varying effect on social justice efforts. Above all, these memorials are dedicated to visibility and remembrance as fundamental conditions in keeping alive the struggle to end violence against women, whether the victims are local women working in the sex trade, women murdered 35 kilometres away in a Vancouver suburb or women murdered in a Montreal university 5,000 kilometres across the country.

MARKER OF CHANGE/À L'AUBE DU CHANGEMENT

Half-a-dozen blocks south of the "cold heart" of Downtown Eastside, at the intersection of Main and Hastings, is Thornton Park, a small green space which often serves as a shortcut from the bus stop at Main Street and Terminal Avenue to the VIA train station (Newton 2002). Here stands a symmetrical ring, 27 metres (90 feet) in diameter and 91 metres (300 feet) in circumference, bordered by fourteen warm pink, construction-grade granite benches, each 1.7 metres (5.5 feet) long and rock-solid like sarcophagi. Each bench is raised 15 cm (6 inches) above the ground, each is inscribed with a woman's name protectively facing the centre of the circle and each has a shallow, oval-shaped indentation sandblasted into its top surface, where rain water gathers. Every second bench bears a dedicatory inscription on its outside face in one of seven languages — Chinese, Swahili, French, Chinook, Hindi, Spanish or English:

THE FOURTEEN WOMEN NAMED HERE WERE MURDERED

DECEMBER 6, 1989, UNIVERSITY OF MONTREAL.

WE, THEIR SISTERS AND BROTHERS,

REMEMBER, AND WORK FOR A BETTER WORLD.

IN MEMORY AND IN GRIEF FOR ALL WOMEN

WHO HAVE BEEN MURDERED BY MEN.

FOR WOMEN OF ALL COUNTRIES, ALL CLASSES,

ALL AGES, ALL COLOURS.

One bench, bearing the name of Geneviève Bergeron, carries a feather etching designed by First Nations artist Susan Point to indicate that the language of its inscription, Chinook, is Aboriginal.

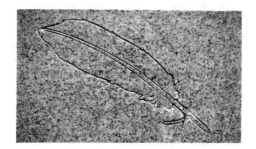

Surrounding the circle of benches is a continuous exterior ring of ceramic brick tiles with over 5,000 names of individuals and groups who donated time or money to the project. Each name is hand letter-punched into the clay — from CÉLÉBRATIONS LESBIENNES to NELSON HOUSE FIRST NATION to MINISTRY OF THE ATTORNEY GENERAL. Tiles inscribed with epitaphs written by the families of the fourteen women are placed across from the benches dedicated to their respective daughters. An orientation stand is located on one corner of the site, closest to the path leading to the trains, with key text written in Braille and raised lettering, in both English and French:

THE WOMEN'S MONUMENT, 1990–1997.

A FEMINIST PROJECT REALIZED BY A SMALL GROUP OF WOMEN

IN COLLABORATION WITH CAPILANO COLLEGE

WITH LOVE FOR ALL PEOPLE.

MARKER OF CHANGE CREATED BY BETH ALBER.

The project that led to the installation of this memorial on December 6, 1997, was initiated in 1990 and led by Christine McDowell, a media student at Capilano College in North Vancouver and a former rape crisis counsellor. Shocked by the events of December 6, 1989, McDowell joined with women from the Capilano College Women's Centre and some women's studies students to draft a proposal for a permanent marker to remember the women murdered in Montreal and to protest violence against women everywhere. Outraged that the whole country knew the name of the women's murderer while the women themselves remained largely unknown, McDowell approached Capilano College for support in inscribing their memories into history. She met with an unusually warm reception from a supportive female Dean, Carol McCandless, and after some months of political processing the proposal was accepted. With the support of her institution, McDowell established a volunteer committee and initiated what would be the long process of planning, decision-making, negotiating, and raising both funds and awareness.

The process they adopted from the outset was feminist, the women's monument committee operating as a collective. This is apparent in the documentary video about the project, *Marker of Change: The Story of the Women's Monument*, by filmmaker Moira Simpson, where the women are seen meeting, cooking, eating, debating and endlessly talking. As one committee member, Janine Carscadden, says, "What happens hand in hand with a lot of the practicalities of a project like this is the philosophizing, and discussion — and there was a *tremendous* amount of discussion. It was *soul searching* in a lot of ways, and redefining language and ideas."[2] Beth Alber, who entered the project much later as the designer of the monument, comments,

> I've never been involved in a process like this one. You know, I've been to a gazillion meetings in my life ... but I've never been in a meeting where

somebody has asked me how I feel, what's going on in my life, and am I comfortable … It takes longer, no doubt, but it has been a very rewarding experience for me, to see things done in this way.

But as Carol McCandless emphasizes, "The way in which the monument was created was as important as the end product. It needed to empower women."

The committee proceeded to negotiate one challenge after another, eventually securing from the park board a conditional offer of Thornton Park as the monument's location.[3] The board delayed full approval pending details of the monument's making as set forth in the committee's design competition guidelines. The key detail came to be the inscription, which took the following wording, to be translated into a number of languages, including Braille:

GENEVIÈVE BERGERON	HÉLÈNE COLGAN
NATHALIE CROTEAU	BARBARA DAIGNEAULT
ANNE-MARIE EDWARD	MAUD HAVIERNICK
BARBARA KLUCZNICK	MARYSE LAGANIÈRE
MARYSE LECLAIR	ANNE-MARIE LEMAY
SONIA PELLETIER	MICHÈLE RICHARD
ANNIE ST-ARNEAULT	ANNIE TURCOTTE

MURDERED DECEMBER 6, 1989

UNIVERSITY OF MONTREAL

IN MEMORY AND GRIEF FOR ALL WOMEN

MURDERED BY MEN.

FOR WOMEN OF ALL COUNTRIES, ALL CLASSES,

ALL AGES, ALL COLOURS.

WE, THEIR SISTERS AND BROTHERS,

REMEMBER, AND WORK FOR A BETTER WORLD.[4]

As the video makes clear, it was over this dedication that, in the words of juror Haruko Okano, "the shit really hit the fan. Because it went public." Pressure was insistently put on the park board through the media to delete

the phrase "murdered by men" and replace it with something more concil-
iatory. "That's when we found out you can't say who's murdering women,"
says McDowell. "Don't say it. It's all right to say women are being murdered
and need to be remembered, but don't say who's doing it." Trevor Lautens, a
columnist for the *Vancouver Sun*, led the objections and expressed considerable confidence in his own assumptions:

> I think that the phrase "murdered by men," precisely because it's so general,
> *unquestionably* stereotypes men, it *unquestionably* is discriminatory, and it
> *unquestionably* suggests, or raises the possibility, of attracting hate to a de-
> terminable group. (emphasis in the original)

"The press were like a hammer ... 'change the dedication,'" recalls McDowell.
"I'd never *seen* a women's group attacked so much in the press. It really hurt
to be told that what you're doing is actually destructive, and the opposite
of what you intend." Elinor Warkentin, a committee member, recalls, "We
got a bomb threat as soon as it started ... And the *irony*, you know, we're
building a monument to remember the women who have been murdered,
and then to be threatened like that ... We were faced with a choice, do we
take out men or not? And you know, with our feminist process, we were
considering it ..." But after long and anguished discussions, the committee
stuck to its original decision. In Warkentin's words, "In order to be true to
the women who were killed, we had to do what we had to do, and what
we had to do is name the reality, and the reality is that women are being
murdered by men."

At the board, as at Capilano College, the committee was fortunate
enough to encounter a well-positioned and sympathetic woman, Nancy
Chiavario, a city councillor and former park board chair who was a sup-
porter of the project. She explains:

> We're very protective in the park board system about monuments, you
> know, and you have to be not offending people, and that kind of thing. But
> it seemed like a good concept. Then somewhere along the way after we go
> from concept to more specifics, we got the inscription, and basically all hell
> broke loose in the media ... It was pretty clear the board wasn't going to
> approve it, with the wording. And the women were adamant that there was
> going to be absolutely not one word changed. I thought, ok, well, that's a
> good place to start. So I said, "I'll take you all to lunch."

At lunch, Chiavario and the monument committee chewed less over the
meal than over the proposed wording, reading and rereading the words

until Chiavario exclaimed, "I've got it! ... We'll just take this paragraph and put it in front of this paragraph!" Her suggestion was to move the sentence "We, their sisters and brothers, remember, and work for a better world" to the beginning of the dedication, immediately following the murdered women's names. As Chiavario pointed out, "It still says the same thing, but it softens it in a way, less as an accusation to all men. So that people right away saw the idea that men and women do support and are acknowledged as supporting this." The committee was elated.[5]

When the proposal went to the park board, according to Carscadden, the committee "went in prepared to really talk about it, and justify it, and I remember going up there and start[ing] to say something, and they took it away, that was it." According to Chiavario, two councillors, Tim Louis and Dermot Foley, pushed the proposal through. Foley remarked, "Who are we afraid of, a bunch of murderers?" and the board voted unanimous approval.[6]

That major hurdle passed, the committee proceeded to assemble a nationally representative, intercultural and interdisciplinary group of seven prominent women jurors, including such luminaries as Black activist and politician the late Rosemary Brown, francophone lesbian feminist poet and activist Nicole Brossard and Asian-Canadian interdisciplinary artist Haruko Okano. They launched a nationwide design competition and stepped up efforts at fundraising the $300,000 needed to complete the project (Mills 1998; Money 1995). In response to a national call for contributions, donations came in from corporations, governments, unions, students, community groups and individuals from across the country, from outport Newfoundland to towns and villages in the Northwest Territories and the Yukon, and everywhere in between.[7] The committee was overwhelmed. According to committee member Cate Jones, "Local women ... knew that the opposition was so strong that if they didn't give, it wouldn't get built," but no-one expected the broad groundswell of support that the monument would receive nationwide. As McDowell remarks, the tiles that circle the monument say it graphically: "You need six thousand groups and individuals to make this happen. That's the truth."

But even at this point, and with this level of support, the installation of the monument was not without controversy. "When I found out that the women's monument was going into Thornton Park I was really disappointed," says Muggs Sigurgeirson, a long-time Downtown Eastside resident. "The Downtown Eastside is the poorest neighbourhood in Canada. It's also the neighbourhood in Vancouver which all the social problems are shoved into, including poverty, street drugs, homelessness." Kam Raj, of the Rape Crisis Centre, argued that, "as a crisis line worker, as a front-line worker, when I'm trying to get a transition house for these women to get *out*, there is no place to go, so my thinking, the way we stand is, that money could have been put to better use than to be building fancy little benches, or tombstones. We didn't buy into that."[8] And victim service worker Marion Dean Dubick, pointing to a long list of murdered and missing local women that includes many First Nations and other non-anglophone or franco-phone names, concurs:

> There's people dying every day down here … The fourteen women in Montreal got massacred and that is horrifying, but look at the names on the list. All these women counted. We don't have Canada-wide coverage of all the women that die right here in the Downtown Eastside. Why is that? We're not university students. We're not across the country. We're right here. We're dying every day.

In a scene in Simpson's *Marker of Change* video, Christine McDowell admits to Cleo Reese and Squamish language teacher Vanessa Campbell, "When we started the project, we didn't know about the Downtown Eastside and what was going on there. And we learned about it. Certainly we had meant for the dedication to mean all women. And it does. But I know that the First Nations women in the Downtown Eastside don't feel included in it, and I understand. It's not enough." At this point, the camera, in close-up on Campbell's face, shows her eyes lowered in a look of resignation. But Vanessa Campbell herself, together with Elders from her community, nevertheless helped with the translation of the dedication of the monument, and its eventual unveiling featured First Nations ceremonials. As Campbell explains,

> For myself and the Elders that took the time to work on the dedication, for us the issue is not what the women look like or where they come from, the issue is that these are all women who suffer because we are not intervening to save a life or cherish a life — a mother, a sister, an aunt, a grandmother, a daughter. When someone in our family is gone, and we hear that someone in another family has gone, in the same way, in our hearts we know the pain they suffer.

MONUMENT AS PUBLIC MEMORY

The women's monument was planned as public art and was designed by Toronto silversmith and jewelry designer Beth Alber, the winner of the competition. It is now perhaps the best known of the many memorials across Canada devoted to the victims of the Montreal massacre. Dedicated eight years after the event, after seven years of planning and fundraising, it was, according to Sharon Rosenberg, "the first national permanent monument" dedicated to them, and to "all the women who have been murdered by men"(2000, 78). As such — *national* and *permanent* public *art* — the monument carves out its place among other national monuments, including war memorials, "writing in stone," as it were, the nation's acknowledgement of the war against women and claiming for itself the cultural cachet of art.

Christine McDowell emphasizes the need for "a monument that's permanent." Haruko Okano calls "this particular monument a sleeper ... It resonates something that is very much needed within the realm of public art and monumental works ... [I]t sets in that [realm] *forever* an image created by *women*." According to Beth Alber, "When I'm here, I look at it and I think that, *these look so strong* ... They're right there, they're in the ground, they're *planted*. And goddamit, they're not going to be moved, you know? I love that." Art critic Gary Michael Dault calls the monument's design "so thoroughly conventionalized and sparely minimalist it is almost styleless — fittingly." It "meets enormity with a structural calm," he argues, "indexed by a rigorousness of design, which transcends, in its affecting logic, its minimalist origins to hearken back to the ceremonial structures of pre-history," entering a realm that is both "beyond or rather *anterior* to composition" and "archetypal" (1998, 21).

The monument, then, enters gendered violence, and specifically the Montreal Massacre, permanently into national public memory. But in doing so, as Josephine Mills argues, it "has to respond to the interrogation of the whole notion of monuments" (1998, 52). Monumental forms tend to glorify "heroic" violence, bury the past rather than keep it alive and provoke what James Young calls "the illusion that our memorial edifices will always be there to remind us," allowing us "to take leave of them and return only at our convenience ... To the extent that we encourage monuments to do our memory-work for us," he argues, "we become that much more forgetful"(1993, 5). Attempting "to redress the virtual non-existence of public monuments in Vancouver that directly relate to women" (Mills 1998, 52) and at the same time aiming to produce an "anti-monumental monument" (Kelley 1995, 10), the design guidelines for the Vancouver women's monument competition asked, "How would a Women's Monument be different?"

In many ways, Beth Alber's design powerfully answers that question. Both an aesthetic object and one that subordinates "design" to political purpose, the monument takes on organizer Christine McDowell's challenge to test the power and efficacy of art. Both permanent and provisional, it asserts its solidity and significance while remaining dialogical, anti-monumental, and, in Caffyn Kelley's phrase, "radically open": "It makes room," she argues, "for a vast range of individual responses, in a space where we might join hands, and make a difference" (1995, 10). The monument eschews the vertical, unitary and phallic form of the traditional public monument designed to elevate the eye. Rather, it incorporates multiple, interactive components laid out on a horizontal and grounded human axis. And, as Rosemary Brown indicated in announcing Alber's winning design, "it employs a circular form used by women for centuries to represent a continuum." "The circle," she said at the dedication ceremony, "is a place of remembering." The fact that the circle is constituted of benches, moreover, "creates the potential for a gathering place," as Josephine Mills explains (1998, 52). It "evokes a feminist style of meeting as well as rituals for healing," reflecting and echoing the feminist processes of the monument project.

This sense is invoked, too, by the circle of donor bricks that surround the benches. Not the standard list of honorary patrons or corporate sponsors, the bricks link the named victims of the Montreal massacre with other living names, and together they constitute "a magic circle and first line of defense for the hallowed memorial ground within," according to Dault (1998, 21). The *Marker of Change* video makes much of this: "The circle of donors," one organizer argues, "represents a voice against violence against women. It's about bringing people together in a common vision, a common bond." Another says, "I love the tiles. They show individuals putting their names behind something, and the courage to do that." Finally, the sense of the circle as healing place is reinforced by the indentation at the top of each bench, a shallow hollow that Frances Fournier describes as "vulva-shaped," designed to catch rainwater and evoke tears. These hollows are also used, on special occasions and by occasional passersby, to cradle flowers.

But the monument is not exclusively about healing circles and the creation of "an occasion for community" (Kelley 1995, 9). It is also about keeping memory alive, active and painful. "That cut that's in the top," asks Alber, "is it a scar? Will it ever heal? No, it will never heal." The fact, too, that the benches were made of *construction*-grade granite from Quebec, granite "removed violently from the earth" (in Alber's words), points to an engagement with *active* remembering rather than a commitment to conventional and conventionalized memorializing as a means of disengagement, of achieving individual comfort and closure. As Alber insists, "It was going to be about work; it wasn't going to be about death." The fact that the benches consciously resemble sarcophagi, together with the fact that they are not just park benches but cold, hard granite benches that are deliberately uncomfortable and discomfiting, also serves to move the monument beyond the realm of contemplative healing. It is difficult to sit or picnic on these benches without being conscious of the violence that underwrites them and the violation of remembering that is involved in cathartic acts of recollection that are attendant upon healing and moving on. This violence and violation, too, are invoked by a reading of the benches' surface indentations, not as wells of tears and rain, but as scars. As Caffyn Kelley argues, the monument potentially opens space for "a different kind of memory — capable of spontaneous combustion, a furious and uncontrollable grief" (1995, 8). Sharon Rosenberg identifies this different kind of memory with a productive rupture serving to *prevent* familiarization, deny "comprehension" and disavow "business as usual" (1997, 2000).

These tensions and others are legible, too, in the most controversial component of the monument: the multi-language inscription that both is and is not "written in stone," translated and multiplied as it is throughout the site. The controversy surrounding the inscription's positioning and naming of men has already been sketched in our discussion of the process by which the monument was created. The tension between the ongoing activation of memory and the healing need to put the past behind us, however, is also evident in the inscription, notably in its uneasy shift of tenses, which move from the past-tense identification of a dateable, locatable and fixed historical event confined to the past ("*were* murdered/December 6, 1989, University of Montreal"), through an indeterminate but active present tense positing a better future ("remember, and work for a better world"), to return to "memory," "grief" and the generalizing, continuous past of "all women who have been murdered by men." But there is another tension that is also legible in the inscription. That is the one between the remembering of individual, named women ("the fourteen women named here") — white university students and staff from 5,000 kilometres away — and the imperative to open the dedication to include "women of all countries, all classes, all ages, all colours," as is also indicated by the use of six international languages plus the indigenous Chinook. Most imperatively, among the larger circle to whom these gestures refer are the many women, most of them disempowered, many of them First Nations, who have been murdered and disappeared each year in Vancouver's Downtown Eastside, the immediate neighbourhood of the monument itself.

The felt need both to name as individuals and to treat as representative the fourteen women murdered in Montreal was a driving force behind the campaign to establish the monument from the outset. In the *Marker of Change* video the organizers articulate their outrage that, as a result of the skewed coverage of the massacre, the name of the murderer was known nationwide, awarding him a kind of fame at the expense of his victims, who remained largely anonymous. Beth Alber, too, articulates in the video a concern for the fourteen murdered women as individuals, going so far as to celebrate the fact that each of the benches bearing a name, "because they're going to be done by hand ... will be different ... It's important," she says, "that these women be respected as individuals." But, like the organizers, Alber also sees these women, and the monument she designed, as representative, reading the tears symbolized by the sandblasted gashes in the benches' surfaces as emblematic, as weeping "for those women and for other women who have died with such violence." The inscription, then, attempts to honour the individuality and the horrific circumstances of the deaths of the women it names, while it nevertheless resists treating them as exceptions, the victims of an inexplicable and isolated act of madness rather than of a societally systemic misogyny. For better *and* worse, as Sharon Rosenberg (2000) argues, it treats them as emblematic.

If at the outset the organizers were unaware of the problems involved in using a memorial to white women of some privilege to emblematize all victims of male violence, they did not remain so for long. Their response to criticism on these grounds, which involved the inclusion of the inscription in Chinook together with its accompanying feather, also involved the writing of one of the donor tiles, using wording that, while still not managing explicitly to indicate race, class or economic conditions that make some women more susceptible to men's violence than others, nevertheless opens the monument's community outwards in more explicit, located ways and gestures to the need for the more localized memorials that are discussed below. That tile, which to us is among the most powerful of those that enclose the circle of benches, reads as follows:

IN LOVING MEMORY
OF THE WOMEN KILLED
ON VANCOUVER'S
DOWNTOWN EASTSIDE

SO MANY WOMEN LOST TO US

WE DREAM
A DIFFERENT WORLD
WHEN THE WAR ON WOMEN
IS OVER

EXPERIENCING MEMORY

What is it like to experience the Marker of Change, to walk through Thornton Park among the benches, to stand encircled by them, to read the inscriptions and to crouch to examine the names and messages recorded in the donor tiles? One visitor imagines herself in the circle of stones and wonders how far they can take her into the depths of memory: "Might the shallow, curved depressions on the surface of each form serve as gestures to the (un)knowable beneath the surface? My memory's skin begin to thin, give way, as tomb after tomb comes into vision, as I stand surrounded by stones to the dead?" (Rosenberg 2000, 87). The experience is no doubt different for different people, and purposefully so, but it would seem, in part at least, to have to do with the visitor's experience of space, place, landscape and history.

For some, the park's location outside the city's central train station will make it a productively liminal site, as will its proximity to the shoreline meeting of land and water on the continent's west coast — a place of meetings and departures, ebbs and flows, tears and joy, and a place coded with change. For others, the park's Edwardian design, the "formal and balanced geometry" cited in the design competition guidelines, will constitute it as a restful and respectful place, ordered for reflection and contemplation and set apart from the busyness of daily life. Such visitors will no doubt appreciate what McDowell (1999b) calls "the great old trees" that surround the monument, the role that the monument played in renovating what had been a neglected park at the city's core, and its participation in what, in a Western tradition, is the calming and regenerative nature of public parks as green space rather than politically charged sites of public gathering or debate. For still others, however, with deeper knowledge of the site's history, or closer engagement with its troubled neighbourhood, the location of the monument will be less comforting. Caffyn Kelley (1995) and Sharon Rosenberg (2000) both draw attention to the largely forgotten pre-1917 history of the park, which Kelley links to the impossible-to-ignore-or-forget contemporary situation of the monument's besieged neighbourhood, which connects to a local history of colonization, of both people and the land:

> In the history of this country, white supremacy is both enabled and justified by the plunder of nature. I have lived in Vancouver now for twenty-five years, but I never knew the city is a gravestone marking the internment of a vast estuarial habitat until I began working on the Women's Monument.

Thornton Park, where the monument [was] built, was once a salt marsh where gooey mudflats supported an intricate web of life. Now it is a flat, square patch of green, made to stand for nature where there was once all that chaotic life and stink. The city gave away the wetland to the Canadian Northern Pacific Railway. By 1917 the swamp was buried.

The underground rivers and the buried landscape are the unconscious image of this city, testimony to a violent culture that would tame nature as it would tame us. In places of vast diversity, in the radical openness of natural communities, what protects your power over the things of the earth? What guarantees your difference from them? What form of forgetting would not remember this? (Kelley 1995, 9–10)

The women's monument committee continues to both remember and work against that violent past, vivifying this memorial as a space of possibility and action. For December 6, 2004, for example, the committee organized a "Peace Is Possible" event, inviting people to come together in Thornton Park to build a communal peace symbol in the middle of the monument. As the poster for the event announced, it was to be a living, usable symbol — made of "flowers, quotes, fruits, vegetables, and other useful offerings such as toys, candles, socks and gloves … these will be left for people who need them" — as well as an occasion for political lobbying. Women's collective efforts to remember the past in order to change the future continue.

CRAB PARK

From one perspective, the ambition of the Marker of Change/À l'aube du changement to be not just emblematic but "national" is exemplary, raising the status and visibility of the struggle against violence against women. From another perspective, that ambition risks giving deep offence. For many First Nations peoples, the very concept of the national — understood as referring to the latter-day nation-state of the European settler colony — (re)enacts the violence of the colonization and subjugation of those Nations that preceded Canada and never ceded their claims to indigenous and independent nationhood. The memorials built and performed in memory of murdered and disappeared women from Vancouver's Downtown Eastside have deliberately eschewed any claim to national representation and remain determinedly local.

The first memorial, ten blocks north of Thornton Park, on the other side of Main and Hastings and right on the waterfront, is in CRAB Park at

THE HEART HAS

IN HONOR OF THE SPIRIT OF THE PEOPLE
MURDERED IN THE DOWNTOWN EASTSIDE
MANY WERE WOMEN AND MANY WERE NATIVE
ABORIGINAL WOMEN. MANY OF THESE
REMAIN UNSOLVED. ALL MY RELAT

ITS OWN MEMORY

DEDICATED JULY

Portside (the acronym stands for Create a Real Available Beach). The monument was first dedicated in 1997 but not fully installed until two years later, by the CRAB Water for Life Society and the organizers of the Missing People website.[9] This monument, surrounded by a clump of bushes, sits at the dividing line between the park's expanse of green lawn and the beach that curves around the bay. It consists of one inscribed boulder and a bench-mounted plaque. Like the Marker of Change, the boulder's inscription attempts to bridge the local and the universal, but it also insists on inscribing a publicly unacknowledged community of women. The insistence is heard in the words "The heart has its own memory," an excerpt from Longfellow, which Don Larson, the non-Native author of the inscription and spokesperson for the organizers, says he found on a drugstore greeting card and used in order to remind people to be compassionate even to those victims of violence he feels society too easily disregards and too readily blames for their own deaths. The full inscription reads as follows:

THE HEART HAS

IN HONOR OF THE SPIRIT OF THE PEOPLE
MURDERED IN THE DOWNTOWN EASTSIDE.
MANY WERE WOMEN AND MANY WERE NATIVE
ABORIGINAL WOMEN. MANY OF THESE CASES
REMAIN UNSOLVED. ALL MY RELATIONS.

ITS OWN MEMORY

DEDICATED JULY 29, 1997

The CRAB Park memorial contrasts with the Marker of Change in other ways as well. While the women's monument was established through a major national fundraising effort and a national design competition, Larson put together a necessarily inexpensive memorial design quite serendipitously. He didn't encounter any opposition to the memorial inscription when the park board and city council reviewed it. He thinks this was because the city was caught off guard by the fact that such a memorial was even being established (Larson 2000). We might also attribute the council's reception to the aftershocks of the controversy created by the women's monument and the all too brief, but intense, media coverage of the missing women this prompted.

The City of Vancouver has surrounded the boulder with approximately 11 metres (35 feet) of soil and a variety of full green shrubs, which simultaneously block, cradle and attract attention to the boulder within. Flowers and greenery are planted at the boulder's base, and visitors leave their own messages written on rocks and driftwood nestled among the shrubs. The dedication is clear from a distance, its inscription sharply etched into a smooth rock surface angled slightly towards the eye, defiant against the soft curves of its surroundings. Both the boulder and an accompanying bench overlook the Burrard Inlet that separates downtown from North Vancouver, with the North Shore Mountains behind.[10] The location's immediate context is contemplative, but it is not unequivocally so, energized and disturbed as it is by the almost constant noise of float planes and helicopters and the deep red robotic cargo lifts that tower in the background. And the welcoming natural curve of the beach is interrupted by signs warning against swimming in the polluted waters of the inlet, as the wharf that shields the beach to the west from Vancouver's downtown carries similar warnings against crab fishing.

The site also carries with it memories and marks of conflict.[11] The CRAB Water for Life Society underwent an enormous struggle between 1984 and 1987 when it (successfully) struggled to attain this section of parkland, the Downtown Eastside's only access to the shore that winds extensively around Vancouver. The park continues to accrue marks of symbolic conflict in its accumulation of First Nations signs and symbols. At its eastern entrance sits a Story Stone, a City of Vancouver Millennium Project installation by artist Fred Arrance, which articulates an internalized conflict for the "Urban Indian" for whom "soup lines replace trap lines," but asserts that "Indian ways are not for sale."[12] To the west of the monument, an Irly Bird Pavillion shelters a West Coast First Nations eagle design painted on a concrete slab. Elsewhere a rusted civic plaque provides an early Native name for the area, "Lucklucky" (Grove of Beautiful Trees), and marks it as the site of Vancouver's first church in 1876, "a Methodist mission to the Indians." Two other signs compete ironically for attention: a coyote alert warns against contact with the animal that is central to many Native spiritualities as a trickster figure; and a Parks Department notice wards off the contemporary homeless: No Person Permitted in This Park 10 P.M.–6 A.M.

The memorial that sits at the centre of the park carries with it complex resonances within this context. The inscription on the boulder, with its careful blend of specificity and inclusiveness ("many were women, and many were Native Aboriginal women") and its concluding phrase "All My Relations" (in symbolic contrast to the Longfellow quotation that brackets it), marks at once its cultural specificity and its openness. The phrase serves as an English equivalent of one familiar to most Native peoples in North America, used to begin or end a prayer, or speech, or story, and to mark not only a close relationship with family and relatives but also a relationship with and shared responsibility for all human beings, animals, and plants—indeed "to all the animate and inanimate forms that can be seen or imagined" (T. King 2000, ix). Although the names and dates of the dead are unlisted on the boulder's inscription, the names are inscribed on the nearby bench's plaque, in contrast and supplement to the boulder's generality:

IN MEMORY OF L. COOMBES, S. DEVRIES, M. FREY, J. HENRY,

H. HALLMARK, A. JARDINE, C. KNIGHT, K. KOSKI,

S. LANE, J. MURDOCK, D. SPENCE & ALL OTHER WOMEN

WHO ARE MISSING. WITH OUR LOVE. MAY 12, 1999

The CRAB Park memorial initiative has consistently contributed to the campaign to bring attention and action to the women disappearing from the Downtown Eastside — a campaign which gathered steam in 1996, when the disappearances that began in the late 1970s escalated exponentially and more and more protesting voices became heard publicly. The memorial serves as a potent site of solidarity and mobilization, at both the personal and the political levels. On May 12, 1999, for example, Maggie de Vries, sister of Sarah de Vries who disappeared in 1998, and Val Hughes, sister of Kerry Koski who disappeared earlier the same year, organized a memorial. About 300 people gathered at the First United Church for a remembrance service for Vancouver's missing women — at that point, a list of twenty-three names — which combined First Nations and Christian ceremonies. The group then marched, with banners and placards, through the Downtown Eastside to CRAB Park to lay flowers at the memorial boulder and hear speeches from family members, social activists and politicians.

At least two mothers are on record attesting to the empowerment they derived from this rally. Michele Pineault, mother of Stephanie Marie Lane, who disappeared in 1997, said "I always thought I was going through this alone. But talking to some of the other moms has made me realize they are feeling the exact same pain as me" (Heakes 1999). Pat de Vries, Sarah's mother, has also talked about the strength in numbers: 150 candles had been brought to the gathering, and they weren't enough. "People had drifted apart from each other because they didn't know how to talk about it," she said; getting together was "a healing experience ... none of us were alone" (2001). And she observes that people visit the bench at other times in place of a grave site.

The impact also contributed to public awareness and official action. Media interest revived once more and, in the words of Roxanne Hooper (2002): "With the cohesiveness of the families that began to gel that day, and with the assistance of Const. Freda Ens (a native support worker for

Vancouver Police), the families were finally able to pressure police to take the large number of missing women complaints seriously and investigate possible links." One result was a poster, listing thirty-one missing women and offering a $100,000 reward for information, issued by the Vancouver police and the BC Attorney General. By fall 2001, the momentum resulted in the Missing Women Task Force, a joint venture of the RCMP and the Vancouver Police Department. This initiative came against the backdrop of sustained pressure and organizing by family members, reinforced by several developments: the *Vancouver Sun*'s eleven-part series on the missing women (which put the number at forty-five); an arrest in Washington State of "the Green River Killer" (a Seattle serial killer, thought to have links to Vancouver area murders); and the wrongful dismissal case against the Vancouver Police Department filed by Detective Kim Rossmo (the inventor of geographic profiling who argued that a serial killer was preying on downtown women).[13]

Through all this, as women's remains began to be discovered in Port Coquitlam, as the numbers of women "officially" missing rose to 69, as murder charges began to be laid, as the Task Force increased to 85 investigative officers, 50 specially trained bone experts and costs above $10 million, CRAB Park continued to serve family members as a site for organized remembrance, a repository for family photographs of their missing relatives, and a place of solace ("Missing Women Investigation" 2002). On February 14, 2005, the CRAB Water for Life Society and Aboriginal Front Door Society jointly held remembrance ceremonies, parallel to the Valentine's Day march happening elsewhere in the city. About three dozen people gathered at CRAB Park, then a smaller crowd at Wendy Poole Park nearby, for soup, coffee, carnations and prayers presented by a Native elder (Larson 2005). Yet, still, all the names can scarcely be spoken. The eleven names on the CRAB Park bench only partly overlap with the twenty-seven women named as of May 2005 on Pickton's first-degree murder charge: Sereena Abotsway, Andrea Borhaven, Heather Bottomley, Heather Chinnock, Wendy Crawford, Sarah de Vries, Jane Doe, Tiffany Drew, Cara Ellis, Cynthia Feliks, Marnie Frey, Jennifer Lynn Furminger, Inga Hall, Helen Mae Hallmark, Tanya Holyk, Sherry Irving, Angela Jardine, Andrea Joesbury, Patricia Rose Johnson, Debra Lynne Jones, Kerry Koski, Jacqueline McDonell, Diana Melnick, Georgina Faith Papin, Diane Rock, Mona Wilson, Brenda Ann Wolfe. The names, the memories and the protests continue to accumulate.

WENDY POOLE PARK

In the course of 1999, Don Larson and his group went on to address the memorial potential of another green space, at Main and Alexander, just one block in from the waterfront, on the south end of the overpass leading to CRAB Park. When Larson heard that the city was planning to renovate the small park, he petitioned city council to dedicate it to Tsay Keh Dene woman Wendy Poole. In 1989, Poole's body was found in a dumpster one block from the park now named for her. She was twenty years old and pregnant, working in the sex trade at the time she was murdered. Her murder is still unsolved, and Larson (2000) believes that it has never been rigorously investigated by police.

After about a year of lobbying, on September 25, 2000, the city agreed to name the park after her, the first park in Vancouver to be named after a First Nations person.[14] The naming challenged the park board definition of an appropriate dedicatee (the guideline that such a person must have made a "significant" contribution to the community usually applied to a public benefactor or organizational luminary) and public protestations that

Vancouver had "enough" monuments to murdered women. Other opponents argued that, because a diverse group of people used the park, it should bear a more generic name. "Where has this United Nations approach been in the creation of memorials to white people?" Larson (2000) asked, rhetorically. His logic won the day; the "Park Naming Report" accepts his argument that Wendy Poole "is representative of a terrible malaise in the area and that the naming will help bring to light the plight of these forgotten women" (Vancouver Board of Parks & Recreation 2000). The rising tide of protest against institutional handling of the "missing women" cases — a "hugely disproportionate" number of whom are First Nations women, according to Terri Brown — presumably added to the pressure for this naming to happen (Fournier 2002a).

If CRAB Park can be experienced as a site of resistance, Wendy Poole Park smacks more of dislocation. Tucked into a corner of Gastown, overlooking an array of train tracks and situated beneath a bridge, the wedge-shaped space has a marginality that resonates powerfully with the story of Wendy Poole. When the city landscaped the park (at a cost of $40,000), they uprooted everything: the drug users and homeless people who had used it as a gathering place, the old trees and benches, any object that provided a hiding spot. New things have been planted: sharp rocks rooted in cement point towards the sky along one edge where the homeless might otherwise find sleep and shelter; lamp poles hover above; irrigated grass spreads between a retaining wall and the freshly painted vivid brick belonging to the neighbouring house next door. Apart from a single park bench, there is no place to rest here. A cement sidewalk winds down the centre of the park inviting the passerby to follow it to the far edge, where the pathway expands into what seems to be a semicircular viewing platform, incongruously overlooking nothing but the train tracks below. As the visitor approaches the street corner where the park is located, she confronts the granite memorial boulder abruptly at the street's edge rather than being led towards it by the pathway that seems designed for the purpose. Not only does the large granite boulder bearing Wendy Poole's name seem dislocated in its own space, it also seems to bear the marks of violence, a major crack on its left side having been somewhat clumsily repaired.

There are two memorial inscriptions on the site. One, designed by Larson, is prominent on the boulder itself, the other is mounted on a small regulation plaque near the ground and to the right of the park's entranceway.

The inscription on the boulder appears beneath a ring of feathers encircling a dogwood flower, and it reads:

WENDY POOLE PARK

TSAY KEH DENE

"Like water, truth embraces
both stone and starlight."

DEDICATED YEAR 2000

"Tsay Keh Dene" (People of the Mountains) identifies Wendy Poole's Nation. What follows, perhaps incongruously, is a Taoist proverb that Larson, who is not Native, borrowed, as he did the imagery for the feather and dogwood design, from a book on Taoism, even as he had borrowed the Longfellow quotation for CRAB Park from a greeting card (Larson 2000). He reports that one park-board member contested the inscription with the concern that it might be read to be commenting on land-claim conflicts, because the dogwood flower, British Columbia's provincial emblem, is surrounded by Aboriginal feathers, an image accompanied by allusion to the distilling of truth, but with no direct mention of Wendy Poole's story. Larson explains that, in his mind, the sentence pertaining to truth refers to the fact that Poole's murder remains unsolved and was not being attended to by the police with due diligence. His hope was that the park would not only represent all of the murdered or missing women in the Downtown Eastside but would also put pressure on the police to solve their cases. Unfortunately, in this inscription, the matter of violence against women — indeed, the fact that Poole was murdered — goes unsaid. Considering the opposition we have seen organizers confront, it is perhaps little surprise that the inscription represents, as Larson admits, a concession to a public that insists on de-politicizing, de-gendering and de-racing memorial intent.

The inscription on the park's plaque, on the other hand, provides official clarity and the discourses of respect, including one line in Squamish:

WENDY POOLE

heʔk̓ʷmətaləm tə siÿém̓
YOU ARE REMEMBERED, RESPECTED PERSON

In September 2000, the Vancouver Park Board dedicated this park to Wendy Poole (1968–1989), a First Nation's woman from the Tsay Keh Dene (People of the Mountains) nation in the north west of the Province. Wendy was known as a kind, trusting person. She was one of a number of British Columbian aboriginal women, who lived and lost their lives in the Downtown Eastside. Her young life was unfairly taken from her, and taken from our world.

Her spirit lives on. Let your visit to this park respect her memory.

Wendy Poole Park was dedicated at noon on February 14, 2001, in a ceremony, closed to the press, at which Musgueam Elder Emily Stoofan performed a traditional Salish healing ceremony and blessing of the boulder, local dignitaries spoke and soup, coffee, bannock and a pink carnation were provided to the approximately thirty people in attendance (Larson 2001).

***

These three permanent monuments to violence against women co-exist in Vancouver within blocks of one another. The first, the work of a dedicated group of white feminists, is a national monument to fourteen female engineering students and staff killed on the other side of the country, and to "all women who have been murdered by men." The second two, the work primarily of a white male environmental activist, are dedicated to local women, particularly First Nations women, who have been disappeared and killed in the city's Downtown Eastside. A fourth, particularly powerful memorial — the most site-specific and the most performative — has been wholly conceived and controlled by members of the First Nations community as an annual Valentine's Day remembrance since 1991. The ritual is described by Caffyn Kelley (1995) in an article framed by the haunting story of the brutal 1971 murder by four white men in The Pas, Manitoba, of Helen Betty Osborne, a nineteen-year-old Cree woman (whose memorial is discussed in chapter 3). Kelley describes "a different kind" of memorializing in the Valentine's Day demonstration organized by First Nations women of the Downtown Eastside, one that involves ceremony, naming, site-specificity and the commitment of active and ongoing pilgrimage. The description (now a decade old) resonates hauntingly with other efforts to make memorializing serve social justice, with the rituals enacted at the Port Coquitlam murder site, and with the unrelentingly lengthening list of Vancouver's "missing women":

> Every Valentine's Day, hundreds of people gather to honour the memory of women who have been murdered in the area — otherwise known as skid road. At a smudge ceremony they name the dead women, and form a healing circle to honour their lives. The group then marches through the streets, stopping periodically at the sites where over forty-eight women have died violently. The Valentine's Day demonstration is a memorial that refuses to produce a happy ending. Instead of telling a seamless narrative, it establishes a dialogical space. The structure of memory that it suggests allows us to keep talking, but also to keep counting. (Kelley 1995, 8)

By 2005, at the fourteenth annual march, the number of local women honoured with "roses and remembrance" had risen to seventy-two.

Chapter 2

CALGARY AND EDMONTON:
LEST WE FORGET

lest we forget lest we forget lest we forget
lest we forget Dawn Shaw - 6, lest we forget
Misty Dawn Boudreau - 13 lest we forget
Mary Zozulak, 12, Carla (Vicky) Cicuta - 31,
Stennia Lovegrove - 31 and daughter Annaleisa - 6
Linda Crocker - 6, Susan Freschi, Sharon Fox - 45
Laurie Wood - 33, Karen Rainey - 31, lest we f
Linda Joe - 17, Krystal Senyk - 29 lest we for
Elsie Shorty - 70s, Annette Lubovicki - 21 lest we
lest we forget Cathy Brown - 23 lest we forget

THE NAMES AND AGES COME CASCADING DOWN THE SILVER COLUMN OF crushed, tattered paper, handwritten in ragged script, punctuated by the haunting refrain "lest we forget." Another face of the monument intones with unbearable monotony "one of the disappeared one of the disappeared one of the disappeared," over and over from top to bottom. Another declares: "Let all lists begin with the 14 women slain in Montreal Dec. 6 1989: Geneviève Bergeron – 21 Hélène Colgan – 23, Nathalie Croteau – 23, Lest Barbara Daigneault – 22, Anne-Marie Edward – 21 Maud Haviernick – 29, Maryse Leclair – 23 Lest we Annie St-Arneault – 22, Barbara Maria Klueznick – 31, Maryse Laganière – 25, Anne-Marie Lemay – 23 Sonia

Pelletier – 28, Michèle Richard – 21, Lest we forg Annie Turcotte – 20 Lest we forget Lest we forget Le."

This sculpture, Lest We Forget by Calgary artist Teresa Posyniak, sits in the main foyer of the brand new Law Building of the University of Calgary, encased in thick glass, catching the traffic between the Law Library and the central staircase to the offices above. Lest We Forget suggests many things, about memorializing violence against women generally, about the possibilities and perils of that activity in this province specifically, about the benefits and costs of institutional endorsement and about the need for and accompanying limitations imposed by protected spaces for memorializing murdered women.

The lessons of Lest We Forget — about institutionalization, containment and survival —are played out graphically across the cityscapes of Alberta's two largest cities. In Calgary and Edmonton we discovered five memorials to women murdered, all of them facilitated by institutional resources, all of them dedicated to making changes for women more than temporary, and all of them intent on building community around that promise. The five suggest a spectrum of political intervention, with Posyniak's sculpture sitting in the central, linchpin position. Three seem more limited in reach than her sculpture, more sheltered by their campus environments; the fifth — sitting in conditions closer to those of the memorials in Vancouver's Downtown Eastside — is more directly exposed to the chillier winds of urban poverty.

LEST WE FORGET, UNIVERSITY OF CALGARY

In 1994, Lest We Forget found a permanent home on the University of Calgary campus, through the efforts of Dean of Law Sheilah Martin and some law faculty alumnae. The piece by Calgary artist Teresa Posyniak remembers and protests violence against women through language, motifs of nature and ominous images of deterioriation and disappearance. The sculpture, which is close to a storey high but with a broken-off top that suggests its reach could be much higher, sits in the airy main foyer of the Law Building. The location was deliberately chosen to encourage members of the legal profession to be mindful of feminist social justice and legislative inadequacies in the protection of women. As Posyniak describes it:

> The sculpture stands seven feet high and sixteen by twenty-four inches at the base which is surrounded by bronze painted leaves. Constructed of wood

and styrofoam, it is covered with thick sheets of handmade paper and painted a luminous, silvery bronze. One hundred thirty-five women's names and ages (some names added from the Calgary area [to Mary Billy's femicide list]) are carefully written on the paper surface, interspersed with the phrase "*lest we forget.*" Although intentionally reminiscent of war memorials, "*Lest We Forget*" differs significantly from traditional heroic tributes to posterity. Its human scale, its intimacy, its personalized script and especially its fragile, organic material suggest impermanence and vulnerability. Ominously, one side of the sculpture is left partially blank for future entries as the violence against women continues. (Posyniak, n.d., 2)

Aiming to juxtapose vulnerability and strength, Posyniak employed handmade, tattered material and architectural reference points reminiscent of ruins to convey a melancholic ephemerality. The fragility and decay of the sculpture imply the vulnerability of any structure (a home, safety, shelter), the "nature of justice for victims of murder" (Severson 1994), and the inconstancy of memory. This display of deterioration, along with the handwritten script, subverts the otherwise traditionally vertical form. In reminding us of phallic war monuments, the work challenges their notions of conquest, heroism, the permanence and righteousness of the status quo. Posyniak's materials evoke the destructiveness of violence to create "a symbol for the collective grieving of women murdered day after day" (qtd. in Beacom 1994, 5). The 145 names of murdered girls and women, ages 6 to 84, descend on the viewer in an unremitting barrage that is both insistent and fragile, as its materials crumble into nothingness. The metallic surfaces seem simultaneously to reflect and absorb light, rendering the piece both bright and dark, a visually destabilizing presence. The piece demands attention, its emotional effects linked intimately with political reflection.

The political impact of the installation in this setting feels finely balanced. On the one hand, it signals both confrontation and outreach. The work's visual challenge to the ordered, institutional context becomes explicit in the information sheet prepared by the university prior to installation: the sculpture "would help to reveal the inadequacies of the legal system and the concomitant responsibilities of lawyers and lawmakers to society" ("Law School" n.d.). The plaque mounted alongside the sculpture also quietly insists on the politics of this artistic statement — "Hand-made paper and mixed media sculpture (1992), dedicated to Canadian women murdered by violent men" — as well as pointing to further information about the

sculpture and the victims in the Law Library. Sherene Razack has critiqued the role of the law in making the space of prostitution violent, partly by legally demarcating "degenerate space" as a separate zone from the protected "respectable space" of mainstream society (2002, 127). In the context of this analysis, this sculpture's challenge, situated at the heart of legal training and scholarship, is considerable.

Moreover, the sculpture's sheer listing of names and ages challenges the protocols of silence around the horrific proportions of violence against women, a fact which came home to Posyniak in 1992 when she read Mary Billy's "itemized, descriptive list of women in Canada who had been murdered by men" (Posyniak n.d., 2). Those names, from all walks of life and economic circumstances (a context supplied by the annotated list in the Law Library), broaden the sculpture's reach well beyond the protected and privileged space of the law school. One line, among all the haunting refrains and accumulating names and ages, particularly reaches out to the woman viewer with a sense of threat: "9 Calgary women whose murderer is still out there." During the time that Posyniak had the sculpture in her studio, she received a visit from the extended family of a woman murdered while working in the sex trade. They brought the woman's small son to see the sculpture on his mother's birthday and took his picture next to his mother's name. Years later, the sculpture now installed on campus, he left a flower and a card at the base of the memorial after a December 6th vigil. In the words of Sheilah Martin, "Nobody touched it for about six months. That spoke a lot about how powerful this memorial is and how respected it is" (Martin 2001).

On the other hand, the sculpture's location contains its political impact in both real and figurative ways. Take its display case, for example. Lest We Forget was first displayed in different galleries around the city in 1993, evoking such a strong response from women in the community (including law school alumnae) that they set about finding it a permanent home. When the university agreed to house the sculpture, it also undertook to preserve it, raising $8,000 to "protect it from vandalism or tampering" ("Law School" n.d.). Given the fragility of the monument's materials, it was an entirely rational decision to enclose the piece in thick glass. Yet that protection withdraws the sculpture further into a sheltered space, removed from city residents, off the beaten track of most students, readily available only to the privileged few accepted into the study of law. The glass case not only distances the memorial from the outside world, from us to whom it speaks, but it also arrests the evolution of Posyniak's vision, since she cannot respond to requests to add names in continued recognition of and protest against women's murders (Posyniak 2001). This is how it would have felt if Harburg-Hamburg municipal officials in Germany had lost their nerve over the disappearing Holocaust monument discussed in our introduction, if they had stopped its unrelenting movement into the earth and kept it a fraction above the ground as a relic of its intent. Such a memento would have deflected attention from the responsibilities of remembrance to the curiosity value of the object itself. Similarly, in the well-lit, brisk and clinically clean atmosphere of the Law Building, Posyniak's sculpture risks becoming a display that invites passive spectatorship and risks losing its capacity to provoke resistant remembering.

Yet those limitations may also be the precondition necessary to the monument's survival. Although local journalists expressed much admiration for Posyniak's sculpture at the time of its installation, it did also come under attack by the province's right-wing press. A columnist for the Alberta Report used inflammatory rhetoric and badly skewed statistics to criticize the sculpture for ignoring murdered men and exploiting "the victims of violence to promote blatant feminist propaganda" (Sillars 1994, 46). He claimed the support of the organization REAL Women of Canada and Calgary Sun columnist Licia Corbella in insisting that violence is never gendered. In light of this onslaught, the protection offered by the Faculty of Law location can seem as much enabling as limiting. On the one hand, professional decorum contains the work's political charge; on the other, could it have survived in a less privileged location?

FACULTY OF ENGINEERING MEMORIALS, UNIVERSITY OF CALGARY AND UNIVERSITY OF ALBERTA

The effects of institutional embrace on memorializing are played out graphically in Alberta's engineering schools. After the murders of December 6, 1989, Faculties of Engineering across Canada struggled to deliver appropriate responses. Activities and initiatives took place on many campuses, some of which are recorded in this book. Some were as simple as a plaque naming the women murdered, some accompanied that remembrance with statements about the need to make engineering schools women-friendly, and some supported those statements with scholarships and lecture series dedicated to the promotion of women engineering students. One of the lessons from the Vancouver memorials is that the makeup of the community that creates a memorial inevitably marks everything about it, including its design and use. Memorial-making groups or individuals in engineering schools do not identify primarily by politics (as with feminist groups) nor by ethnicity (as with First Nations groups) but by profession. The designs, language, placement, ideologies of their memorials inevitably, then, speak back to that profession. This is the case with all the memorial structures on the university campuses of Calgary and Edmonton — all are ultimately contained by the protocols of the profession— but they are different enough to demonstrate a meaningful spectrum of possibilities.

In 1999, student memory-making was boosted by the Canadian Engineering Memorial Foundation (CEMF), when it launched a competition for students to create an outdoor or indoor bench or equivalent in memory of the fourteen women murdered in Montreal.[1] The guidelines blended skills training, consciousness-raising and community healing. Student teams were required to engage in the full engineering process — budget, construction, installation and utilization — and were given $1,000 to cover the costs of doing so. The guidelines also specified that submissions must name the women murdered and create a space for ameliorative dialogue, "while demonstrating the successful integration of a human-made structure with the environment." The guidelines spoke to a real need for publicly acknowledging this tragedy (more than one student confessed to not previously knowing of the killings) but did so in a language of regret and healing, using the vocabulary of "tragedy" and "loss" rather than the language of anger and outrage that feminist and Aboriginal activists would have used (CEMF 1999). The Faculties of Engineering at the University of Calgary and the University of Alberta took first and second places, respectively, in this competition.

COMMEMORATIVE WORKTABLE

In Calgary, a team of six students diverse in race, gender, engineering specializations and artistic skills came together with faculty and staff.[2] In just over a month they designed and built — with some technical assistance from local companies — a worktable, proposing that "it better fa-

cilitated communication and teamwork" than did a standard resting bench ("Submission" 1999, 2). The table can accommodate one to three working groups, with twelve attached stools and room for two wheelchairs. The tabletop is biomorphically shaped, a curvilinear form in Canadian maple with twenty-seven brightly coloured, angular geometric shapes fitted together as the centrepiece of its polished surface. Fourteen of these shapes are engraved in brass with the names of the women murdered in Montreal; the other thirteen shapes represent those who were injured in the shooting that day.

The students were inspired by the geometrical abstractionism of Wassily Kandinsky's *Accented Corners* of 1923, with its energetic explosion of shapes and colours. They believed that abstraction would "permit viewers to appreciate and interpret the memorial in their own meaningful way without being influenced by any images we present" ("Submission" 1999, 2). Yet their design does encourage certain symbolic links. As they explain in their proposal:

> The pattern represents the diversity of engineering applications as well as the people who make up the profession ... The light colour of the table, and the black finish of the supports, makes it appear as if the table is floating above the dark floor. The strength and durability of the materials can also be taken to represent the mathematical and scientific principles upon which

engineering is built, and the contrasting colours reflect the ethical behaviour which an engineer must uphold as part of her/his ongoing responsibility to society. ("Submission" 1999, 2)

The explicit recognition of murder, the design leaves to the user.

The worktable's location renders its message at once sheltered and interventionist. The piece sits within the main foyer of the engineering complex, a light-filled modern space which feels well kept and well resourced; a leafy, sun-dappled courtyard provides a backdrop that is visible through the floor-to-ceiling window against which it is set. Dean of Engineering S. C. Wirasinghe (1999) publicly endorsed the choice at the table's unveiling: "The location is very important. It is at the main entrance to our Faculty. It signifies our ongoing and central commitment to the equality of men and women in engineering." This kind of official endorsement, however, threatens to obscure the remembrance itself. The memorial is well off the main university beats of the general student population, and a large brass plaque on a nearby wall (not part of the students' design but donated by the administration) also detracts from the worktable's referential minimalism.

The language of the worktable's plaque euphemizes the murders, commemorating the fourteen women "who lost their lives" (as if the women were agents of their own deaths). It also carries so many institutional logos, titles and acknowledgements that institutional self-congratulation threatens to overwhelm the act of remembrance. Perhaps the most pointed and productive feature of the memorial is that it sits among other carrels and student work spaces. When students huddle around it to confer on projects, to catch up on studying or simply to chat, the brass names stare up in sharp contrast to the brightly coloured surface, insisting that attention be paid, speaking directly and on a daily basis (if without explanation) to the profession's next generation.[3]

REPLACING REMEMBRANCE

Three hundred kilometres north of Calgary, on the large, opulent and well-groomed campus of the University of Alberta, students working to the same competition guidelines produced a rather different memorial. Particularly in light of its subsequent fate, this work seems a little more challenging in its reach to a wider student population. Working on the project between their classes and job interviews, eight engineering students (three women, five men) from civil, environmental and computer engineering programs constructed a bench and a boulder as a memorial. It won second place in the CEMF competition, earning their school the $5,000 prize.[4]

While the result was hardly confrontational or disruptive, it took up space quite thought-provokingly. The memorial sat at the southern end of the largest quadrangle on campus, a green expanse with a great deal of student bustle and a strong sense of the historical pomp and circumstance of the university. Bordered by a phalanx of imposing, early twentieth-century red-brick buildings, each elegantly landscaped with mature trees, the quad is criss-crossed by four paved walkways designed to channel students from the Student's Union Building to other main buildings on campus. At the southern end, the castellated facade of Pembina Hall faces the west wall of the Civil/Electrical Engineering Building, an equally massive building but of a more minimalist brick-and-glass 1960 design, with a mural representing human progress through technology.[5] The memorial was positioned between these two buildings and spoke back, to a degree, to their triumphant monumentalism.

The bench sits at an intersection of walkways, in a triangular area, approximately 6 metres by 5 metres (20 feet by 16 feet), covered with limestone gravel and overlooked by a large birch tree. Under its sheltering branches, the slatted wooden bench seating fourteen people formed a somewhat angular semicircle around a memorial boulder, giving the sense that, as the tree sheltered the installation, so the seat curved protectively round the stone. The low boulder bore a large copper plaque, on which was written

IN MEMORY OF THE 14 WOMEN WHOSE LIVES WERE TAKEN

ON DECEMBER 6, 1989 AT L'ÉCOLE POLYTECHNIQUE

The plaque listed the names and professional specializations of the fourteen women in two columns. Along the bottom was a quotation from nineteenth-century American writer Oliver Wendell Holmes: *"What lies beneath us and what lies ahead of us are tiny matters compared to what lives within us."* In the centre, a photograph of fourteen female students standing in a semicircle in the same space was acid etched into the plaque, the faces sanded to obscure their identities and create a silhouette. In the words of the proposal, "The fourteen silhouettes serve to remind the public of how we are not immune to tragedy and how personal it can be" ("Dean's Millennium Award Project" n.d.).

These design features, in that particular place, made an intervention. Although the language of the dedication is euphemistic in its circumlocutions (describing lives being "taken" instead of women being murdered), its reference point is noticeably different from the triumphant progressivism of the towering engineering mural opposite. In a nicely suggestive positioning, the mouth of the semicircle presented the plaque and its remembrance directly to the Engineering Building; someone sitting on the bench would have the mural and the plaque in the same sightline. As mandated by the competition guidelines, the plaque was intended to serve as a focal point for discussion. In the words of one of the student designers, "With its almost ideal location, everyone on campus that walks by or sits on the bench is reminded about the tragic event that happened in Montreal" (Dempster 2001). And the plaque inserted women's names, specifically, and bodies, generically, into an institutional space still dominated by men.

That figurative insertion became literal every December 6th, when the December 6th Memorial Committee organized the annual vigil at this site: women predominated in the ceremony, the 1999 program included photographs of the fourteen women murdered in Montreal, and it listed "Fourteen things that YOU can do to make a difference," one of which was "Discuss the Memorial in your classes, at work and with your friends and family" ("Uniting for Change" 1999). However hedged in the memory-making was by male-dominated presences — the university structures, the mural, the notably conservative choice of Holmes for a quotation — there was an insistence on remembering the actual women. As the male president of the Civil Engineer Student Society commented, "When we started this, I had very little exposure to the event and to tell the truth, it was a day that had come and gone. Now I think of each individual as a separate woman rather than an event. There are 14 individuals and 14 supports and without those the monument would fall"(qtd. in Dey 1999).

But the monument *has* fallen; the boulder and plaque were removed in 2004. Only five years after installation, they were so badly weathered and vandalized that they no longer seemed "respectful."[6] The Engineering Students' Society and faculty agreed to install a new plaque in the student commons of the engineering teaching complex. While they are developing a contemplative space around the plaque, it seems a retreat into a much more standardized form, with minimal language and a reduction of the memorial's reach, sheltered in a location typically traversed by only one segment of the campus population. Ominously, in our view, the memorial's removal has been closely followed by a decision to cease public on-campus vigils on December 6th, administrators citing lack of interest from the university community (McMaster 2004). It is more negative evidence, if more were needed, of the crucial part memorials play in sustaining awareness of and resistance to violence against women.

What remains publicly visible on campus is a model of academic decorum. The University of Alberta's official December 6th memorial, installed in 1994, sits centrally and yet anonymously, effacing not only the ugly fact of murder but even the gender of the victims. In front of the main University Administration building — a street bustling with buses, cars and pedestrians — there is a large boulder, capped with a plaque, at the edge of a small, kidney shaped garden of mixed brush. The plaque reads:

> THIS COMMEMORATIVE GARDEN
> IS DEDICATED TO THE MEMORY OF
> THE FOURTEEN STUDENTS FROM
> L'ECOLE POLYTECHNIQUE WHOSE
> TRAGIC DEATHS IN 1989 WILL FOREVER
> SERVE AS A REMINDER TO ALL WITHIN
> OUR COMMUNITY OF THE IMPORTANCE
> OF LIFE AND OF OUR COMMITMENT TO
> DIGNITY AND RESPECT.
>
> DECEMBER 6, 1993

While the inscription is dedicated to remembrance, to our eyes its language is thoroughly informed by avoidance. It speaks of tragedy in terms that suggest natural disaster issuing in a cycle of renewal. There is no agent — male or otherwise — responsible for the deaths. It does not name nor specify the gender of the fourteen women, it does not recognize that not all of them were students, and it does not acknowledge that they were murdered because they were accused of doing men's work. Without these specificities, the commitment to entirely admirable principles of community behaviour feels ungrounded and abstract. Despite the central location, the memorial is not easily noticed because it blends in so seamlessly with the landscaping around the building. Only a few feet away stands a two-storey, metallic, abstract, bird-like sculpture marking an industrial company's donation to the university.[7] Overshadowed by this neighbouring commemorative sculpture, the garden and boulder feel ominously obscure, the official endorsement doing more to contain and erase memory and grief rather than bring it alive in active and activist terms. The site design and plaque inscription ultimately render the memorial inert, a classic example of what Michel de Certeau theorizes as the recording of past events to make them manageable, forms of entombment which keep the dead dead.

Institutional sponsorship always brings institutional containment. What the four campus-based memorials tell us is the power of making the silences audible, the gaps visible. Blank spaces provoke questions and scrutiny in a way that the discretely unsaid does not: the face of Lest We Forget not (yet) filled with names, the unnamed shapes on the University of Calgary table, the anonymous women's faces on the copper plaque (now absent) at the University of Alberta. These visible gaps promise to take remembering beyond institutional limitation, to transcend — to different degrees — institutional embrace and its celebratory agenda.[8]

A VISION OF HOPE: MARY BURLIE PARK, EDMONTON

Twenty blocks northeast of the University of Alberta campus, but a world away in terms of economic resources and communication lines, three figures rise from a bleak and raw-looking green space. This is Mary Burlie Park, a small space with a pavilion, benches, young trees and plantings, without any of the elegance, pomp and circumstance of the University of Alberta quad across the river. The park is pressed in on all sides by life in the poor end of the city. On the day of our visit, three women loll in the empty lot on one side of the park; a busy, construction-heavy street at the edge of Chinatown stretches across the other; the city's prisoner remand centre looms behind; the vivid graffiti covering the low brick buildings nearby is only a chainlink fence away. A man stumbles up the stairs into a small pavilion and passes out on a bench, while two others settle themselves at a picnic table to get high. In the midst of this scene rises the sculpture A Vision of Hope, at once a commitment and a contribution to eradicating violence against women, the result of three years of labour by a subcommittee of the Sexual Assault Committee of Edmonton (SAC).[9] Created almost simultaneously with the students' bench on the University of Alberta campus, this sculpture too remembers the fourteen women murdered in Montreal on the tenth anniversary of the killings, yet neither organizing group knew of nor collaborated with the other. The gap in communication signals other differences. A Vision of Hope protests violence against women in explicitly political terms. It connects with the city community directly in design, language and location. And, although its creation did have institutional support, it enjoys little of the environmental protection afforded the other memorials in Edmonton and Calgary. In other words, this sculpture in this location represents an entirely different political and artistic dynamic.

A Vision of Hope is a 3-metre (9-foot) high Ciment Fondu™ sculpture — stone in texture, bronze in colour — of three women representing three degrees of suffering and survival. It was created by francophone artist Michèle Mitchell, a graduate of the University of Alberta's fine arts department. Nick Lees, writing in the *Edmonton Journal*, described it this way:

"I've used three life-size figures of women in different positions of sufferance," said Mitchell. "They represent the three phases women go through when they are abused."

The first figure is called Despair and has a woman in the fetal position with a clenched hand. The second is named Grief and the figure is bent

over on her knees. And the third has a woman looking at the sky with her hand raised. It's called Hope.

"People must raise their eyes to the third figure and are comforted by the message of hope," says Mitchell.

A 108-mm gear wheel depicted in the sculpture has 15 shattered teeth, representing the 14 women who died plus an extra one for all other women who lost their lives through abuse. "The wheel represents the wheel of life and the circle of abuse that returns constantly," says Mitchell.

There is an I-beam shaft in the middle of the work that represents the lightning-bolt speed that shattered the women's lives. (Lees 1999)

The contrasts and convergences with Lest We Forget say much about the possibilities of feminist public art. The two art works occupy tellingly different cultural spaces. The sheer rigours of Edmonton's climate meant that Mitchell's outdoor sculpture had to have durability and visibility; the poignant effects of Posyniak's design depend on a protected, indoor location. Culturally, Mitchell is speaking to a very different audience. While Posyniak's minimalist, conceptual design does, as we have seen, communicate effectively with a wide range of people — often through their attachment to the names incorporated into her column — Mitchell's is much more firmly situated in the populist tradition of heroic figurative art. Her figures are closer to Soviet-era social realist celebrations of muscular working men and women than to Posyniak's delicate techniques. Ultimately, however, both women's sculptures speak back to the masculinist traditions they invoke. In Mitchell's work, women achieve the vertical posture conventionally associated with masculine triumph. They redefine the meaning of the posture by performing the stages by which and effort with which they undergo that transformation, thereby also reminding the viewer of the cycle of abasement and despair that always threatens to overwhelm women once more.

Mitchell's work — again like Posyniak's, though again in much more vernacular accents — is also accompanied by strong political statements. The dedicatory plaque in front of the sculpture is direct, specific and activist in its orientation:

A VISION OF HOPE

ARTIST, MICHÈLE MITCHELL

A MONUMENT TO HONOUR THE LIVES OF WOMEN

14 OF THE TREES IN THIS PARK ARE TO HONOUR
THE VICTIMS OF THE MONTREAL MASSACRE
AND THE 15TH TREE IS IN RECOGNITION OF ALL WOMEN HURT BY MEN.

GENEVIÈVE BERGERON
HÉLÈNE COLGAN
NATHALIE CROTEAU

Barbara Daigneault
Anne-Marie Edward
Maud Haviernick
Maryse Laganière
Maryse Leclair
Anne-Marie Lemay
Sonia Pelletier
Michèle Richard
Annie St-Arneault
Annie Turcotte
Barbara Klucznick Widajewicz

A la douce mémoire.

Killed because they were women
December 6, 1989

In memory of all women abused, raped and killed by men
in Edmonton, Alberta and Canada.

May all who gather here remember, grieve, honour women's lives
and renew their commitment to ending violence against women.

Fifteen young chokecherry schubert trees are planted on the periphery of the park, intended by the monument committee as an extension of the sculpture's troublingly double signification of the cycles of abuse and of life: "The new buds remind us of growth and change ... reminding of the universal face of abuse ... But the trees, as vibrant as young lives lost, also signal change ... The transfer from remembering to living is embodied in a monument alive with movement, and growing" (Ringma 2000). Each of the fourteen trees dedicated to the women murdered in Montreal has a plaque at its base noting a name, along with the name of the person, family or organization that sponsored the tree. The Institute for the Advancement of Aboriginal Women sponsored the tree to Barbara Klucznick Widajewicz. The Boyle Street Co-op sponsored in the name of Mary Burlie. One sponsor chose to replace her own name with a dedication to her mother and mother-in-law. The fifteenth tree is dedicated to

ALL WOMEN ABUSED,

RAPED AND KILLED

IN EDMONTON,

ALBERTA AND CANADA

CANADIAN UNION OF PUBLIC EMPLOYEES
LOCAL 3341

The sculpture stands near the centre of the trees on a cement block, edged by rocks and dwarf roses, in which the title and the artist's name are boldly stamped. Contributors of labour and materials are also listed here. The overall effect speaks of both effort and solidity. The sculpture's weight and texture signal fixity (the artist reports that it took ten people to make each of the four cement pours in its construction), while the naming of so many sponsors and contributors indicates an engaged network embracing the sculpture's mission, much as the donor tiles around the Marker of Change symbolize an established, protective, proactive circle.

The prime mover behind the sculpture's erection was the SAC monument subcommittee. Conceiving of the memorial as a permanent gathering space for women's events, especially the December 6th vigil, the committee surveyed local women about their preferences. Determining that majority opinion favoured an outdoor setting, they approached the city. Here, despite the dedication's explicit wording, they encountered much more support and a much speedier approval process than did the women's monument committees in Vancouver and across Ontario. Part of the difference was structural. In Edmonton, parks and recreation is integrated with the community and family services department, so the values and protocols involved in approving public monuments are much more informed by a commitment to the disenfranchised and victims of abuse.[10] The committee proceeded to conduct a local design competition and fundraising campaign for $10,400. The city added four trees to the eleven in Mary Burlie Park. After three years in process, including a year for the sculpture's creation, the memorial was unveiled on the tenth anniversary of the Montreal murders, with about 250 attendees who ended the ceremony by scattering long-stemmed red roses over and around the monument.

The selected location puts the memorial sculpture firmly in the urban arena. Mary Burlie, after whom the park is named, was a social worker known for her social activism who died of cancer. This is a deprived part of the city, with few images of beauty. As the committee's booklet says, "Ironically or symbolically, the park is in one of the most beaten-down areas of town and is next door to many community agencies and groups working for change" (Ringma 2000). Dell Marlow (2001), the committee's driving force as well as SAC director of education, envisions the sculpture's location as also contributing to local change. She hopes "that survivors in the neighbourhood feel a sense of women's community." Committee members managed to convert at least one skeptical journalist who came to throw her support behind the initiative: "I hope the sculpture becomes a point of inspiration, not just once a year, but a daily reminder to the living that they need never be alone" (Faulder 1999). The dangers of the location make the need for such community and commitment more urgently evident. As Judy Allen (2001) of parks and recreation, community and family services explains, "it's not someplace you'd go to at night ..., not if you value your life," and that threat is visible in the graffiti covering the picnic tables: warnings of gang violence, death threats mixed with milder insults addressed to "bitch" and "tits." The reminder to any woman sitting in the park that she, too, is a potential target of violence is considerably more graphic, more visceral and more immediate than the gestures to women's vulnerability in the campus memorials.

That vulnerability to attack was political as well as physical. During the process of the memorial's creation, one of the sponsors requested that the organizers remove the phrase "war against women" from their original inscription, a request to which they complied for fear of losing much-needed funding. They were also subject to a nasty campaign by MERGE (Movement to Establish Real Gender Equality) which campaigned to get the memorial plaque replaced, on the grounds that it violated Alberta's human rights law. MERGE even accused Dell Marlow of "being like Marc Lépine" and manipulated a distorted analogy between race and gender to represent the memorial as racist.[11] However fraudulent their logic, they clearly hoped to play on the potential that (predominantly white) small business owners and city council members would fear being perceived as bigoted.[12] It was yet another demonstration of how, the more open memorial art is to the community, the more open it is to attack.[13]

***

The five memorials across the campuses and cityscapes of Calgary and Edmonton echo each other, to a point, in intent and design. All conceive of public monuments as leading to social change in terms of gender equity. All blend art, nature, utility and language to stabilize memory while pointing towards lived action. And all combine elements of natural recycling (trees, leaves, paper, wood) with manufactured materials (various metals, glass, Styrofoam) to produce forms that are at once permanent in their heft, elevation or protected locations and symbolic of cyclical flux — the female figures representing movement through levels of despair and hope, the column both a lasting marker and a deteriorating relic, the bench dented and corroded with the effects of weather and time, the table facilitating generations of use. All represent a continuous and cyclical remembrance of violence that leads to protest and healing.

What signals the world of difference among them is location. The student memorials came out of and speak back to the engineering profession, the need to maintain diversity within it and the imperative for engineers to act ethically in the world. In contrast, Posyniak's and Mitchell's sculptures strive to embrace the epidemic proportions of gendered violence and to emphasize a greater degree of transformation. These memorials are not limited to a remembrance of the Montreal massacre as an isolated event impacting on a single profession, and their concern is not with creating a "work space" with the same emphasis on utility. But of the five memorials discussed here, Mitchell's is the only one sitting in close proximity to life below the poverty line. Lest We Forget, like all the campus memorials, is both more protected and more contained than A Vision of Hope. Posyniak's sculpture is secured in a well-monitored foyer and within a glass case; A Vision of Hope organizers have already had to replace vandalized lights that illuminate the sculpture at night. One enjoys a private and privileged audience, while the other is relegated to a public but marginalized space at the edge of town. In the end, all five memorials speak to demographically restricted communities, from those struggling to survive on the wrong side of town to the professional faculties with their established privileges and protocols.

As we left Edmonton, driving through its streets one intermittently sunny day, the word SEXIST — scrawled across billboards advertising a local newspaper and a Hooters franchise — leapt out at us. Especially for women visitors to the city, hyperconscious of the province's ultra-conservative profile, the graffiti summed up graphically the gendered struggle over public space. The memorials we have seen, however, suggest that the struggle is neither simple nor clearly polarized: the same institutional forces that enable the memorializing of women murdered can also limit its potential for social change; but more confrontational memorials (and those associated with their making) become vulnerable to physical and political onslaught. The question is how the politics of resistant remembering might tip the balance.

Chapter 3

WINNIPEG AND THE PAS:
IN MEMORY OF HELEN BETTY OSBORNE

I carve the letters BETTY OSBORNE on this yellow page.
Surely the paper must bleed from your name.
Why doesn't it bleed for you, my throwaway sister?
The sister I never met except in my dream, my obscene
*   nightmare.*
Betty, do I betray you by writing your name for people
*   to see who will not love you?*

— Beth Brant, "Telling" (1989; 2001)

On National Aboriginal Day 2001, on the grounds of the Manitoba legislature, the name of Helen Betty Osborne brought together memory, justice and public policy. The trustees of the Helen Betty Osborne Memorial Foundation gathered in the Women's Grove Memorial to announce the first two recipients of scholarships for Aboriginal residents of the province engaged in post-secondary study.[1] This was a powerful and profoundly layered rhetorical moment, reclaiming political space in order to connect the memory of a woman murdered to the drive for social reparation. All memorial-makers working against violence against women aim to make an impact on public policymakers. In Manitoba, the connection is peculiarly direct, with permanent memorial space carved out from the official seat of provincial power (the only such example we have discovered) and the memory of femicide palpably affecting the language and actions of elected politicians. Memory-making in Manitoba also impinges on race relations, a history which has been officially acknowledged to be scarred by "racism, sexism and indifference." We have probed in the case of Vancouver the difficulties and shortcomings involved in white feminists producing a memorial that tries to include First Nations women. This moment in Winnipeg signals a different dynamic, a layering of Aboriginal and non-Aboriginal memorializing in which the more privileged community creates a space that can enable without appropriating the search for justice by diverse cultural communities.

WOMEN'S GROVE MEMORIAL, WINNIPEG

The creation of the Women's Grove Memorial was motivated by the murder of the fourteen women at l'École Polytechnique, but early in the process it took on an inclusive, cross-cultural perspective. Since the 1980s, according to Keith Louise Fulton, there had been vigils in Winnipeg for women killed by their partners. The murders of December 6, 1989, provoked yet another vigil, in the rotunda of the Manitoba legislature, but on this occasion the building proved too small for the crowd that turned out. "We decided we needed a place where we could continue to explore the thoughts and feelings shared that night, a place of permanence, growth, resilience, and continuity" (Fulton 1999, 318). A group of about a dozen women — including politically active women attached to the Universities of Winnipeg and Manitoba — began to coalesce as the December 6th Women's Memorial Committee and to organize discussions with women's groups in Winnipeg and throughout the province about establishing a permanent memorial.[2]

During this period, local artist Lin Gibson mounted her own temporary memorial to the Montreal Massacre. She fashioned fourteen brass plaques, each "engraved with the name of one of the murder victims, and the inscription, 'Murdered by Misogyny, December 6, 1989, Montreal.' (In some cases the inscription was in French.)" (Yeo 1991, 9). Part of her aim was to subvert a form of remembrance "customarily used to commemorate men of status" (11). Working with Plug-In Gallery, she won the agreement of fourteen public sites across Winnipeg to display a plaque for one year from the first anniversary of the murders. Many of these sites had established institutional prestige and all were avowedly dedicated to "the betterment of the community" (9). The plaques' visibility and purpose were reinforced when they served as focus points for ceremonies in remembrance of the fourteen women murdered.[3]

In several ways, the Women's Grove Memorial reads like an extension and expansion of Lin Gibson's installation. Like her, the December 6th committee worked to locate a memorial in a prominently public place, to make a strong political point by bringing women's vision to traditionally male forms of power, but also to go further in providing sustenance on a more permanent basis and to be as culturally inclusive as possible. Setting their sights on the Manitoba legislature, they won the support of the late Gerrie Hammond, then minister responsible for the status of women, and the Manitoba Women's Advisory Council, eventually winning permission from the provincial government for the establishment of a memorial garden on the grounds of the Legislative Building. In 1992, Myra Laramee, a First Nations educator (and now Elder) blessed the site for the garden. After an additional three years of fundraising, on September 24, 1995, the garden was dedicated.[4]

The garden is close enough to the legislature, on the northeast corner of its grounds, that the seat of provincial power is constantly in view, a link that was emphasized at the dedication by the presence of Rosemary Vodrey, Minister Responsible for the Status of Women, who accepted the garden "on behalf of the people of Manitoba." Eight meters (26 feet) in diameter, the memorial is made of limestone and paving stone laid out in the shape of a four-spoke wheel. There is a light in the centre and a low limestone wall around parts of it.[5] Each quadrant is planted with a different mixture of flowers and plants, designed to bloom continuously, with blue and green Colorado spruce providing a partial shelter on the perimeter. In attendance at the ceremony was Keith Louise Fulton, one of the driving forces behind the garden's creation. She explained how landscape architect Cynthia Cohlmeyer, working in consultation with the December 6th committee, designed the garden to signal and enable "a community of power, respect and entitlement for women":

> That respect is written into this Memorial Grove in the public symbols of a garden welling up from our earth, raised like a burial mound, encircled by the limestone of Manitoba's deep sea past. The circle is open, for the garden is not a fortress. Its paths lead from the four directions to a sacred space where all may enter. Our determination is solid as a rock, our goal engraved in stone, our presence a claim on the highest goals of democratic government and public purpose. The flowers are prairie perennials whose life span includes many winters; time in the sun must nourish them for time under snow. From their roots in the earth, they return again in the spring. And so it is for us. Those who stand here today, those who visit, can do the work to end violence against women in places that we come from. But, we don't have forever, so we had better get to work. (Fulton 1999, 319)

In that description, we can hear the influence of Aboriginal forms on the site's construction and the desire to make the space appropriate and welcoming to women from different cultures and social situations. The inscription reinforces that embrace of difference. Two identical stone posts low to the ground, joined by the curve of the limestone wall, mirror the other through the inscribed wording in French, Cree and English — each inscription similar but not identical:

LE JARDIN DES FEMMES

UN ENGAGEMENT VIVANT

 PC PᵔPƆᑕᒥ Δᵔᑊ·ᐊ·ᕁ

WOMEN'S GROVE

A

LIVING COMMITMENT

HONOURING THE

LIVES OF

MANITOBA WOMEN

DECEMBER 6, 1989

LE JARDIN DES FEMMES

UN ENGAGEMENT VIVANT

PC PᵔPƆᑕᒥ Δᵔᑊ ᐊ·ᕁ

WOMEN'S GROVE

A

LIVING COMMITMENT

TO END VIOLENCE

AGAINST WOMEN

DECEMBER 6, 1989

This wording resulted from lengthy deliberations by the group, as they struggled to create a permanent statement that would be both inclusive and activist, injecting a broad consciousness of violence against women into the priorities of the legislative policymakers close by. They decided not to commemorate specific names of women murdered because "where would the list begin and end?" (Fulton 1999, 319). Moreover, they wanted to support "the work of creating equality and justice for *all* women," to insist that eliminating violence against women involves changing the social climate so that "*all* women are honoured as full and equal members of society" (318, 321). In this spirit, at the garden's first dedication and in its subsequent use, the date on the inscription signalling the murders of the fourteen women in Montreal is joined with the citation of Manitoba women murdered — fifty-nine killed by male violence between December 1989 and September 1995.

The memorial's linkage of local femicide with violence elsewhere set the pattern for how December 6 is observed within and beyond the legislative assembly, supporting a political analysis of systemic violence against women.[6] In the 1999 observance, for example, the connection was front and centre:

> The Manitoba Women's Advisory Council, who organize the December 6 candlelight vigil at the Women's Grove Memorial on the Legislative Grounds, commemorate the Manitoba women who have been murdered by their partners during the year as well as the 14 women killed in Montreal.
>
> The council calls the Montreal massacre a political crime in that it was a crime of sexism and that it highlighted, and continues to highlight, the fact that threats of violence, or recourse to violence can be the result of any woman who "dares" to step beyond traditional female roles. "The Montreal massacre was the event that has heightened our awareness of the vulnerability of women to violence. And it's not just an isolated act of a madman but a reflection of what's happening (to women everywhere)," says Sue Barnsley, executive director of the council. (Ramsey 1999)

HELEN BETTY OSBORNE MEMORIAL, NEAR THE PAS

The name that was spoken repeatedly on June 21, 2001, in the Women's Grove Memorial and that had been reverberating in the Manitoba legislature off and on (depending on the priorities of the party in power) for thirty years, was Helen Betty Osborne. On November 13, 1971, Helen Betty Osborne, a nineteen-year-old Cree woman from Norway House First Nation, was abducted from the streets of The Pas by four white men. She was driven out to Clearwater Lake, repeatedly assaulted, stabbed over fifty times with a screwdriver and left dead, naked except for her boots, in the bush. For sixteen years, the RCMP failed to apprehend her killers, who were protected by townspeople of The Pas. In 1983, Constable Robert Urbanoski vigorously reopened the case and succeeded in identifying the four men involved in the killing: Dwayne Archie Johnston, James Robert Paul Houghton, Lee Scott Colgan and Norman Bernard Manger. In December 1987, Johnston was convicted and sentenced to life imprisonment, Houghton was acquitted, and Colgan, having received immunity from prosecution in return for testifying against Houghton and Johnston, went free.[7] Manger was never charged.

The handling of Helen Betty Osborne's murder provoked calls for a judicial inquiry. Three months later, those calls redoubled when J.J. Harper,

executive director of the Island Lake Tribal Council, was shot and killed by a City of Winnipeg police officer whose innocence the department rushed to declare the following day, conspicuously flouting the requirement for a full-fledged investigation. Under pressure to explore how the justice system treats Aboriginal people, the Manitoba government launched the Aboriginal Justice Inquiry which, three years later in 1991, produced a wide-ranging report on policing, legal counsel, court processes, jails and post-sentencing treatment of Aboriginal people, on the killings of Helen Betty Osborne and J.J. Harper, and on how "the relationship between Aboriginal people and the rest of society must be transformed fundamentally … based on justice in its broadest sense" (Aboriginal Justice Inquiry 1991).[8] The report officially acknowledged that the response of the police and the courts to the murder of Helen Betty Osborne was marked by "racism, sexism and indifference."

During the preparation of this report and its subsequent languishing, other efforts at bringing attention to the case of Helen Betty Osborne were underway. In 1989, Winnipeg reporter Lisa Priest published *Conspiracy of Silence*, a book which told the story of the murder and charged the townspeople of The Pas with engaging in a cover-up of the murderers' identity until Bob Urbanoski forced the issue. The CBC adapted the book as a two-part miniseries of the same title in 1992; it won seven Gemini Awards and has been widely viewed in Canada and the United States.[9] Also coming into public office during this period was Eric Robinson, an NDP Cree politician who was highly instrumental in spurring the government into action in the Helen Betty Osborne case.[10] In late November 1999, with a newly elected NDP government in power, the Aboriginal Justice Implementation Commission was finally created to develop an action plan based on the original recommendations from 1991. The commission produced its report in June 2001. In 2003, however, a petition to the government of Canada still charged that "little, if anything has been done to implement the recommendations of the inquiry."[11]

While the government dragged its heels, Robinson continued to work closely with the Osborne family, pressing for justice in the specific case of Helen Betty Osborne's killers and for wider changes in social and judiciary attitudes to Aboriginal people. One result of these efforts came on July 14, 2000. Justice Minister Gord Mackintosh, on behalf of the Manitoba government, formally apologized to Helen Betty Osborne's family, represented by her sister Cecilia, in front of a crowded legislature and a throng of Winnipeg media. The press quoted Mackintosh: "On behalf of the government of Manitoba, I wish to express my profound regret at the way the justice system as a whole responded to the death of Betty, and to apologize for the clear lack of justice in her case" (Taillon 2000). "A tearful Cecilia Osborne trembled and held the hand of Manitoba's justice minister as she thanked his government for apologizing for the way officials handled the 1971 murder of her sister Helen Betty Osborne. 'Well, for me I guess it's sort of letting go,' Osborne said in a quiet voice in Winnipeg" ("Manitoba Sorry" 2000).

Another link between Osborne's memory and social change — and again a development centrally driven by Eric Robinson and members of the Osborne family — came in the provincial *Helen Betty Osborne Memorial Fund Act* of December 15, 2000, which initiated the Helen Betty Osborne Memorial Foundation. "The life of Helen Betty Osborne will be recognized," declared Mackintosh (Le Moal 2000). In describing its aim, the newly formed Foundation echoed that intention: "The Act acknowledges Helen Betty Osborne's goal of becoming a teacher before her untimely death in 1971. The events that followed resulted in concerns about the relationships of the justice system and Aboriginal people. The report of the Aboriginal Justice Inquiry concluded these events were marked by racism, sexism and indifference" ("Helen Betty Osborne Memorial Foundation" 2002-2003). The provincial government committed $50,000 to help establish the fund, which would grant bursary awards to "all aboriginal residents of Manitoba — First Nation, Métis and Inuit — enrolled in post-secondary studies" and who wished to apply.

The scene in the Women's Grove Memorial, which opened this chapter, represents the culmination of these efforts. The group that gathered in the garden to announce the first two scholarship winners represented an astonishing cross-cultural coming together around the memory of Helen Betty Osborne. It included representation from her family, the First Nations community, white and Aboriginal MLAs, a white university professor and the chair of the Foundation, Sgt. Bob Urbanoski, the police officer who had forced the murder investigation nearly twenty years earlier. Sara Goulet, 2002 scholarship recipient, subsequently wrote to the trustees in words that demonstrate how Helen Betty Osborne's memory continues to inspire the Foundation's work:

> I feel privileged to receive this award, which honors the memory of the late Helen Betty Osborne. She suffered unfairly in her life. Although this injustice can never be corrected, her memory can serve as a reminder of the needless pain and suffering that many of our people face each day. Her memory will serve as a reminder to me to "walk the good road" and serve the people of my community with the love and respect that Helen Betty Osborne deserved to receive. (Goulet 2002)

Such institutional efforts to produce better conditions for Aboriginal people in the name of Helen Betty Osborne persist. In 2002, for example, construction began on a new K-12 School in Norway House bearing Helen Betty Osborne's name.

Far from the formal language and stiff rituals of the legislature, but during the same period of attempted reparation, Aboriginal students at the Ma Ma Wechetotan Centre of Keewatin Community College in The Pas were working to reclaim the memory of Helen Betty Osborne in their own memorial terms. Early in 2000, a group of them travelled to Norway House to ask Mrs. Justine Osborne for permission to undertake a memorializing project and, in the subsequent months, they sustained close consultation with the family in developing plans for a monument and the celebrations that would accompany its unveiling (Keewatin Community 2000). Through a number of fundraising events, students gathered $9,000 for a memorial made of a bronze circular plaque within a stone wheel, mounted on a base about 1 metre (3 feet) high, to be installed in the middle of Guy Hill Park, 25 kilometres northwest of The Pas/Opaskwayak Cree Nation. Two days after the provincial government's public apology, with about eighty people in attendance, "the family and friends of the late Helen Betty Osborne joined in with the rest of The Pas and Opaskwayak in A Celebration of Life, honouring her birthday with the unveiling of a memorial plaque." Master of ceremonies was Aboriginal and Northern Affairs Minister Eric Robinson, "the only political leader allowed to speak on behalf of the Osborne family" (Cooper 2000). The plaque carries an impression of Helen Betty Osborne as a smiling young woman and, next to this image, a dedication shaped to follow the curve of the circle:

HELEN BETTY OSBORNE

JULY 16, 1952 – NOVEMBER 13, 1971

THIS PLAQUE IS IN MEMORY OF
HELEN BETTY OSBORNE WHO DIED AT THE
YOUNG AGE OF 19. BETTY ATTENDED SCHOOL
HERE AT THE GUY HILL RESIDENTIAL SCHOOL
IN 1969, PRIOR TO ATTENDING MARGARET BARBOUR
COLLEGIATE, THE PAS, MANITOBA.

BETTY LIVED LIFE FULLY AND WAS THE EMBODIMENT
OF LOVE AND GENEROUS SPIRIT.
SHE DREAMED OF BECOMING
A TEACHER TO SERVE HER COMMUNITY
OF NORWAY HOUSE, MANITOBA.

WE PRAY THAT HER LIFE SERVES AS AN EXAMPLE
FOR PEOPLE AND COMMUNITIES TO LIVE AND
WORK TOGETHER IN TRUE FRIENDSHIP, PEACE
AND HARMONY.

PLACED BY THE STUDENTS OF
THE MA MA WECHETOTAN CENTRE OF

KEEWATIN COMMUNITY COLLEGE,
THE PAS, MANITOBA, WITH GENEROUS SUPPORT
OF THE PEOPLE IN THIS COMMUNITY AND
SURROUNDING NORTHERN COMMUNITIES.

DEDICATED JULY 16, 2000

After the unveiling, the crowd travelled to the college for a traditional Feast of Life, performances and a give away of gifts.[12]

With these events the First Nations community reclaimed Helen Betty Osborne in their own terms. The image on the plaque and the traditional forms of address and performance literally re-embody her memory. While the memorial-makers welcomed non-Aboriginal co-operation and participation and while they wrote the dedication in English, in both the memorial's inscription and the events surrounding its unveiling, cultural power remained firmly located within Aboriginal forms of identity and expression. Much of the significance of this memorial event cannot be grasped by non-Aboriginal commentators such as ourselves,[13] but some of its impact can be measured against long-standing derogatory images of First Nations women. Emma LaRocque, a Métis professor of Native Studies at the University of Manitoba, wrote to the Aboriginal Justice Inquiry on this matter:

> The portrayal of the squaw is one of the most degraded, most despised and most dehumanized anywhere in the world. The "squaw" is the female counterpart to the Indian male "savage" and as such she has no human face; she is lustful, immoral, unfeeling and dirty. Such grotesque dehumanization has rendered all Native women and girls vulnerable to gross physical,psychological and sexual violence ... I believe that there is a direct relationship between these horrible racist/sexist stereotypes and violence against Native women and girls. I believe, for example, that Helen Betty Osborne was murdered in [1971] by four young men from The Pas because these youths grew up with twisted notions of "Indian girls" as "squaws" ... Osborne's attempts to fight off these men's sexual advances challenged their racist expectations that an "Indian squaw" should show subservience ... [causing] the whites ... to go into a rage and proceed to brutalize the victim. (LaRocque 1990)

The commission also heard from the Canadian Coalition for Equality and the Manitoba Women's Directorate about the media's continued stereotyping of Aboriginal women. These groups compared lurid newspaper coverage of the Helen Betty Osborne murder in The Pas to more straightforward and sympathetic coverage of a young non-Aboriginal woman murdered in Winnipeg. In the context of those dominant images, the history of ugly race relations between The Pas and Opaskwayak Cree Nation on either side of the Saskatchewan River, and the particular facts of Helen Betty Osborne's murder and its aftermath, it is remarkable that the First Nations people who participated in the memorializing — the students, the family, the performers, all who attended — chose to move forward in the name of love, respect and community.

The site of the stone and its identification on the plaque create another layer to this highly nuanced memorial work, and again one that can be only partially appreciated by non-Aboriginal researchers. Guy Hill Park is the site of the former Guy Hill Residential School, one in the vast system of boarding schools owned by the federal government and operated by the Church — in the case of Guy Hill, Roman Catholic priests and nuns — between the 1870s and the 1970s.[14] These residential schools were specifically designed to assimilate Native children into the dominant culture, by tearing them away from their families, forcing them into a highly foreign system of regimentation, dress and appearance, and forbidding them their own language, their spiritual beliefs, their cultural practices and their emotional ties to family members even when they attended the same school. These institutions are now a byword for the colonization and abuse of First Nations people. Cree writer Tomson Highway and several of his siblings attended Guy Hill Residential School during the same years as Helen Betty Osborne. In his novel *The Kiss of the Fur Queen* (1998), Highway represents the experience as a hell of furtive rape and sexual assault — inflicted on children as young as six years old — joined with the more open physical, spiritual, cultural and emotional violations. The residential schools' eradication of embodied cultural memory worked, together with sexual violence against First Nations women and myths of cultural authenticity and racial purity, as a material agent of real and cultural genocide.[15]

In the same years as activists in Manitoba attempted to bring justice to the province's Aboriginal people, efforts were being made on a national scale to bring recognition and redress to residential school survivors. Eventually the federal government responded with, first, a Royal Commission on Aboriginal People, then a report recommending an annual allotment of at least $1.5 billion, next an action plan which acknowledged the federal government's culpability in the residential school system and apologized for its abuses. Finally, in 2001, then prime minister Jean Chrétien announced a new department entitled Indian Residential Schools Resolution Canada along with the allotment of $350 million as a healing fund for residential school survivors — a considerably smaller amount than that recommended by the Royal Commission.[16]

Throughout this process, as residential school survivors struggled to make the government accept responsibility and dedicate appropriate resources, Aboriginal spokespeople repeatedly emphasized the centrality of memory to their "healing journey." Phil Fontaine (1993), who attended the Fort Alexander Indian Residential School in Manitoba — and subsequently became Grand Chief of the Assembly of Manitoba Chiefs and National Chief of the Assembly of First Nations — has spoken publicly and at length about his experience of abuse. He addresses forced forgetting as a central mechanism of colonization. He recalls that as children in residential schools, "we were taught to forget who we were and to accept everything about the outside so we could emulate the non-Indian" (50). Remembrance becomes a central tool of cultural revival: "When you put something to rest it doesn't mean you forget about it. You remember it in different ways, in ways that give you strength ... We should never forget what was done to us. It must become a part of the public record" (55, 59). In another context, Laguna/Pueblo scholar Paula Gunn Allen (1986) writes of "re-membering" as the healing of individual and cultural *dis*memberment, and as the province of woman.[17] Residential school survivors lobbied hard for the resources to sustain their own healing circles and healing journeys. Dan Highway, for example, who attended Guy Hill Residential School for thirteen years, initiated a healing journey which has become the annual Guy Hill reunion and spoke in 1995 of plans "to create a permanent healing gathering centre on the site" (Lowery 1995, B2). He said, "We have proven people can heal from this experience" (Ferguson 1998).

Reconstructing this context, especially the emphasis on the healing journey, brings alive some of the resonances of the Helen Betty Osborne memorial for the non-Aboriginal visitor. At the unveiling, Eric Robinson reiterated the importance of memory-making to personal and cultural survival. He thanked the student memorial-makers for "their contributions in helping the Osborne family in their ongoing healing journey" and for breaking some of the silence — in the wording of the plaque — around residential school history: "What most people don't know is that before Helen Betty attended school in The Pas, she attended the Guy Hill Indian Residential School here in this field — but there is no evidence that the school ever existed" (Cooper 2000). This field and the brush at Clearwater Lake where Helen Betty Osborne was murdered had long served as the destination of pilgrimages, personal, familial and political, by First Nations people for whom returning to the site of injury and death holds particular spiritual meaning in the healing process. At Clearwater Lake, the family had erected a simple wooden cross carrying Helen Betty Osborne's name; others left their own private memorials.[18] The plaque brings permanent and public recognition to multiple memories and cultural histories, making some of them available across lines of racial difference for the first time.

James Young has argued that Holocaust counter-monuments "reanimate amnesiac sites" in Jewish history (1997, 869; 2000, 3). For those of us outside the First Nations community, the Helen Betty Osborne memorial similarly reanimates the site of a history that the dominant culture has preferred to forget.[19] It is intensely moving that the pain of destruction — the murder of a Cree woman and an abusive educational system forced upon Aboriginal people — should be countered by a memorial designed by Aboriginal students, both female and male. This seizing of cultural power is further inflected by the lobbying of one woman student, Odell Ballentyne, to change the name of Guy Hill Park to Helen Betty Osborne Park and to paint the plaque's foundation with the four sacred colours (Cooper 2000). Memory, Aboriginal women's agency and a strongly grounded vision of healing come together here in a literal transformation of the meaning of place.

***

When Champion Okimasis, protagonist of Tomson Highway's *The Kiss of the Fur Queen* (1998), moves to Winnipeg, deeply scarred from his years in residential school, he becomes haunted by figures who are and are not Helen Betty Osborne. His lonely wanderings through the city's nights are punctuated by the murders of Northern Cree women, reported in the *Tribune* as found naked and mutilated, one picked up by "four teenaged men with Brylcreamed hair" (106), another "skewered in the sex by fifty-six thrusts of a red-handled Phillips screwdriver" (216). Another figure, "the Madonna of

North Main," with the calf-length boots that were always noted in reports of the discovery of Helen Betty Osborne's body, fades in and out of his life, on the street, in bars, at the powwow (216). The silent figure is swelling and swelling with a pregnancy that never proceeds to birth — five months, ten months, twenty-seven months — the life slashing and stabbing inside her, as if she holds all the pain of Aboriginal existence in a world dominated by white patriarchy. In 1998, as the novel was being published, Tomson Highway spoke of his own reaction to the murders in Montreal:

> I remember hearing about the fourteen women who were killed in Montreal. December 6th, that's my birthday, I'll never be able to forget it. All my plays are about that in some way, the terrible way misogyny has split the world ... why are women treated like this? God is a man, Jesus was a man. Until we conceive of God as female, women will not have that power to be treated with respect ... In the Cree language, there's no gender. The world isn't divided into that kind of gendered hierarchy. But along the road in history, God as man met God as woman and raped her. And that's where that line comes from [in Highway's play *Dry Lips Oughta Move to Kapuskasing*], the one that so many people reacted so strongly against, that they couldn't stomach: "Because I hate them, them fucking bitches. They took the power the ones with the power." That's Big Joey's line.[20] He can't stand being impotent in the face of women, and he blames women. (Schmidt 1998)

Eerily enough, the character first spoke that line in full performance in 1989. Highway's images of agony and his systemic analysis of gendered violence powerfully render the conditions addressed by the memorials discussed in this chapter. From their different cultural positions, and in their different cultural accents, these memorials remember women murdered in order to end violence and make change, a healing process that their makers have had some success in persuading public policymakers to recognize and support.

Chapter 4

CHATHAM:
IN MEMORY OF THERESA VINCE —
STOP SEXUAL HARASSMENT

On June 2, 2001, a large and diverse group of mourners, friends, activists, fellow workers and immediate family members of Theresa Vince gathered in the pouring rain beneath the Centennial clock outside the large indoor mall in downtown Chatham, Ontario, where she had worked at the Sears outlet, and where she had been murdered by her male supervisor. As the crowd huddled beneath umbrellas to await the beginning of the fifth anniversary service commemorating her life and protesting the circumstances of her death, members of her family and of the local Women's Shelter and Sexual Assault Crisis Centre, who organized the service, welcomed supporters and handed out purple paper roses which we inscribed with messages and taped to the doors and windows of the mall. They also circulated, for use later in the ceremony, long-stemmed red roses and small bits of paper to which strings were attached and on which were written fragments of the story of Theresa Vince's life and death.

Once the group had assembled, we moved in silent procession around the periphery of the mall to gather around a small table/altar outside an anonymous window on Fifth Street at the side of the Sears department store — the window of the office, now renovated to serve as a storeroom, unmarked and unrecognizable, where she was killed. Midway through the service, the curtains were anonymously drawn from inside the store, closing off even symbolic access to the site of the murder, after Sears Canada, for a fifth straight year, had refused the family members' request to bless the place where the woman who had been their spouse, mother and grandmother, had been murdered.

Facilitated by Vince's daughter Catherine Kedziora, the service that ensued included testimonials, stories, angry critiques of Sears, and critiques of a more general corporate neglect of sexual harassment. The remarkably participatory, inclusive but nevertheless women-centred event also featured tributes from women friends and family (including Theresa Vince's other daughters and granddaughters), as well as participatory songs, hymns, the lighting of candles, "affirmations of hope and love" pronounced to the almost liturgical refrain of "we will re-member" (program), and a ritual laying of roses by everyone in attendance.

A narrative of Theresa Vince's life and death was also read out, during which we were invited, while our inscriptions were read as part of the narrative, to tie the fragments of text that had been circulated earlier to a cluster of purple helium balloons, each participant taking responsibility for a fragment of her memory. When the narrative came to its close, one of her granddaughters released the balloons, and we watched in rapt silence as they rose high over the heads of the crowd through wind and rain towards the heavens, finally disappearing to the north.

THIS CHAPTER TELLS THE STORY OF ONE WOMAN'S MEMORIALIZING AS A MODEL of effective activism. Theresa Vince's community remembers her murder in ways that join reflection and action, family and community, privacy and performance. Key to this integration of personal grief and political protest is the maintenance of multiple, mutually supportive memorials. In addition to private space dedicated to the memory of Theresa Vince at the Chatham-Kent Sexual Assault Centre and the Chatham-Kent Women's Shelter,[1] there are two public memorials to her in Chatham. The first is the dynamic service, described above, performed annually at her workplace where she was murdered. The second is a reflective rose garden at a church some distance away. The former maintains the ongoing struggle of the Vince family to keep her memory alive, together with the continuing struggle of the family in collaboration with the local women's community against sexual harassment and gendered violence in the workplace. The latter provides the consolations of nature and faith to a family and community in pain.

Chatham is a small, rural Ontario city (population 43,000)[2] where Theresa Vince grew up, where she lived with her husband Jim, four daughters and one son, and where she had worked for twenty-five years at the local outlet of Sears Canada. For the last several years of her employment, working in the personnel department, she had been the victim of persistent sexual harassment by her supervisor, Russell Davis, and of uncomfortable teasing about it by her fellow employees. Having been unable to obtain relief from this situation from the management at Sears, she decided to take early retirement at the age of fifty-six. She was desperate to escape harassment that had left her unable to eat or sleep; in the words of her daughter Jacquie Carr, "all she could do was curl up into her self protective ball and wish for her hell to be over" (Carr et al. 2004, 4). Two weeks before that retirement was to take effect, on June 2, 1996, the last Sunday she was to have worked, Davis detained her after work, shot and killed her, and then turned the gun on himself.

In the weeks following Theresa Vince's murder, and in the face of considerable community resistance, the Chatham-Kent Sexual Assault Crisis Centre, the Chatham-Kent Women's Centre and the Chatham District Labour Council, in solidarity with the Vince family, formed a coalition to lobby for an inquest. According to Michelle Schryer (2000) of the Sexual Assault Centre, "people felt badly for the family," but many in the community opposed the inquest, noting that "Sears is a major downtown business anchor ... We were accused of hurting the entire community, and destroying the downtown core." Opposition to the inquest took several forms. A rumour was circulated that Theresa Vince may have had an affair with her murderer that had gone wrong; the women's organizations involved in the coalition were denounced ("the crisis centre was accused of using Theresa's death to exploit her family and to meet our own agenda"); and the organizers of the coalition came under personal attack. Nevertheless, "at the end of the day we were completely vindicated" by the findings of the inquest in December 1997, which showed that Sears had not acted to investigate Theresa Vince's complaint (lodged sixteen months prior to her death) and had not followed its own sexual harassment policy (Verdict 1997; McCrindle 2000). At the request of the coalition, the inquest jury asked that the first week in June be declared Sexual Harassment Awareness Week in Chatham-Kent (Verdict 1997).[3]

At the first anniversary of Theresa Vince's murder, Chatham's Sexual Assault Crisis Centre decided to create a reflective garden in her memory, and on June 2, 1998, the second anniversary of her death, the Theresa Vince Memorial Rose Garden was dedicated. There was controversy here, too, over the wisdom of remembering an event that many in the community wished to deny or forget, and in part over the location of the garden. Several settings were suggested, but it was felt by the organizers that the women's shelter would be overly exclusive, while a public park would be lacking in personal resonance.

The memorial was finally installed in the gardens behind St. Ursula's Catholic Church, several kilometers to the northeast of the city's centre, where Theresa and Jim Vince were parishioners. The garden is planted with six roses (one for each of her children and one for her husband) and ten forget-me-nots (one for each of her grandchildren) in a 1-square-metre (10-foot-square) plot set in the middle of a lush green lawn between the church and a neighbouring school. It features a rectangular plaque mounted on a stone monument with a simple dedication:

THERESA VINCE

MEMORIAL ROSE GARDEN

1998

Since the dedication of the park, the family and the women from the shelter and assault centre have brought new "gifts" annually to the site. A small boulder was added in 1999, and in 2000 a bench of wrought-iron and varnished wood with another simple dedicatory plaque: "In Memory of Theresa Vince." The plaques tell the visitor nothing of her story, nor even acknowledge that she was murdered, but the garden nevertheless remains controversial for some in the community, who feel that it serves only to keep the pain of her passing alive and to inhibit healing. But for the family the garden site remains central. Jacquie Carr (2001) says:

> It is important to me to have a living memory that requires continuous care and attention — it is a concrete way of cultivating a new positive energy to replace the destructive energy that took Mom's life ... It's a conscious decision to create a living space that promotes beauty, healing and hope. She laid down her life in a cold business office without any of her loved ones near her. I've always felt Mom and the family were robbed of being able to honour the place where her body lay. We were never permitted near it, there

were no flowers, no prayers in that space. It was remodelled, rearranged and covered over. For me it's left a void.

The garden is maintained by Jim Vince as a labour of love and *active* remembrance, a simple distinction from otherwise similar memorial gardens — such as the December 6th rose garden at Conestoga College in Kitchener, Ontario — which are less local and immediate in their reference and which are anonymously maintained by institutional or municipal grounds crews. Jim Vince, moreover, in a gesture of inclusivity different from those of symbolic monuments to "all women" which threaten to erase significant differences in material circumstance, has left space in the garden for additional flowers to be planted in memory of other murdered local women.

In contrast to the memorial garden, whose function is primarily private and reflective, the annual service held in Theresa Vince's memory is both public in presentation and activist in intent. The occasion which the authors of this book attended was exemplary in many ways, enabled as it was by a strong women's community and a loving and supportive family with the dedication, social position and resources to continue to fight against societal indifference and neglect. It was actively engaged, public and performative in ways that were quite different from the physical and reflective detachment and safety of the rose garden that complements it on the other side of town, to which participants retreated after the service. The service differed from most December 6th rituals in the immediacy with which it evoked the memory of a local woman, and from most tributes to victims of femicide in the close and apparently uncomplicated co-operation it modelled among feminists, family members and the larger community.

The ceremonies paid tribute to Theresa Vince, honoured the site of her death as a sacred space through ritual procession as rite of passage and provoked a rare conjunction of calls for both grief and outrage, remembrance and action against gendered violence. Within a largely conservative community, family, feminists, social activists, friends, co-workers and others were brought together in what, for a memorial vigil, was a notably aggressive occupation of public space and private property, as when our messages on purple roses were taped to the glass doors of the mall. That this was felt to be an invasion is indicated by the fact that the messages had been removed from the doors before they could be recovered as memorials at the end of the afternoon, and by the fact of Sears closing its curtains during the ceremony to shut their employees and customers off from the events outside. The occasion, moreover, cut across stereotypical communities of difference, as burly men in workclothes shed tears and sported buttons featuring purple ribbons that linked memory with change — In Memory of Theresa Vince—Stop Sexual Harassment — while standing shoulder to shoulder with feminist activists and family members who embraced publicly in heartfelt mutual support.

In the wake of the inquest, the family and feminist community sustained the political pressure by keeping Theresa Vince's memory alive and grief over her death active and performative. The local press reported that "others found the courage to come forward with complaints [about sexual harassment] and change their situations" (McCrindle 2000, 3).[4] Moreover, "letter writing campaigns are launched here," remarked Michelle Schryer at the memorial service. On May 1, 1997, another rally against sexual violence and workplace harassment was organized in memory of Theresa Vince. Marchers carried a long purple ribbon to the office of the Member of Provincial Parliament (at that time, Jack Carroll), wrapped it around the building and tied it in a bow at the front door (Schryer 2005).

A talk given at the fourth anniversary memorial service in 2000 by Pat Hoy, subsequent MPP for Chatham-Kent-Essex, included a commitment to the introduction of a parliamentary bill to include sexual harassment under the province's Occupational Health and Safety Act. The bill was drafted in consultation with feminist lawyer Geri Sanson and with the Vince family, the Chatham-Kent Sexual Assault Crisis Centre and the Chatham-Kent Women's Centre. It was introduced to the House on June 7, 2001, for first reading in the fall legislature and again in 2003 (Hoy 2001; Barlow 2005). Then, in October 2004, a hefty report on workplace violence and harassment was released at Queen's Park, culminating in eleven pages of recommendations for everyone touched by workplace harassment: from women who are harassed to their co-workers, managers and union representatives, to police, the Ministry of Labour and human rights commissions. The four authors, who include Jacquie Carr, "dedicate this report to Theresa Vince whose death in 1996 changed the views of many people in Ontario about sexual and workplace harassment," and they open with a painful account detailing her experience (Carr et al. 2004, 3).

The memorials to Theresa Vince are unusual among those that we have researched. The existence of two memorials — one a performed and performative pilgrimage to the site of her death, the other a private contemplative space — perhaps enables a combination of activist effort with therapeutic healing that is more conflicted in memorials that try to combine individual grief and reconciliation with social engagement and productive rage. The space provided by the rose garden for retreat and comfort after the more activist event can even be understood as making the latter possible. Perhaps, too, because Theresa Vince's death was the result of workplace harassment rather than intimate femicide in a domestic setting, efforts to pay tribute to her memory have produced an unusual degree of solidarity. Surviving family members, feminists, front-line workers in the fight against violence against women and members of the larger community all face violence and harassment in the workplace as a common, systemic enemy. Perhaps these two circumstances have produced an unusual degree of convergence between the often discrete imperatives of memorializing and working for change that are linked together quite naturally in the slogan In Memory of Theresa Vince — Stop Sexual Harassment.

The productive interplay between memory and action continues in Chatham. As of 2005, plans are afoot to make the Theresa Vince garden more explicitly aligned with activism. It will be moved to a site currently in the making, the Chatham-Kent Peace Garden Park, to sit alongside a December 6th Monument of Remembrance and Hope, among other memorials. From legislative debate to public policy recommendations to community protest, it is noteworthy that, of all the memorial sites and events of which we are aware, those dedicated to Theresa Vince have issued most directly in political action aimed at ending violence against women.

Chapter 5

LONDON:
THE WAR AGAINST WOMEN

*Grief for you has rebellion at its heart, it cannot
simply mourn.* — ADRIENNE RICH[1]

VICTORIA PARK IS THE CLOSEST THING LONDON HAS TO AN OFFICIAL
repository for public memory. A vast, leafy expanse, it is situated downtown, in the heart of the unofficial capital of southwestern Ontario, with its
entrenched reputation for social, political and cultural conservatism. What
the park remembers is war. From the entrance at the southeast corner, dominated by the light sandstone Whitehall Cenotaph to the central towering
Boer War monument to the Holy Roller tank on the north side, the site
is one of unremittingly masculinist images of battle, conquest and domi-
nation. This is the company that the London Women's Monument chose
to keep, its creators determined to insert remembrance of violence against
women into the busiest, most visible location in the city. The monument's
detractors were equally determined that such a memorial would not find
a home among the august symbols of national glory. When the Women's
Monument was unveiled on December 6, 1994, at a public ceremony in
Victoria Park, it was a triumph of political know-how, teamwork and commitment.

The city has three other memorials to murdered women, all located
on the edge of town, on the main campus of the venerable University of

Western Ontario and at its Catholic affiliate, Brescia University College. None of these memorials involved the political process demanded by the Women's Monument, but they tell valuable stories. At Brescia, women also organized around the felt need for "something concrete" to memorialize women murdered. Within an institutional context that explicitly values women's spirituality, however, their process and product are much less troubled by traces of struggle. On the main campus, two memorials were produced within much more individualist models of action. Partly for that reason, we suggest, their visibility is declining, shrouded by the kinds of institutional norms and protocols sketched in chapter 2.

Among other things, the London stories tell us why women's community is crucial to the production and maintenance of resistant remembering. We have famous cases of women inserting their alternative visions into the masculinist mythologies of war: Maya Ying Lin's Vietnam Veterans Memorial in Washington DC; the Greenham Common women camped next to the missile base in England; and Lori Clermont's Monument to Marlene Moore closer to home, in Halifax (discussed in chapter 7). What the women in London achieved is an intervention of the same order. In the words of one organizer, "Nothing is more important than a lasting visible symbol to remember." And nothing is more telling than the myriad ways in which that lasting visibility can be threatened.

The London Women's Monument, Victoria Park

It was a seasoned group of feminist activists who got together to plan the London Women's Monument. Under the auspices of the Women's Education and Research Foundation, Margaret Buist and Lorraine Greaves gathered around them a core group of sophisticated organizers with networking and lobbying experience, among whom were feminist lawyers, grassroots activists and a university administrator.[2] One thing they knew from experience was the need to move fast, before controversy could gather. They had been through enough battles lost and won to know that the more public attention the project attracted, the greater would be the public opposition. Especially for feminist projects, inviting broad public consultation often amounts to inviting backlash. Their advice to organizers of similar initiatives was to quietly bring together the movers and shakers who shared a feminist vision and make it happen before objections could be orchestrated — "do it quick and

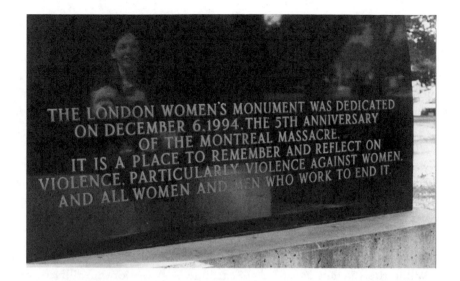

dirty," in their ironic summary. They worked quickly — very quickly — to plan and raise funds for the monument. It took them only six months from their first planning meeting to the day of the dedication.[3]

Their process involved planning, fundraising, a design competition, negotiating official sanction with the City of London and the installation of the monument. The first few stages were hard work, but the process went relatively smoothly. It was the final stage — acquiring official sanction from the municipal government — that posed the most difficulty, because of political roadblocks placed in their way. Organizers had to call on their supporters to lobby city council, hard. And it worked, as some of the organizers recall: "The faxes, remember we just jammed the fax lines, we jammed the phone lines"; "We had several councillors tell us that they had never been lobbied so hard on anything in their entire career"; "People told us they had never seen such a strong lobbying before in the city, we got everybody we knew." The messages of support poured in for the monument and, in particular, for its installation in the city's downtown Victoria Park.

Before approving the installation of the monument, the city debated issues concerning its location, inscription, artistic merit and the degree to which it was representative of the people of London. The proposal ran the gauntlet of multiple municipal bodies — the Arts Advisory Committee, Community and Protection Services, the Public Utilities Commission, as well as city council — each of which challenged some aspect of the project. The debate about the location of the monument was heavily influenced by local war veterans, who believed that Victoria Park should continue to be reserved for war memorials. In response, local women made the point that a monument acknowledging the war against women fitted completely with the park's focus. In a reader call-in to the *London Free Press* in November 1994, Patricia Maurice asserted that

> Victoria Park is an appropriate place for a memorial to violence against women. Some have stated that Victoria Park is a war memorial and shouldn't have a memorial for violence against women. Violence against women is a war, it's a declared war against women and the 14 women who were killed in Montreal were killed because they are women. It would be a memorial to them all and to all women who have died at the hands of men. Our society is in denial about this epidemic. (Coad 1994, B1)

While the veterans advanced the strongest opposition, hostility to the monument came from additional, often unexpected sources. Some argued against the installation at Victoria Park on the grounds that "the park is for everyone," implicitly suggesting that war is the provenance of the community and the field of male valour while violence against women is shameful, should be kept hidden or is the concern of "special interest groups." Even a group of local women who wanted to turn Victoria Park into a Victorian garden did not want the women's monument to disturb their peaceful, perhaps nostalgic, vision of nineteenth-century contemplative space. It is indicative of the overwhelming preserve of the military armoury already mounted in the park that the same women failed to register any concern about the armoured tank or cannons.

Victoria Park was crucial to the organizers' vision, however, partly because it was the established location for December 6th vigils and Take Back the Night marches, together with International Women's Day and Gay/Lesbian Pride celebrations. The park is also a central location where people working in the downtown core eat their lunches, and where community festivals are held. The organizers wanted there to be a visible symbol to commemorate the women massacred in Montreal, and they wanted to raise broad public awareness of violence against women in the most prominent location possible. After the torrent of lobbying and strategizing, site approval finally "squeaked through city council by only one vote" (Money 1995, 10). Still, the organizers had a lingering unease, because they had been told that the monument would very likely be dug up and moved at some future point. Now, years later, they gain considerable satisfaction from having won this battle, too. When installing the monument, they made an on-the-spot-decision to dig a huge pit to ground it permanently, asserting, like their colleagues working on the Vancouver women's monument, that this, "goddammit," would not be moved: "We purposely sank a seven-foot concrete base, it cost a lot of money, very, very expensive; we jacked that bugger right in there." They gave the monument the most substantial anchor they could and have since rested assured that it would be extremely difficult for anyone to quietly dig up and displace this memorial so deeply grounded in the earth and the women's community of London.

That community solidified and celebrated itself at the monument's unveiling, still remembered as "a very, very moving ceremony" and "a real victory." Intimations of struggle remained in the heavy police presence spurred by a death threat. But women seized the space, converting it into "public theatre," wheeling the monument in on a decorated flatbed truck, with music, a ringing bell, speakers, women from many different groups each putting a rose in a vase in the centre of the monument. And there were the small, palpable gestures of mutual support — like those which occur every day when women help one another in the face of overwhelming and oppressive structures of dominance — such as when the young designer of the monument, too nervous and afraid to speak, was supported and given voice by one of the organizers, Louise Karch. Later that evening, their victory was celebrated in a party thrown to honour two of the primary organizers, Margaret Buist and Lorraine Greaves, who were presented with a painting of a labrys by a local artist.[4] Finally, after all the struggle, the London Women's Monument was in place: "Little pretty tiny little snow flakes falling ... that was such an evening. That was fun."

In terms of the monument's continuing presence, its physically and symbolically central location in Victoria Park — downtown, near city hall, sharing public green space with war monuments and military memorabilia — continues to be one of its most notable features. It seems to bask in perhaps unintended official sanction as a war memorial, the violence it memorializes (by implication if not intent) officially endorsed as "war against women." The organizers who fought for the existence of this monument clearly won a major battle within a conservative community by achieving permanent physical recognition of that war in prime civic space. In practice, nevertheless, there are lingering intimations that the hard-won approval of the monument by the civic authorities was grudging. The lack of *explicit* sanctioning by the city that is accorded other monuments in the park by way of plaques, the monument's unobtrusive occupation of what seems to be as little space as possible, and its placement in the northwest corner of the park — "it couldn't be near the tank, it couldn't be near the cenotaph," so it ended up near the garbage dumpsters and portable potties that are installed for public events — can be read as the continued societal marginalization of the concerns of half the population as "women's issues." In this context, the city's routine neglect of basic maintenance speaks volumes about the monument's civic status. One organizer spoke in utter frustration about the simple matter of burned-out light bulbs, installed to illuminate the site at night: "I have to tell you I have been phoning for six months trying to get the light bulbs replaced. I personally offered to pay for the light bulbs. I'm going to take a screw driver and go and do it myself." Shrouded nightly in darkness, the monument's effect is checked once more.

The monument was designed by Leigh Ann Ramsey, a fine arts student at London's University of Western Ontario. The design appealed to the

committee on aesthetic, feminist and localist grounds, as well as for economic reasons. The two perpendicular oval slabs of charcoal grey granite that constitute the monument, imported from a quarry in Quebec, face one another, their polished, inscribed sides angled inward in a way that is at once protective, inviting and exclusionary. From a distance, and particularly from the park's western periphery, the monument, presenting only its rough exterior, is inscrutable. Unlike the war memorials with which it shares the park, which stand erect in a kind of celebratory phallic splendour, visible from a distance and drawing the eye upward in apparent awe, this monument hugs the earth, and draws the eye downward in grief and contemplation.

In order to read its inscription or appreciate its design, a visitor is required to make the commitment to entering what feels very much like its private space within a public park. For women, the space is welcoming, private, secure; for men, entering the intimate oval sheltered by the granite stones can feel like a violation. That space nevertheless opens outward to the park's interior, offering an invitation to the interested viewer and an opportune focal position (complete with firm, concrete base) for speakers and organizers at the December 6th, Take Back the Night, and other events and demonstrations that are held at the site. Especially on December 6, in the ice-cold heart of winter, the stone pulls shivering participants into its orbit, hugging them into a human circle of warmth, which is both literally and symbolically protective.

But on less charged occasions, the casual visitor, drawn in to the enclosed space created by the mutually reflective slabs of the monument, discovers herself falling deeper into the experience of violence than she had anticipated. Reading the inscription situated on the bottom of the otherwise clear and polished left-hand slab, she finds herself reflected in the mirrored sea of diverse and intercultural young and old women's faces etched in the stone opposite, and therefore included in the most local of ways. The viewing female self is seen reflected as one among many potential and real victims of the violence that the monument memorializes. This design, like the location of the monument, had met with some opposition. A male member of the city's Arts Advisory Committee, the first hoop the organizers had to jump through in negotiating Victoria Park as a location, disparaged the design by describing it as resembling the two buns of a hamburger. In spite of such opposition, the organizers managed to convince the committee that the monument did, indeed, have artistic merit, and approval was eaked out. The inscription framed by this provocative design reads as follows:

THE LONDON WOMEN'S MONUMENT WAS

DEDICATED

ON DECEMBER 6, 1994, THE 5TH ANNIVERSARY

OF THE MONTREAL MASSACRE.

IT IS A PLACE TO REMEMBER AND REFLECT ON

VIOLENCE, PARTICULARLY

VIOLENCE AGAINST WOMEN,

AND ALL WOMEN AND MEN

WHO WORK TO END IT.

Although the images of women on the monument's northern slab are heterogeneous, suggesting a variety of ages, ethnic, racialized and cultural features and qualities, the inscription explicitly cites only the fourteen here unnamed women murdered in Montreal on December 6, 1989. In naming no local women or women across specific differences, and in moving from the symbolic Montreal massacre to the general (including the generality of the "women and men who work to end" the violence), the monument risks effacing the raced, classed, sexualized, local and daily character of abuse, rape and murder. It was a risk that the organizers knowingly took: "We wanted it to be generic." They also aimed to keep alive the specific naming of local women as participatory vocal utterances at the annual ceremonies, which invite both the formal speaker and members of the crowd to speak names known to them. And of course the wording used was to some extent a strategic compromise with institutional forces. One male councillor threatened to withdraw his support unless the monument acknowledged men, too, as victims of violence. The organizers were unwilling to make such a concession — as one later exclaimed, "We didn't want to put men in there, they have the tank to remember them!" But they did add an acknowledgment of (some) men as workers against violence to partially accommodate the objection; "it was a small price to pay, considering all the other victories we won."

What finally makes the monument's cultural work distinctively power-ful is the combination of the inscription and the design. Together, they negotiate the gap between the symbolic importance of December 6th and more generalized (or generalizable) violence, "particularly violence against women." Their combined impression moves from the specific, histori-cal event that was the Montreal Massacre through the mediation of the grounded and local reflected images of individual viewers to general re-flection. Sympathetically understood, the reflective conceit enacted in the monument's design and read against its inscription is extraordinarily effec-tive. It provokes reflection about the provenance and potentiality of gen-dered violence in contemporary Canadian society. It places all women as potential victims of male violence. It includes the female viewer reflected among the sea of diverse faces as potential victim. And it reflects — per-haps disturbingly to some city councillors — the male viewer as potential brother, father, partner or perpetrator, as inclusion slides into implication and attribution of responsibility

14 DANCING WOMEN, FEMMES DANSANTES, BRESCIA COLLEGE

On the same date as the Women's Monument dedication, a memorial sculp-ture was installed in the foyer of the main academic building of Brescia University College, situated on a hilltop on the edge of the city to the west of Western's main campus. Brescia has a different relationship to the com-munity than the feminist organizers of the London Women's Monument or the sheltered preserves of the main university campus. A women's college, it houses The Women's Circle Centre (known as "The Circle"), part of whose vision is to nurture community within the institution while negotiating a relationship between the college's particular mandate and society at large. In its goal of memorializing women murdered, this group has been remarkably successful.

The memorial sculpture — entitled 14 Dancing Women, Femmes Dansantes — was commissioned by The Circle's art committee and de-signed by Windsor artist Elaine M. Carr, a graduate of Western who has degrees in both fine arts and culture and spirituality.[5] According to Sister Patricia McLean, speaking at the dedication ceremony in 1994, the need for the sculpture emerged from the "Re-membering Ritual" held at noon each year on December 6th, which "both honoured the women slain and

allowed us to rededicate ourselves to finding ways to take positive steps towards eradicating violence against women." Participants in the vigils needed something concrete, "something they could see and touch and use" (McLean 2001). Pauline Maheux (2001), former acting director of The Circle, said it was important to have "something tangible to be around all year." The second impetus emerged from one of The Circle's yearly themes, "Creativity and Craft as an expression of the Sacred." At the dedication, Sister McLean pointed out that this "led us to the realization that art has the ability to transform at both a personal and public level. It was then we knew we wanted a piece of art to serve as a permanent symbol of Remembrance." In commissioning the sculpture, the committee followed The Circle's "over-arching principles":

> Explore the role of the sacred in women's lives. Create a space to accommodate this continued investigation. Work with ritual as a tool for transformation. Commit ourselves to taking action that helped inject the positive female energy into the world. Create links with other groups with similar motivations. (McLean 1994)

The sculpture was funded by individual donors in the community and by the Ursuline General Council (the religious order affiliated with the college) from Chatham. The organizers received overwhelming community support — some of it from unlikely and unwelcome sources such as Herman Goodin, the anti-feminist journalist at the *London Free Press* who objected to the downtown location of the London women's monument, and saw the more removed Brescia sculpture as preferable. They also met opposition in the form of a bomb scare before the inaugural ceremony, which prompted pressure from faculty to cancel the event. There are lingering fears of vandalism, but to date there has been none, and the sculpture continues to generate positive energy. As Carol Brooks, manager of Brescia College's Centre for Women and the Sacred, points out, "The walk by the sculpture is a walk to a sacred place and symbolizes the way people want to bring about change ... We're capitalizing on our sense of grief, but we're changing the energy from grief into action" (qtd. in Richer 1994, A3).

The artist herself was motivated by impulses similar to those of the committee. She had created an earlier version of the sculpture in the days immediately following the femicides at l'École Polytechnique because, as she says, "I was in shock." Since then, she has created a new sculpture to commemorate the event each year, sculptures which are now housed in private collections in the United States. In response to the commission from Brescia in 1994, Carr revisited her original design. "It is so important to have markers of where we are and where we come from. We see these statues of men on horses everywhere, and prime ministers in front of big government buildings. They mark everything we do" (Carr 2001). And, she said at that time, "I wanted to show them [the fourteen women] as young women who had a lot of life ... When it first happened my reaction was very raw and painful ... There has been more of a healing in the five years since the event. The pieces have changed. This one is about regenerating life" (Richer 1994, A3). In the commemoration ceremony pamphlet, Carr voices her commitment to giving form to community: "I want to give visual expression to our longing for justice, liberation and spiritual freedom."

14 Dancing Women, Femmes Dansantes rests atop a waist-high 450-kg (992-pound) block of white Windsor granite in a prominent location to the left of the main entrance to the building, which is attractively decorated with greenery. The organizers intend the location to encourage reflection and preserve the quiet dignity of grieving. The sculpture consists of a communal cup fashioned out of bronze, 46 cm (18 inches) in diameter and 30 cm (12 inches) high, resembling both a household bowl and a baptismal font. The cup is (intentionally) cracked, and a seedling sprouts through the fissure entwining itself around the figures of the fourteen women, who dance in the relief that forms the vessel's periphery, holding it aloft in celebration. Framed in glass on the wall behind the sculpture are the "Artist's Words of Description," which explain the association of sculptured form

with engineering and encourage viewers to transform the copper-bronze by touching it: "i believe it is important that a memorial piece be touched because the event involved all of us and touching involves a deeper interaction with the piece." Carr also reflects on her choice of a limestone base full of crystal shards, which she found in a quarry in Amherstburg, Ontario. The material echoes the college's own construction, and it reflects the dancers with a vivacity that granite, with its conventional funereal association, would not have provided. The stone's unusual shape, she writes, resembles "the shapes of the stone cairns in scotland where i was born. from earliest times stone has symbolized permanence and all that is unchanging. stone pillars have been used as sacred objects, markers of sacred places. cairns are often used to mark a memorial site or to honour a memory." All these associations and evocations embrace women's communal life. The sculpture of

"14 dancing women" ... has resisted all attempts to tame her. with the alluring power released when women dance together, she invites us to join her, to experience her, but to know that each time we meet, she will speak a new word to us. she enlivens us with the energy generated by such a communal experience, promising it will always be there when we join arms and stand together. she reminds us in her plurality, she is SACRED; in her communal life she is one life which simply is. And so, out of respect for her persistent refusal to be tamed and domesticated she is "14 dancing women," "14 femmes dansantes." she waits to converse with all who approach as she dances on her swollen stone. may she bless us with the word we need to hear in that moment. and in that moment may we touch the depth of union we share with all that is. (Carr n.d.)

Clearly, the convergence of purpose and intent among the community-building, spiritual, celebratory and memorializing goals of the sponsoring group with those of the artist issued at Brescia in a sculpture and an annual memorial service that are extraordinarily clear and uniformly focused. To this extent, at least, however non-controversial and devoid of overt radical activism, the sculpture and the rituals that attend it seem to have played a positive cultural role in solidifying a sense of community among women, promoting women's spirituality and modelling at once strength, permanence and individual and social transformation.

ENGINEERING SCIENCE BUILDING, UNIVERSITY OF WESTERN ONTARIO

The first of London's memorials to be installed, and one of the first December 6th memorials in the country, seized the least space or attention. The initiative of a single male faculty member in engineering at the University of Western Ontario, this memorial shows again — as at the University of Alberta and other engineering schools — how institutional context and professional protocols can muffle the politics of remembrance. Particular developments at Western demonstrate how the ultimate logic of that institutional dynamic erases the fact of murder or even of death. Potentially (however unintentionally), such effacement of femicide, combined with so many other occasions on which this reality is obscured, can enable the war on women.

The Montreal Memorial Garden is situated to the left of the front entrance to the Engineering Science Building on the main campus. It consists of a long, narrow, curvilinear garden, approximately 30 metres by 4 metres (98 feet by 13 feet), in which are planted fourteen flowering magnolia trees of four different varieties, which make a considerable display for the week in spring each year when they bloom. The garden was designed and planted in the spring of 1990 by Hugh Peacock (2001), then a member of the Department of Civil Engineering, who explains that "I wanted to bind some ties between Quebec and Ontario," and "I really wanted to have nobody ever forget."

At the front edge of the garden, at the centre, is a small boulder bearing a plaque (Ardyth Leitch, the secretary at the time to the dean of engineering, wrote the inscription for Peacock, who couldn't decide on appropriate wording):

> THESE 14 MAGNOLIA TREES HONOUR
> THE MEMORY OF THE 14 WOMEN
> SLAIN AT L'ECOLE POLYTECHNIQUE,
>
> MONTREAL, IN DECEMBER 1989.

In 1999, as part of the CEMF competition (discussed in chapter 2), students added a wide wooden bench to the left of the boulder with another plaque:

> THIS MEMORIAL BENCH IS DEDICATED
> TO THE MEMORY OF
> 14 WOMEN ENGINEERING STUDENTS
> SLAIN ON DECEMBER 6, 1989
> AT ECOLE POLYTECHNIQUE, MONTREAL

Following these words are the names of the women murdered in two columns and an acknowledgement of the donor: "Courtesy of the Canadian Engineering Memorial Foundation Dean's Millennium Award."

The cultural work performed by the memorial in raising awareness or producing social change cannot easily be seen as activist. Perhaps reflecting the urgency in the immediate wake of the murders, the initial inscription — the mixed, part-nationalist part-memorializing initiative of one male faculty member and the work of an administrative secretary — is oddly imprecise about the date of the murders. The boulder and bench inscriptions "honour" women "slain," but identify no agent, male or otherwise, and make no claim to any wider social resonance for the event. The bench, installed ten years after the events it remembers, gives the significance of the women's status as engineering students equal weight to their gender and again (like one memorial stone at the University of Alberta) forgets that one of the fourteen was a staff member. However, the plaque does (in accordance with CEMF competition guidelines) list the names of the women killed, and the memorial may well have made an impression on the local engineering faculty with, for example, the 1991 establishment of an annual memorial lecture series in science and engineering featuring prominent women speakers. Perhaps this installation goes as far as an individual initiative can, in an institution which long resisted women entering the engineering classroom and in which, according to Hugh Peacock, only six of the forty-five engineering faculty members agreed to wear symbolic white ribbons in the wake of the murders in Montreal.

More disturbing than the relatively conservative work done by the nevertheless prominent memorial at the front of the building is a young memorial tree around the corner to the east, at the roadside amidst a group of trees marking the passing of three engineering students. One male student died from cancer, one female died in a motorcycle accident. The third tree intends to remember Lynda Shaw, a University of Western Ontario engineering student who was murdered in the spring of 1990 when returning from her cottage to write an exam after the Easter weekend. After a search involving her fellow students, Shaw's body was found a week later, after the snow melted. In August 2005, fifteen years later, Allan Craig MacDonald was named her murderer. According to the chair of her department at the time, Dr. John Tarasuck, with whom Shaw was planning to work on a project the following year, "everybody was still in shock over Montreal and this just added to it." A memorial service was held by the university, which Tarasuck describes as "very full and touching and therapeutic," and students and faculty raised money to plant a tree and rose garden in her memory at a ceremony from which the press was barred. In a form familiar to this genre of memorializing — and, again, with an intention to protect private grief — the plaque identifies the tree's variety more prominently than Lynda Shaw. It does not provide the date of her birth or death, or the fact of her murder:

TULIP TREE

LIREODENDRON TULIPIFERA L

EASTERN NORTH AMERICA

PLANTED IN MEMORY OF

LYNDA DIANE SHAW

APRIL 23 1990

Such tributes are not without value. Indeed, they may well have a therapeutic effect on the profession and contribute to its gradual change. But they are a long way from the confrontation of violence against women enacted by the London Women's Monument and planted deep into the earth of Victoria Park, and a long way from the "rebellion" named by poet Adrienne Rich. The silences of the campus plaques fit too easily into an institutional logic that ultimately erases resistant remembering. Tarasuck reports that a man tried to chop down the Lynda Shaw tree for unknown reasons less than six months after it was planted. Recently, a university construction crew, unaware of the significance of the December 6th garden's magnolia trees, ripped out and threw away two of them to gain easier access to a renovation project. Precisely because it was inadvertent, the act symbolized, to us at least, a recognizably gendered recklessness and disregard for natural life. (The trees have since been replaced.) In ways that run the gamut from heartening to disturbing, London demonstrates how crucial it is to prevent ostensible remembering from devolving into actual forgetting, to prevent the war against women from taking ever more diverse forms.

Chapter 6

GUELPH:
TAKE BACK THE NIGHT

WOMEN UNITE!

TAKE BACK THE NIGHT!

WE HAVE THE RIGHT

TO WALK AT NIGHT!

— Marching Chant

This book began in Marianne's Park in Guelph, literally and conceptually. At one time, all five members of our collective lived and worked in the vicinity of the park, and our different relationships to it as a memory-making place brought us together in search of other memorials to women murdered. As residents of Guelph, we are touched by the everyday significance of its memorial sites. We experience them in action to a degree that is difficult to replicate for other communities which we have visited as researchers. In particular, we know more intimately the symbiotic relationship between design and use: how the characteristics of a memorial space influence the ways in which it gets used, and how its use can shift the associations of its design. We also know how little room can exist for resistance in any public space that is necessarily hemmed in as it is by municipal requirements and community pressures. And we know that activist memorializing is neither easy nor secure: the slippage from opposing to supporting the status quo can be as small as a word spoken or kept silent, a name remembered or forgotten, a subtle shift from active to passive voice.

The City of Guelph is an hour west of Toronto, population 106,000, with an attractive downtown and parks system traversed by the Eramosa and Speed Rivers and a thriving university campus "up the hill" on its southside. Within this topography, there are three memorial gardens associated with violence against women: Marianne's Park and the Reflection Garden, opposite each other on the south and north banks where the two rivers converge; and the Cactus Garden in the Thornbrough Building for engineering sciences on the University of Guelph campus. The constituencies that use these spaces to remember violence against women overlap with one another, and yet the memorializing takes a significantly different form in each place, and the political messages a distinctively different reach. Also distinctive, but ongoing in each case, is the influence memorializing has on those spaces. Together, these three sites suggest how participatory memory-making can change a place and how that dynamic can feed larger changes — personal, professional, social or explicitly political.

MARIANNE'S PARK

Marianne's Park is the most complex and compelling of the three sites, primarily because it brings together individual grief and collective action, private trauma and public outrage, conformity to municipal protocols and support for resistance to the status quo. The park is an unassuming triangle of grass, bushes and trees, wedged between the Speed River on its north side, a scruffy truck-rental lot on its south and Gordon Street on its west, one of the main north-south arteries (for cars and pedestrians) connecting the university campus with the town centre. The eastern tip of the rough triangle blurs into scrubby woods that stretch along the Eramosa River for a way, cutting this space off from the groomed fairways of a private golf course. When the park was first dedicated, the edge abutting Gordon was also shrouded with large shade trees that made it possible to pass, on foot or car, without noticing the small green space. The potential for it being overlooked was further exacerbated by its marginal position on the very edge of the city's parks system. Since then, the city has cut down the old trees, planted saplings that regularize the outline of the park and begun to expand the space into the adjacent lot so that it becomes much more open —

welcoming or vulnerable, depending on your point of view — on its west side. The overall impression has shifted from a quite dense and secretive refuge to a trimmer, more sprightly space.

A defining feature of the park, both practically awkward and symbolically powerful, is the geometrical garden at its centre. As the centrepiece, it is a bit ungainly, turned at an odd angle to the park's overall shape. The garden itself is rectangular, with narrow diagonal brick paths emphasized by spiky hedges cutting through the flower-and-shrub plantings to converge in a circle within the centre. The effect is neat or scruffy, colourful or drab, depending on the time of year, but the design always funnels visitors towards its centre in ones or twos, encouraging private, individualized interaction. It feels like a formulaic design that neither sits easily within the "V" of the park nor provides a felicitous space for larger gatherings or rallies.

The diagonal paths lead the visitor towards the central boulder with a bronze plaque and, on the plaque, these words:

MARIANNE'S PARK

MARIANNE GOULDEN WAS A WOMAN WHO GAVE HER ALL
AND HAD TREMENDOUS STRENGTH TO OVERCOME HARD TIMES.
HER GENEROSITY TOUCHED AND LIFTED EVERYONE WHO HAD
THE PRIVILEGE OF SHARING IN HER LIFE: HER FAMILY,
HER FRIENDS, AND HER COLLEAGUES AT GUELPH-WELLINGTON
WOMEN IN CRISIS AND THE GUELPH CORRECTIONAL CENTRE.
HER FAMILY CAN STILL FEEL HER GUIDING THEM IN THEIR LIVES
INTO MAKING THE RIGHT DECISIONS AND BEING THE BEST
PEOPLE THEY CAN POSSIBLY BE.

"YOU LOOK LIKE YOU NEED A HUG," ARE WORDS
REMEMBERED BY A LITTLE GIRL, GROWN NOW.

MARIANNE, WITH HER FAITH, AND DOWN-TO-EARTH CARING
UNDERSTOOD WHAT THAT CHILD NEEDED AS SHE ENTERED
THE SHELTER. SHE KNEW THAT BY ONLY LOVING EACH OTHER
AND WORKING TOGETHER COULD WE MAKE OUR COMMUNITY
A SAFER PLACE FOR WOMEN AND CHILDREN.

DEDICATED DECEMBER 6, 1993

Much is left unsaid by this homage to a caring mother and selfless worker for the community. Marianne Johanna Goulden was one of the earliest clients of Guelph-Wellington Women in Crisis (WIC), when she fled a violent marriage and moved into the tiny basement shelter with five of her six children. After establishing herself and her family in independent housing, she became a volunteer with the organization, having such an influence on the women whom she supported that WIC named the shelter Marianne's Place and found the means to employ her as paid staff for the next five years. Seven years later, Marianne was dead, murdered in Guelph on January 21, 1992, by her common-law partner Timothy Weldon.[1] Marianne was in her forty-eighth year, a mother of six children and a grandmother of six grandchildren.

At about the same time, WIC managed to purchase a new, more commodious shelter for women and children, and the old one was demolished.[2] The organization approached city council to create a park on the grounds of the previous shelter and to name it Marianne's Park. WIC members wanted

the space to honour Goulden and keep her memory alive while reminding the community of the costs of violence against women and children and the need to keep working for change. In time, two more memorials to Marianne Goulden were established in Guelph — a tree was planted in her name in the university's arboretum[3] and a housing complex was called Goulden Place — but only the park's naming was contentious.

The lobbying for the dedication of the park is yet another story of exhaustion and tenacity. WIC workers struggled to win over a reluctant city council and jump the requisite bureaucratic hoops (one lot to get the park approved, another to have the sign approved) in the stolen moments from their daily work. In the words of Justine Howarth (2000), WIC's then-executive director, "Getting that little hunk of land named Marianne's Park was not a straightforward thing." The organization well knew the civic sensitivities around making femicide in the community visible, and the approach it made to city council was not explicitly feminist, nor even directly tied to violence against women. In fact, the negotiations were never openly political at either end. Dedicating the park to Marianne would be a good and logical move, WIC argued, because she had been part of an important local organization and because the site had housed a building named Marianne's Place. Resistance to the dedication was also ostensibly apolitical: "If we do this," the committee argued, "we would have to do the same for every local organization."

Eventually backroom dealing won the day.[4] When the park was finally dedicated on December 6, 1993, the ceremony brought together civic officials, Marianne's family, WIC workers and feminist activists in a show of unity against violence against women. The fact that the grounds were only partially dug over at that point and the park unfinished and exposed in the steadily falling rain, suggests some of the fragility and incompleteness of that hard-won alliance. Local newspaper coverage stressed the sombre atmosphere: "A dreary rain washed away the tears, but it could not hide the sadness that prevailed Monday as friends and family gathered to remember Marianne Goulden" (Hill 1993, 1).

Once you know these stories, the park seems heavily coded with their traces. The most resonant echo is carried by the oddly placed rectangular garden at the centre, which approximates the shape of the shelter — Marianne's Place — demolished not long after Marianne's murder.[5]

For people who know the connection, the garden becomes literally coterminous with the shelter, continuing some of its work by other means, bringing what is necessarily shrouded in protective secrecy into a more public, potentially politicized domain. The space also feels marked by the negotiation and compromise endured by the lobbyists. On the one hand, the park bears Marianne's name prominently on a large wooden sign situated on a busy thoroughfare. On the other hand, the city park's design and plantings, along with the lack of facilities for gatherings, threaten to fold the park back into the system at large, just another garden for individualized retreat and recreation.[6] In the same way that the physical space fractures group activity, the fact that so much of the park's history and provenance goes unsaid — information remains available only to those in the know — can work against the building of an activist community.

The plaque, too, is finely balanced between celebrating an individual life of achievement — an understandable goal of family and friends, as well as a desirable image of the local community for city council to promulgate — and acknowledging the larger systemic social circumstances and causes of her death, an act of resistance for which women activists struggled. The veiled narrative only hints at violence, in the mention of WIC and the haunting date of the dedication. But the wording also provokes a participatory response, a first step towards action and activism. It is striking that, while the plaque is silent about many features of Marianne's life and about her murder, the text explicitly strives to represent her voice. As the dedication moves from the quotation of her speech ("*You look like you need a hug*") to the first person plural ("could we make our community"), the hope is legible that contact with Marianne's voice will move the reader towards identification with the community in which she participated and which she here represents. Similarly, the shifts between past and present tenses bring her life and work into the reader's consciousness as an ongoing impetus for action.

What tips the balance between the park's capacities for containment and resistance is its periodic use. The park and especially the plaque figured prominently in efforts by Marianne's family to gain public support for their concerns about her murderer's review hearing which threatened to free him to return to Guelph. Linda Reith, a counsellor of abused women, describes another kind of empowerment: she has used the park on several occasions as a "powerful space" in which to support women who are trying to move forward, through ritual or individual counselling. For her, the fact that the park is where the shelter used to be makes it "about violence against women and about the power of women's work, what women working together can achieve ... it's a place that I can point to that says there's energy for fighting violence against women" (Reith 2000).

At least twice a year that energy becomes public, collective and explicitly political — when the park comes alive with Take Back the Night gatherings and marches every September and the annual December 6th vigils. At Take Back the Night, noisy rallies of women muster their demands for safe streets, gathering around speakers who do their best to forge solidarity among the groups scattered among the park's awkwardly dissected spaces, before the crowd moves into march formation, taking to the night with banners and noisemakers. On that night, the park energizes sentiments that remain half-spoken and cryptic for much of the year, a staging ground that encourages women to raise their voices loudly and together:

> Women Of The World
> Who Can Not Speak
> We Shout Tonight
> To Shake The Streets

The rituals of December 6th are quieter and more contemplative, but still politically charged, insisting on the need to acknowledge and resist violence against women as a systemic wrong sewn deep into the fabric of society. Again, the ingenious use of recalcitrant space contributes to community building: one year, for example, we gathered around the edge of the rectangular garden while the First Nations woman who opened the ceremony spoke from a central position next to Marianne's plaque, while around the edge of the central circle candles of remembrance were lit. Most powerful of all, in terms of what the park and these rallies bring to each other, Marianne's murder is spoken of in explicit and angry terms that lose none of the private grief or public recognition of her achievements. Often a family member or friend speaks of Marianne's life and death, a story followed by the reading of the names — and sometimes circumstances of the lives and deaths — of all women in Ontario murdered in the past year. None of this activity ultimately escapes the mechanisms of social control and municipal protocols with which the park's sponsors struggled all along: rules and police escorts contain the march that begins and ends in the park; the tensions around difference and privilege within the women's movement do not magically disappear. Nevertheless, these annual rituals remake the park into a space of collective resistance, of politicized community forged out of individual griefs, and of private knowledge and trauma funnelled into public outrage and demonstration.

REFLECTION GARDEN

The power of Marianne's Park as a space of resistance — however fragile, incomplete or downright awkward — is made graphic in the contrast with the much more decorous space across the river, named Reflection Garden. Although it is a short hop across the confluence of the Eramosa and Speed Rivers, the north bank has undergone enough rustic revival that it feels economically and aesthetically distinct from the more ragged space to the south. The area is marked by a covered bridge, hand-built by the community in imitation of the nineteenth-century Mennonite original; a boat-house tearoom, renovated into a popular afternoon and evening spot from a dilapidated scout hut; and, between them, a small park perched right on the river bank. Reflection Garden commemorates the fourteen women murdered at l'École Polytechnique, and it is shaped into a much tidier, more self-consciously artistic design without the fissures and awkwardnesses that can function as spaces of resistance in Marianne's Park. This garden is neatly oval with two borders curving in towards each other: on the south, a line of

large seating stones and decorative plantings shaped to the bend of the river; on the north, a curved wrought-iron sculpture made of two screens, each consisting of seven rose stems. According to the design plan, "the buds on the top of the stems symbolize the lives of the 14 women, about to bloom. The buds will never open ... as the fourteen women were never able to blossom to their full potential" (Colter, Coates and Schearer 1999). This theme continues in a plaque on a low stone to one side of the oval:

REFLECTION GARDEN
WISPS OF CLOUDS
LEAVES IN THE WIND
REFLECTIONS ON WATER
MIRROR HOPES UNACHIEVED
BRIGHT PROMISES UNFULFILLED.

WE REMEMBER
14 MONTREAL WOMEN
SHINING POTENTIAL SHATTERED
IN A RAIN OF BULLETS
DECEMBER 6, 1989.

DEDICATED IN THEIR MEMORY BY
CANADIAN FEDERATION OF
UNIVERSITY WOMEN/GUELPH
AUGUST 2000

REFLECT AND REMEMBER.

There is no naming of names here and no anchoring of violence against women to the local community. The plaque speaks of grief, regret and remembrance in metaphors of nature that threaten to normalize the Montreal murders as part of some inevitable stage in the larger harmony of the life cycle.

As the name signifies, the garden was not intended for action but for passive reflection leading to healing: the local landscape architect was "alluding to the reflection found in the confluence of the two rivers, and an opportunity for visitors to the site to reflect on the meaning of the garden" (Colter 2001). This garden came into being much more rapidly and with much less resistance from city council than Marianne's Park. The millennium project was the brainchild of the local chapter of the Canadian Federation of University Women, a national, voluntary, non-profit organization of women university graduates, an overwhelmingly middle-class group with strong links to the local business community and with very different politics and mandate than WIC. The group won support from Parks and Recreation and from city council at record speed and raised funds from local companies and individuals, $10,000 in all, to commission the sculpture.[7] The dedication date August 16, 2000, marked not the murders but the first ever meeting of the national CFUW in Guelph. This space fosters woman-centred collectivity, but not in terms that resist the status quo or the protocols of silence and repression that protect established power relations within the community.

The proximity of Reflection Garden has inevitably drawn some focus away from Marianne's Park. When road construction blocked access to the park one year, both Take Back the Night and December 6th gatherings moved to Reflection Garden, and December 6th memorializing has remained in the garden. While many carefully conceived activities and speeches have been delivered on those occasions and attendance has been high, the garden's design and its lack of local historical connections produce a heightened sense of containment. Physically, there is less sense of the space itself helping to bring together the individual and the collective, the local and the distant, across tense lines of difference. At the first December 6th event in the garden, the First Nations speaker stood behind the grill of wrought iron stems rather than beside Marianne's memorial stone; at the next, the candle lighting and other memorializing activity also took place behind the grill, so that the effect was more of a performance for viewing than action inviting participation. In other words, the aesthetics of the space tend to rein in the politics of the gathering.[8] Marianne's name has remained unspoken in the new location; there are fewer layers of local history resonating that could potentially add to the activist energy. When Marianne's Park resumed its function as gathering space for Take Back the Night, the march skirted Reflection Garden without finding a way to incorporate it into the rituals of resistance.

The garden's primary use is normative and familial. The local press characterizes it as a space of "solace and peace," quoting a CFUW officer: "Yesterday I watched as a family came and sat here. I could see they were affected by it" (Shuttleworth 2000, A5). The garden has quickly become a favourite summer spot for children and adults with ice creams, and its good press has been rewarded with further civic beautification. This development has spilled across the river to bring Marianne's Park more securely into the parks system, in terms of horticultural attention and resources, than was previously the case. In political terms, of course, the "upgrading" of Marianne's Park is a very mixed blessing.

THORNBROUGH BUILDING, UNIVERSITY OF GUELPH

Up the hill, in the engineering building on the University of Guelph campus, the cycle of remembering and forgetting, the reciprocity between memorializing and community-building, happens in accelerated form. Guelph's engineering school has a reputation for being women-friendly at both the student and faculty level, and it regularly raises funds for WIC as well as donating resources to December 6th vigils in Marianne's Park.[9] Its memorial, however, like many in engineering schools, has had a more limited mandate, one that focuses on gender equity in the profession rather than on feminism or larger questions of social justice and broad political change. Set to one side of an airy, second-floor corridor in the modern and quite elegant Thornbrough Building, the December 6th Cactus Garden is a rectangle of soil planted with fourteen cacti of different varieties. In the midst of the garden is a boulder and plaque:

> THIS MEMORIAL SERVES TO REMIND US
> OF THE TRAGEDY THAT CLAIMED THE LIVES
> OF OUR COLLEAGUES AT
> ÉCOLE POLYTECHNIQUE IN MONTREAL,
> DECEMBER 6, 1989.

DEDICATED BY
UNIVERSITY OF GUELPH ENGINEERING STUDENTS
DECEMBER 6, 1990

The silences on the plaque echo those on institutional memorials at other campuses: the language effaces both murder (the terrible act converted into an inevitable, agent-less "tragedy") and the victims' gender.

Of the three memorials against femicide in Guelph, and again in a familiar pattern for engineering faculties, this one was created most quickly — indeed, it is among the first group of Montreal memorials in Canada — and with least struggle or even debate. The then director of the School of Engineering, who had been involved in attracting the high proportion of female engineering students and believed it was incumbent on this school to lead the way in creating a memorial to sustain awareness, enjoyed the means to act swiftly and unilaterally. He used discretionary funds to establish the garden, at that time in the building's ground-floor lobby, designing it in-house with his chief technician to be affordable and low maintenance. He then handed over "nominal ownership" to the student engineering society, which chose the wording for the plaque (James 2001).

What happened next is endemic to the cyclical relationship between memorials and communities of remembrance. Because generations of students pass through the institution so rapidly, personal memory of the murders in Montreal began to fade. For students who had barely entered public school in 1989, "the event was tragic but not burned in their memories," in the vivid words of Professor Valerie Davidson (2003). With its elegiac and unspecific language, the memorial's power to provoke remembering waxed and waned. While women from the engineering society continued to hold small ceremonies at the garden on the anniversary of the massacre, the logic of its design became blurred. At one point, in an attempt to revive the garden's aspect, the society added new cacti. It was a well-meaning effort but, unattached to particular acts of femicide (as in Ottawa's Enclave, discussed in chapter 9), the addition threatened to erase further the specificities of the fourteen murders (and their lessons about power relations). Eventually, many students forgot the garden's meanings, and a creeping lack of community commitment — what one student calls "a sense of ownership and pride in the garden amongst the students" (Webb 2003) — turned into vandalism. All the new plantings were stolen and the garden deteriorated into a depleted state, with fewer than its original fourteen cacti surviving.

But the cycle is turning again. Some women students recently formed a new group, Women in Science and Engineering (WiSE), and made one of its published goals "to adopt the December 6th Memorial." The garden and the group are each gaining an increased profile. With faculty support, the group obtained funds to move the garden to a more central location, revive its physical state, and enhance its lighting: in other words, to seize more space and visibility. The remembrance ceremony has become a more prominent event on campus, more clearly women-centred and more linked to larger social inequities. In 2004, the ceremony both returned the fourteen names to the garden, with each name being written on a white ribbon that was planted in the soil, and aligned itself with the larger analytical reach of the international campaign, "16 Days of Activism Against Gender Violence." Campus guides for prospective students now include an explanation of the garden, a memory which stayed with at least one student as an effective reminder of "what women have faced and overcome, both in engineering and society in general" (Lindsay 2003).

Beyond the glass windows backing the cactus garden, another reminder nicely suggests the possibilities of community meaning-making. The cannon is a famous sight on campus, encrusted with generations of symbols painted on by student groups of many political stripes and a staging-ground for so many celebrations and protests and alternative events that, over the decades, it has taken on historic resonances of activism. The cannon is also where the engineering students do their annual fundraising for WIC. Like the cannon, the garden is being remade, literally and politically. The latest memorial initiative enlarges the politics of memory so that the invocation of nature becomes oriented less towards the transcendence that can shade into forgetting and more towards the remembrance that sustains awareness and action. As all three memorials in this chapter demonstrate, resistant remembering depends on a process of mutual and continual reinforcement: a memorial site can help to consolidate a community of remembrance and action; equally, especially in an area so coded by covert allusion and silence, that community is needed to keep animating and, when necessary, reshaping the memory-making force of the site.

Chapter 7

HAMILTON:
END THE VIOLENCE

Silence and invisibility go hand in hand with powerlessness.
— AUDRE LORDE[1]

THE YELLOW-GREEN LEAVES OF A HARLEQUIN MAPLE TREE DANCE IN THE sunlight, a sprightly presence in the stately Avenue of Trees at Hamilton's Royal Botanical Gardens. It is the slenderest and brightest tree in the boulevard, most of which is made up of grander horsechestnut, Norway maple, and ancient ash, all pruned and groomed to perfection. Several are dedicated to the memory of family members — a nickname here, an aunt there — or upstanding members of the community. The slender maple also has a standard dedicatory plaque:

ACER PLATANOIDES 'DRUMMOND II'
DRUMMOND – ENGLAND – PRE 1903
HARLEQUIN MAPLE
MARLENE MOORE MEMORIAL

The shock of realization is sudden. This dedicatee is no mourned mother nor member of the business fraternity. This is Marlene Moore, a woman destroyed by Canada's correctional system, "constitutionally dubbed Canada's Most Dangerous Woman all 90 lbs. of her," and put under threat of indeterminate sentence, a threat which ended only with her suicide.[2] This tree — in its location, its tending, its aspect, the decorous company it keeps — represents all that was denied Marlene Moore. The plaque's silence is eloquent, since it is not Marlene so much as everything she did not have that the memorial represents.

The shock of dissonance delivered by the Marlene Moore tree epitomizes the workings of women's memorials in Hamilton. Situated in Ontario's "Golden Horseshoe," Hamilton is a steel town of half-a-million, which wears its industrial roots and post-industrial effects on its sleeve. The place does not immediately bring the notion of decorum to mind; indeed, it has been touched by a number of brutal, high-profile femicides. Yet, of all the cities we have visited, Hamilton boasts the highest concentration of distinctly decorous memorials, heavily invested with images of a healing nature. Not coincidentally, the three memorials discussed in this chapter sit in institutions of considerable cultural cachet: the Royal Botanical Gardens, McMaster University and city hall. As we have seen throughout this book, seizing institutional space involves accommodating its protocols. Invoking images of nature makes memorializing violence against women acceptable by fitting it into a standard form of remembrance, but the associations of nature can also deflect attention from a systemic critique of or challenge to the status quo. In terms of the hinge between memorializing and activism, the question these memorials pose is, to what degree does nature enable and to what degree inhibit the infiltration of systemic protest into places of power?

MARLENE MOORE MEMORIAL TREE

The case of Marlene Moore stretches conventional definitions of femicide and the conventions of nature as healing remembrance. In strict technical terms, Marlene committed suicide on December 3, 1988, age thirty-two, in the Kingston Prison for Women.[3] Everything about her treatment from childhood onwards tells us that she was a victim of the social, penal and justice systems. Abused sexually, physically and institutionally, she was locked up at thirteen before ever committing a crime, incarcerated for 80 percent of her adult life, repeatedly victimized by prison policies and finally destroyed with the state's label of "dangerous offender," a grotesquely inappropriate classification for a woman who, as her lawyer argued, "didn't come close to displaying the type of threatening behaviour that would qualify a man as a dangerous offender" (Kershaw and Lasovich 1991, 129). The Elizabeth Fry Society also challenged Marlene Moore's designation and, at her inquest, tried to get attention for the systemic problems surrounding women prisoners.[4] The Society cites this case as one of the most heinous in the prison system, dating its public tally of prison suicides from Marlene's death: "Between December 1988 and the spring of 1992, 7 women committed suicide at P4W. Six were First Nations women and the seventh was the first woman to be declared a dangerous offender and sentenced to an indeterminate sentence."[5]

There have been several angry, protesting memorials to Marlene Moore. Twelve days after her funeral, "just before dusk on a bitterly cold Sunday afternoon," forty people gathered for a candlelight vigil in Kingston, in a parking lot across the street from the federal penitentiary: "They stood silently as speakers denounced the Prison for Women: Marlene's suicide, they said, was the tragic consequence of 'evil' conditions inside the walls" (Kershaw and Lasovich 1991, 198). During the inquest into her death, "JUSTICE FOR MARLENE" was spray-painted on the wall of the august Kingston court house. And in 1992, Lori Clermont, artist, friend and fellow inmate at the Grandview School for Girls, created Monument for Marlene Moore, an outdoor installation placed near the War Memorial in Halifax, Nova Scotia, as an intervention during the week of Remembrance Day. Clermont incorporated references to Moore's incarceration, her self-mutilation (the obsessive "slashing" of her skin) and her sexual abuse as a child. In her statement she writes:

> The monument itself is created from a discarded piece of gravestone granite which I then gouged to hold a glass enclosed Duraclear photograph of a rose. At the top corner of the photograph, a razor blade is inserted between the glass, cutting into the photograph. Behind the granite block is a cup of water, situated such that when the light shines through the photograph, the water appears red, symbolizing blood. In front of the granite block is a glass enclosed copper framed statement which lies on the ground. (Clermont 1992)

The statement also includes June Callwood's newspaper article on Marlene Moore's life and death, "Woman of 1,000 Cuts," and, handwritten in gold, the words "While the adult world fights on land, sea, and air, children are defenseless victims of violence in an undeclared war with no visible end."

The Elizabeth Fry Society's memorial intervenes in the public consciousness in a very different way. The members of the Hamilton branch of the society took Marlene into their halfway house on her 1983 parole from prison. After her death, they dedicated a harlequin maple in the Royal Botanical Gardens Arboretum to her memory. They aimed, with this memorial act, to bring home all that is denied women in conflict with the law: "We chose to plant a tree in honour of incarcerated women as a symbol of freedom and growth and a symbol of the one thing they miss so much, the sun, the wind, the air, all essential to our own mental health" (Elizabeth Fry Society, n.d.). Their memorial potentially reaches an audience that might not be attracted to vigils, protests or experimental art exhibits — the mothers with young children, the school groups, the Sunday strollers who frequent the arboretum. The risk, of course, is that the standardized plaque renders the woman's reality invisible. Annually, during Elizabeth Fry Society Week, the memorializers revive the maple's meanings with a "tree ceremony" on the Saturday before Mother's Day. The ritual includes the Joan of Arc speech from George Bernard Shaw's *St. Joan* and a First Nations "sage ceremony," "to pay tribute to the disproportionate representation of native women in our jails" (Elizabeth Fry Society, n.d.). The number of participants has ranged from twelve to sixty-five: one to five dozen people remembering what killed Marlene Moore, becoming the repository of her memory, becoming indeed the memorial that fills in the blanks.

NINA DE VILLIERS MEMORIAL ROSE GARDEN, McMASTER UNIVERSITY

Abutting the southern edge of the botanical gardens is the main campus of McMaster University, where a memorial harnesses nature even more decorously than the Marlene Moore tree. A considerably fuller text accompanies this site but, rather than opening up memory to social protest, the language deflects activism into acceptance, memorializing into contemplation, ultimately suggesting a closed community of memory-making.

The Nina de Villiers Memorial Rose Garden was created in memory of a nineteen-year-old woman, at the time a biochemistry student at McMaster University. In 1991, she was shot in the head by Jonathan Yeo while jogging in Burlington, her body then stripped and thrown off a bridge on High-

way 401 into a marshy lake near Kingston (Feschuk 1991). The garden is immaculate, its rich pink blooms ordered into a symmetrical design made up of bushes, walkways, benches and a boulder with a memorial plaque as its centre. The rectangular plot is quite prominent on campus: surrounded by a gated wrought-iron fence and shaded by large oak trees, it sits at the end of a major thoroughfare, in front of the stately, neo-Georgian facades of Gilmour and University Halls. As the publicity at the time of the garden's creation stressed, the university poured considerable resources into this commemorative process.[6]

The emphasis on institutional effort dominates the main dedicatory plaque, attached to the central boulder. Headed with the McMaster crest, the text reads:

THE NINA DE VILLIERS GARDEN

DEDICATED ON SEPTEMBER 15TH, 1993 TO
NINA DE VILLIERS,
MCMASTER STUDENT 1990–1991.

A JOINT EFFORT OF MCMASTER UNIVERSITY,
MCMASTER STUDENT'S UNION,
AND MANY FRIENDS,
THIS GARDEN IS A SYMBOL OF
OUR COMMITMENT
TO HARMONY AND RESPECT OF ALL.

AS THE GARDEN RENEWS ITSELF,
LET IT REMIND US OF WHAT WE CAN DO
TO MAKE THE WORLD A BETTER PLACE.

To us, the wording disproportionately celebrates the sponsors' co-operation: for the one mention of Nina, there are four of the university, and no murder nor even death is named. Other inscriptions in the garden are equally elliptical, and one wonders why they are here, as they bear no mention of Nina. Benches at either end of the garden carry small metal plaques. One, dedicated by the victims' rights group CAVEAT[7] that was headed by Priscilla de Villiers, Nina's mother, omits the naming of gender:

DEDICATED

TO THE MEMORY

OF

ALL VICTIMS OF VIOLENCE

———————

CAVEAT

The other, dedicated to a history professor, omits naming her murder:

DEDICATED

TO THE MEMORY OF

EDITH MARY WIGHTMAN

1934 – 1983

———————

DONATED BY HER FRIENDS

Adding to the weight of the unsaid are two unidentified wrought-iron rose trellises and two rosebushes, apparently memorials from the City of Hamilton in honour of Nina de Villiers, Edith Wightman, Joan Heimbecker (a McMaster graduate student killed in March 1994), Janet McKnight (a McMaster nursing professor killed in January 1994) "and all victims of violence" ("Dedication and Renewal" 1994). And, of course, beyond the embrace of the garden — outside its gated precincts and its coded inscriptions — are all the local women unconnected with the university whose murders are gestured to in the most general of terms. Women such as Debra Ellul who, in 1990, was stabbed twenty-one times with enough force to cut into her bone by her male partner, who was subsequently acquitted of any criminal charges.

The garden's use also suggests how the prettification of memory obscures the horror of violence. From the first, its envisaged use was contemplative: "The garden will provide the University community with a formal setting for rest, relaxation and quiet contemplation" ("Memorial Rose Garden" 1992). The garden continues to be heavily used, but its origin is not well remembered: "When Cynthia Hill asked people passing or sitting in the garden if they knew anything about its origins or meaning, very few did. They just appreciated the rose garden as a pleasant and protected place to visit. When the weather is good, it is a favourite setting for photographing weddings and other celebrations" (Bowerbank, Corneau and Hill 2000). When commemorative events are held at the garden, they rarely voice protest. For example, at least one of the dedication ceremonies, which attracted more than 400 people, emphasized a community turning in on itself to transcend its horror. After a series of addresses dominated by university members — a group expanded only by Priscilla de Villiers and Hamilton's mayor — the university chaplain closed the ceremony with the words, "Let the pain we feel change us and change the world we live in from the inside out" ("Dedication and Renewal" 1994).

All of this together — the discreet inscriptions, the groomed, enclosed garden, the emphasis on institutional presence — ultimately feels exclusive.[8] For all the gestures to "all victims of violence," there is little to trigger remembrance of those who fall beyond the norm of the university's image of its own community.

CITY HALL MEMORIAL

Hamilton's most explicitly resistant memorial — and therefore the one that most suggests the tension between political protest and institutional containment — is downtown, at city hall. In 1989, three well-publicized murders of local women occurred in Hamilton, yet it took the shock of murders elsewhere to organize women's anger into action. Once mobilized, they moved quickly, creating one of the first memorials in the country to name the Montreal murders as part of a larger systemic pattern of violence against women.

Shortly after the murders in Montreal, out of "grief and frustration," Donelle de Vlaming, then president of the board of directors of the Women's Centre of Hamilton, posted notices around town for women who wanted to "do something."[9] About eight to ten women came to this first meeting. Not all of them identified as feminists, but all had some experience of men's violence and were deeply disturbed by the Montreal massacre. They came to form the December 6th Committee, a minimally institutional group aiming to produce a memorial which would not be owned by any particular organization (although the Women's Centre, which provided meeting space for the group, took ownership for insurance purposes).

The committee arrived at an evocative vision: to plant a gravestone in a wild flower garden tended by women. They took this proposal to city council, borrowing the slogan "First mourn, then work for change" to articulate their intention. They also approached Parks and Recreation about establishing the garden in Gage Park, one of the most publicly accessible green spaces in the city centre. City council proved to be the more supportive body, providing an even more central location than the park — Hamilton Place, the plaza in front of city hall — while decreeing that the memorial must take the shape of a plaque and small boulder. The women were jubilant at the authorization of their project. In the words of Renate Manthei, co-ordinator of the December 6th Committee, this location is "central to the city ... a place of power ... to be present there means women have a presence in a place they might shy away from." They moved speedily, agreeing on an inscription marked by a woman's symbol, which was created in Montreal, and producing stone and plaque for only $500. By the first anniversary of the murders, they were ready to unveil the memorial:

END THE VIOLENCE
IN MEMORY OF THE WOMEN MURDERED IN
MONTREAL
DECEMBER 6, 1989

AND

IN MEMORY OF ALL WOMEN WHO HAVE BEEN
VICTIMS OF VIOLENCE

END THE VIOLENCE MONTREAL MASSACRE MEMORIAL COMMITTEE
DECEMBER 6, 1990

The dedication ceremony attracted nearly 200 people, and the site has remained active as a gathering point for annual December 6th vigils.

Some sense of tension does mark the design that resulted from this speedy process. Fitted to the requirements of the city hall site, the garden seems somewhat reduced from the women's original imagining: a smaller plot, overseen by Parks and Recreation employees, more regular and institutional in design — tamer, in fact — than the original vision of a wild garden and gravestone tended by politically committed women. The 2-by-3 metre (6-by-10 foot) rectangle of dainty flowers sits off to one side in the expanse of concrete, the low-lying boulder overshadowed by more prominent memorials, one to Ukrainian pioneers and a massive bronze piece to injured workers, which celebrate the city's ethnic and industrial roots. The ease with which the women's memorial can be overlooked was demonstrated when we first went looking for it in Hamilton. Back in 2001, a city official responsible for culture and events whose office was practically adjacent to the stone, was unaware of its existence.

However, occupying such a prominent location on busy Main Street West, en route to the Women's Centre of Hamilton, is no mean feat. This is one of only two memorials to women murdered we have discovered at city halls across Canada. Moreover, the language of the memorial is unusually direct and forceful for such an institutional site: it demands change, explicitly in the name of women murdered. This demand, lurking in the pretty garden, can offer a salutary shock to the casual passerby strolling among the standard civic gestures of the plaza. What the Marlene Moore tree communicates covertly, the city hall memorial makes explicit. Like the Q in "END THE VIOLENCE," the intimate relation between violence and women — women prisoners, women students, women workers, women in poverty — is sprung upon readers, triggering a double-take of awareness.[10]

Chapter 8

TORONTO:
WOMEN WON'T FORGET

And although I woke at night screaming and soaked in sweat,
which I thought was blood falling from the mouth of the mon-
ster above me, I was not afraid to fight the force by day — the
system that presumed to define justice for me. A community of
women with a history of activism and resistance supported me.
Feminism and a belief in social justice sustained me.

— Jane Doe, *The Story of Jane Doe* (2003)

When "Jane Doe" went around her neighbourhood in 1986 posting warnings to other women about the "balcony rapist" who had assaulted her, she represented only the most extreme example of the need to take matters into your own hands when it comes to violence against women in Toronto. Neither the city nor its major institutions have been notable for their support of efforts to take action on violence against women let alone memorialize those whose confrontation with violence takes their lives — women murdered. Although there have been temporary installations and fundraising arts events mounted in response to the femicides of December 6, 1989, as well as ongoing, so-far unsuccessful efforts by the Women's Memorial Society of Ontario since 1993 to "commemorate the names of those females of Ontario who have died in family violence or intimate femicide since 1980" (M. King 2000), we have found only two permanent memorials to gendered violence in Canada's largest urban centre.[1]

Both memorials are on university land, neither was initiated by the university and both depended on underfunded or grassroots organizations rather than institutional support for obtaining start-up funding, which did not include ongoing maintenance. But the sites are otherwise quite different from one another in the process of their implementation and in their design. The memorial at Ryerson University, proposed and installed some time after the events at l'École Polytechnique that it commemorates, has been non-controversial, institutionally approved and relatively self-contained from the outset. The memorial on University of Toronto land, the initiative of a grassroots organization in the immediate wake of the Montreal Massacre, has been more controversial and conflicted, but broader in both appeal and application.

TREE OF HOPE, RYERSON UNIVERSITY & WOMEN WON'T FORGET MEMORIAL, UNIVERSITY OF TORONTO

On December 6, 1994, a sculpture memorializing the murders at l'École Polytechnique was unveiled outside the centre doors of Ryerson University's engineering department. Two years later, an explanatory plaque was installed. Ryerson is a downtown university, situated just to the east of the busy intersection of Toronto's Dundas and Yonge Streets. But its memorial site is protected from the crowds (as they are from it) through its location in a grassy, shaded area within the relatively peaceful Kerr Hall quadrangle, across from a raised playing field and symbolically marked as the province of Ryerson's engineers. The sculpture was proposed and designed by Alexandra Leikermoser, then a fourth-year interior design student at Ryerson. Named Tree of Hope, it is a simple but elegant outline of a stylized young tree cut from the centre of a 2-metre (7-foot) tall, 9-metre (3-foot) wide weathered steel slab, mounted vertically on a base, flush with the ground and angled slightly towards the building's entranceway. The design is striking, combining "nature and sculpture to create a piece of work that communicates feminist issues and environmental consciousness ... without the use of gory or painful images," according to Cara Scott-McCron, the chair of Ryerson's December 6th Memorial Committee.[2] On the ground below, a 20-cm (8-inch) circular plaque explains the sculpture's significance in small lettering; it is practically invisible from the cobbled pathways that navigate the quadrangle or from the entranceway to the building. For the curious who

cross the grass to investigate, the inscription, when not obscured by snow, stresses the educational role of memorializing as imagined by the designer and donors:

TO SINGLE OUT AND BLAME IS NOT THE ANSWER
TO EDUCATE IS

FOR THE 14 WOMEN MURDERED ON DECEMBER 6, 1989
AT L'ÉCOLE POLYTECHNIQUE IN MONTRÉAL

TODAY WE PLANT A TREE THAT WILL NOT DIE;
A TREE OF HOPE AND GROWTH TO EDUCATE AND CREATE AWARENESS
OF ALL ACTS OF VIOLENCE,
ESPECIALLY AGAINST WOMEN AND CHILDREN

DECEMBER 6, 1994

DESIGNED BY:
ALEXANDRA LEIKERMOSER

DONATED BY:
RYERSON'S
DEC. 6TH MEMORIAL COMMITTEE

Further north in the city, also protected from the rush of nearby Bloor Street and Avenue Road, is the most prominent memorial in Toronto. Dedicated on the first anniversary of the Montreal Massacre, it is located along Philosopher's Walk on the campus of the University of Toronto campus. The small engraved plaque, a large pink granite boulder from the Scarborough bluffs just east of the city and fourteen red oak trees constitute the memorial. They blend seamlessly into the grassy slope at the western edge of the pathway that leads from Bloor Street to Hoskin Avenue. The site is not far from Ontario's legislative buildings at Queen's Park, and is situated on a diagonal line between the Edward Johnson Building housing the university's Faculty of Music and the Varsity Arena. The location again blurs the memorial's impact. At some point after its installation in 1990, the university planted an additional six trees on the site without warning or apparent awareness of the significance of the initial fourteen. Now it is impossible to tell where the memorial begins or ends. Its scope, to all intents and purposes, has shrunk to the plaque and boulder, the last of which was also reduced when its top was mistakenly lopped off to accommodate the plaque that now stands independently before it, facing a gentle slope leading down to Philosopher's Walk. To read the plaque so as to determine the memorial's significance, a visitor must approach it up the slope — a pleasant enough stroll in summer, but unlikely in winter, when both the plaque and boulder are often buried beneath the snow.

If the visitor is persistent in her efforts, however, or is at the site to attend the annual December 6th vigil, as is more likely to be the case, the plaque's rewards are considerable. Its wording negotiates in an exemplary way many of the tensions between the local and global, the specific and symbolic, the contemplative and the activist, the past and the future that are evident in memorial sites across the country. At the same time, it refuses to allow necessary accommodations to efface the gendered nature of the violence or let the onlooker off the hook:

THESE FOURTEEN TREES ARE WITH SORROW PLANTED IN MEMORY AND IN HONOUR OF FOURTEEN SISTERS SLAIN BECAUSE OF THEIR GENDER IN MONTREAL ON DECEMBER 6, 1989. MAY COMMITMENT TO THE ERADICATION OF SEXISM AND VIOLENCE AGAINST WOMEN BE LIKEWISE PLANTED IN THE HEARTS AND MINDS OF YOU WHO STAND HERE NOW AND OF ALL WHO COME AFTER. IT IS NOT ENOUGH TO LOOK BACK IN PAIN. WE MUST CREATE A NEW FUTURE.

CES QUATORZE ARBRES SONT PLANTÉS AVEC CHAGRIN EN MÉMOIRE ET EN HOMMAGE DE QUATORZE SOEURS ASSASSINÉES À MONTRÉAL LE 6 DÉCEMBRE 1989 À CAUSE DE LEUR SEXE. QUE L'ENGAGEMENT ENVERS LA SUPPRESSION DU SEXISME ET DE LA VIOLENCE FAITE AUX FEMMES SOIT DE MÊME PLANTÉ DANS LE COEUR ET DANS L'ESPRIT DE VOUS QUI ÊTES ICI MAINTENANT ET DE TOUS CEUX ET CELLES QUI VIENDRONT APRÈS. REVENIR DOULOUREUSEMENT SUR LE PASSÉ NE SUFFIT PAS. NOUS DEVONS CRÉER UN NOUVEL AVENIR.

THIS MEMORIAL CREATED BY "WOMEN WON'T FORGET" DECEMBER 6, 1990

Unlike its Ryerson counterpart, this plaque focuses less on the design, designer or donors than on the cultural work to be done, less on inclusive and somewhat ill-defined faith in the ameliorative role of education than on the responsibilities of the viewer, and less on avoiding the placement of blame than insisting on the taking of responsibility. The most prominent feature of the Ryerson inscription — "TO SINGLE OUT AND BLAME IS NOT THE ANSWER/TO EDUCATE IS" — that opens the quote and is set in large letters, denies social value to issues of accountability. Indeed, it places in opposition a relationship between education and accountability, which might more productively be understood to be mutually reinforcing. In its exclusive emphasis on contemplation and healing, this inscription runs the

risk of alienating any woman who has been through the ordeal of attempting to take her attacker to court in a fight for accountability and of failing to acknowledge the ruptures of rage and grief felt by many for whom systemic gendered violence is an everyday fact of life. The combination of care and confrontation voiced by the Women Won't Forget plaque resulted from that group's feminist, collective and exhausting processes: "We argued over every word until the very last moment and then we compromised" (Lewis 2001). The inscription insists on accuracy ("slain because of their gender"), on the relationship of the murders in Montreal to systemic "sexism and violence towards women" and on itself playing rather than merely gesturing towards the educational role of explicitly oppositional memory-making.

There are significant differences, too, in the designs of the memorials. Ryerson's Tree of Hope functions effectively as an eye-catching aesthetic object, and one which in its materials and construction cites the link between the host institution and the chosen profession of the murdered women. But it is difficult to see how it negotiates the relationship between feminism and ecology as intended by its designer. In fact, without knowing that intention, we would not have identified the sculpture as feminist. The viewer sees in the cut-out shape of the stripling tree an absence at the centre; she literally sees *through* the steel sheet to the walls and windows of the institution that back it, perhaps at the same time seeing through the designs of the institution itself. The sculpture's symbolism, as explicated on its plaque, seems confused: it is unclear how "a tree that will not die" can nevertheless function as "a tree of hope and *growth*" (our italics). The effect, especially in conjunction with the plaque, is closer to cool formalism than to impassioned outrage. In contrast, the sheer messiness of the Women Won't Forget under-designed and under-realized memorial seem refreshingly enabling, drawing attention to the site's function and use rather than self-consciously to its own design. The site's lack of clearly-defined borders, moreover, open it out to the world, to interpretation, and to use in ways that the formalist containment of the Tree of Hope resists.

The different emphases of the designs of the Toronto and Ryerson memorials and of the wording of their inscriptions are the results of very different processes taking place with different degrees of proximity to the event that prompted them. The Ryerson process, which occurred five years after the murders it remembers, is perhaps reflected in the clean and self-contained elegance of its design and the relative consensus about the sculpture's memorializing function. These more collected responses were not readily available in the midst of the shock, horror, outrage, pain, confusion and ineffable grief that prevailed among women across the country in the immediate wake of the femicides in Montreal. These reactions are perhaps more closely reflected in the confusions and tensions legible in and around the University of Toronto site.

The establishment of the Ryerson site was initially proposed and "sparked to life by the vision of one brilliant student," its designer (according to Scott-McCron). The project was eagerly embraced, not only by the already extant Ryerson December 6th Memorial Committee (which may have recognized the project's perhaps embarrassing belatedness) but also by the university's vice-president of administration, Linda Grayson. Like a number of well-placed women administrators who played enabling roles across the country, Grayson took up the project "like a mission," marshalling approvals through the university's board of governors for the location and wording, which the December 6th committee drafted from ideas submitted to it. Although the two-year delay in mounting the plaque is attributed by Scott-McCron to slow approval for the final wording, ultimately no changes were required. Grayson ensured that Ryerson would continue to groom the site, but most costs were covered by fundraising and voluntary labour.

The committee raised the initial $1,000 for the sculpture and the subsequent cost of the plaque from university employees, students and alumni, and the university charged it with maintaining the sculpture and plaque on an ongoing basis. The sculpture was mounted by Physical Plant Operations and the instructor and students of a civil engineering course and, later, the plaque was installed by a retired member of the university's Campus Planning Committee.[3] In a final show of institutional support, the university's then-president, Terry Grier, performed the ribbon-cutting ceremony for the sculpture. The process — like the location, design and wording — sounds consensual, non-confrontational, uncontroversial and unobtrusive. In real and figurative terms, of course, Ryerson's Tree of Hope appears to have cost the university almost nothing.

Institutional negotiations have been much less smooth for Women Won't Forget, the group responsible for the fundraising, design, dedication and implementation of the Philosopher's Walk memorial and for organizing and funding the annual December 6th vigils held there. Women Won't Forget is a small, grassroots feminist organization formed on December 8, 1989, in the immediate wake of, and in response to, the Montreal murders. "We initially got together to share our grief, sorrow and outrage. We also wanted to find a focus for our feelings. We called ourselves 'WOMEN WON'T FORGET.' We did not know each other then and we came from all walks of life" (Women Won't Forget, n.d.).

The group's first project was to organize the donation and creation of wreathes which they displayed in December 1989 at a Toronto YWCA and then shipped to l'École Polytechnique in Montreal for its memorial service. "Out of this effort, our commitment to continue fighting on behalf of women and children in our society, strengthened." The group met weekly thereafter at a donut shop at St. George's and Bloor Streets, close to the eventual site of their memorial, and over time developed a focus for their work: "The creating of a permanent memorial to commemorate the lives of the 14 women and all women who die from male violence. The memorial would be a symbol of our struggle to end the continuing violence against women" (Women Won't Forget, n.d.).

The group initially raised money at the International Women's Day Fair (March 8, 1990), and subsequently contacted people at various levels of government, sending letters to the city of Toronto and to its universities requesting the donation of a site for the memorial. The University of Toronto at the time was planning to relandscape the Philosopher's Walk area in part to provide better safety for women, and members of Women Won't Forget used this for leverage, "piggy-backing" on this framework to push the project further. The university agreed to set aside a corner of the newly designed green space for the memorial. The site was designed by Women Won't Forget in consultation with the university's grounds department, who vetoed the planned planting of birch trees because of underground piping. The group managed to solicit donated materials for the memorial itself, but student engravers mistakenly shaved off the top of the boulder that had been selected by the organizers when they were attempting to install the plaque, then, as previously indicated, the university added trees which make it impossible to distinguish the fourteen symbolic trees cited on the inscription.

Since the memorial's installation, moreover, relations with the university have been less than smooth. The institution has, it seems, worked to keep the organization marginal rather than embracing it as a "community" or "private sector partner," in the rhetoric used to define co-operation between campus and corporate organizations. In fact, the university takes advantage of public good will accruing from the fact that a memorial service is held annually on its grounds, while avoiding taking responsibility for any controversy over its use and vetoing proposed improvements to the site.[4] Eventually, according to Janet Lewis of Women Won't Forget, "we got tired," but plans are continuing for completing the memorial by creating a visual connection between the fourteen trees and the boulder, perhaps through the installation of a flagstone pathway.

While both Toronto memorials accommodate gatherings comfortably, and both serve as a focal point for December 6th vigils, the scope and resonance of these events are, like the designs of the memorials and the processes of their implementation, quite different. Since the ribbon was cut on Alexandra Leikermoser's Tree of Hope in 1994, the sculpture has served as the focal point for December 6th memorial observances that are by-and-large intimate, in-house, contemplative affairs. "Holding the services outside in the cold and the elements adds a poignancy to the ceremonies, allowing attendees to reflect on the loneliness and horror those murdered in Montreal must have felt, and the cold way in which they were murdered," says Scott-McCron. The December 6th Memorial Committee organizes these events as part of larger educational outreach. With its fund-raising in the Ryerson community, the committee has endowed an education project grant that supports not only the memorial sculpture itself and the annual service but also panels, speakers, theatrical productions, photo and art exhibitions and a December 6th Memorial Award for Ryerson's Safe House to help women there continue their studies.

The Women Won't Forget December 6th vigils are notably assertive and explicitly activist, and they take full advantage of the University of Toronto's institutional indifference. The messiness of the Philosopher's Walk memorial shows traces of the uneven process that developed it and reflects a lack of interest and commitment on the part of a university that did not, like Ryerson, take ownership of the site. But the organization turned that lack of institutional support into a liberating act, creating a politically productive plaque that the university did not see as an official representation of its position and a well-attended unruly annual event that operates without the university's official stamp of approval.[5] Meticulous planning produces an event that is more sprawling and less contained, physically and politically, than is its counterpart at the smaller Ryerson space. Participants have come from well beyond the university community, and with 200 to 700 participants, this vigil is among the most heavily attended and most explicitly activist in the country. Having carefully recorded the names of usually thirty to forty women murdered in the province in the previous year, the organizers give them symbolic internment as part of the ceremony. Massive numbers of candles, large and small, spill throughout the area, while music, speakers, a sweetgrass ceremony, a placement of roses, a reading of names and an acknowledgement of the unknown names of unreported victims are all performed. Climactically, a moment of silence is followed by a huge and resonant scream of rage.

Fundraising materials and flyers in several languages have circulated political commentary by dozens of women from different cultures, communities and sexualities over the years. Among the comments have been those from well known women, including Audre Lorde, Andrea Dworkin, bell hooks, Rosemary Brown and Chrystos. Quotes have been cited from Paula Gunn Allen: "The root of oppression is the loss of memory"; Lee Maracle: "For us [First Nations women], rape is not an oddity, but a commonplace. I've had to fight over and over again for my life. My life"; and Nicole Brossard: "Women's memory is torrential/when it has to do with torture." And there have been comments from lesser-known women. "Mary," who killed her abusive husband in self-defense, wrote, "How is it a crime to save your own life?" An anonymous woman, who was a former stripper, commented:

> When men think a woman is a whore, it's open season on her. They can say anything to her they want, they can do anything they want, they can be absolutely as crass and vile and violent and cruel and uncaring as the darkest part of their personality wants to be. And it's O.K. They don't have to afford the woman an ounce of respect for being a human being. She's not a human being. She's a thing.

One program historicized sexual violence and deflated myths of progress by printing parallel quotations and political cartoons from the nineteenth and twentieth centuries. In the 1990s, these cartoons focused on Ontario's Progressive Conservative premier Mike Harris. One featured a violent husband screaming at his wife: "You heard Mr. Harris! You bloody women are a special interest group! He's not gonna cater to you anymore. He's gonna cater to me!" Another program cover featured designs from a fundraising T-shirt. Above the title, Harris Government Policies & Cuts: Making Sure Women Have No Way Out, are two drawings: the first, "Mike Harris Stays Here," pictures a genteel Georgian home; the second, "Assaulted Women Stay Here," features a graveyard.[6]

Chapter 9

OTTAWA:
WOMEN'S URGENT ACTION

Memory is all we got, I cried, we got to remember. We got to remember everything ... We got to remember to be able to fight. Got to write down the names. Make a list. Nobody can be forgotten. They know if we don't remember we can't point them out. They got their guilt wiped out. The last thing they take is memory.

— MERIDEL LESUEUR, *The Girl* (1936)

IN 1991, IN RECOGNITION OF THE ANNIVERSARY OF THE MONTREAL Massacre, the federal government in Ottawa declared December 6 a National Day of Remembrance and Action on Violence Against Women. The National Capital, nevertheless, is home to no official monument on Capital Hill or on any other land owned by the National Capital Commission to the fourteen women murdered or to violence against women more generally. Indeed, the events at l'École Polytechnique in 1989 are explicitly remembered in Ottawa only through a small plaque at the University of Ottawa's Faculty of Engineering, dedicated December 6, 1990.[1] The more compelling monument in the city is the one dedicated on December 6, 1992, to "all women abused and murdered by men." While the dedication date links the memorial with the murders in Montreal three years earlier, the monument's primary orientation is much more local and ad hoc in the best of senses. It was an explicitly activist measure taken by a collective of shelter, sexual assault and community health workers known as Women's Urgent Action, who came together in immediate response to a series of horrific murders in Ottawa and its suburbs in 1990 and 1991. Strikingly, the monument design incorporates the urgency of action, and the ongoing need for participation and activism; for a time, it continued to change and grow in response to each new femicide.

The Women's Monument, entitled Enclave, is a standing granite boulder on city property in Ottawa's Minto Park, located just east of downtown in the residential heart of Ottawa's Centertown heritage district. Unlike most memorials to violence against women, which by accident or design come to serve as the sites for vigils, memorial services and other women-centred events within their communities, Enclave came about as a direct result of, rather than an occasion for, such events. In June of 1990, in the wake of the murder of fifty-five-year-old Pamella Behrendt, whose husband hacked her to death with a chain saw in Ottawa South, a group of women gathered in Minto Park to plant a tree and install a small (and still extant) plaque "To all women suffering from abuse, and to those who have died." In April 1991, another gathering and another tree planting remembered thirty-year-old Reva Bowers, killed by her estranged husband in Gloucester.

Two months later, yet another vigil and another tree honoured four-teen-year-old Sharon Mohamed, who, along with her mother, Shadikan Mohamed, had been horrifically tortured — by deliberate dousing with boiling water — and repeatedly stabbed by Shadikan's male partner, Alton Royer. Sharon died, her mother was confined to hospital and Royer, charged with second-degree murder and attempted murder, was released on $5,000 bail into the care of his elderly mother. When the police refused to provide protection for Shadikan at a local hospital, the increasingly politicized wom-en who had gathered to hold the vigils since the murder of Pamella Berendt objected publicly to the release of Royer and organized a roster of women to stand protective guard over Shadikan. After the first all-night shift, which provided her with her first deep sleep since the attack, the women contacted the media, whose extensive coverage of the story led to the granting of a twenty-four-hour police guard over Shadikan and eventually to the conver-sion of Royer's charge from second- to first-degree murder.[2]

In the wake of these events, the organizers of the vigils and the hospital roster named themselves Women's Urgent Action, becoming an informal collective focused on *action* whose mandate was "to respond swiftly and in an organized fashion to injustices against women, and when a woman was murdered, to hold a vigil within a week of her death" (Johnson 1999, 315). They did not have long to wait. The vigil to Sharon Mohamed was followed in the same year by vigils honouring Charmaine Thompson, who was stabbed to death in August at the age of twenty-three; Rachel Favreau, twenty, who was shot to death, also in August; and Patricia Allen, thirty-one, who was killed by her estranged husband with a crossbow in November while she was on her way to a routine dental appointment. Intimate femicides had brought women together in mourning six times in less than eighteen months, and Patricia Allen's murder had drawn international media attention, primarily because Allen had been a lawyer, according to Women's Urgent Action founding member Donna F. Johnson. Her murder illustrated, as Johnson said, "that wife abuse is a problem among all social classes," and the attention it attracted showed that "in our society some women's lives are seen to have more value than others" (Johnson 1998, 7). Over 500 people attended two separate vigils in Patricia Allen's honour — one organized by Women's Urgent Action and the other by her professional colleagues — both in Minto Park. By contrast, only thirty people bore witness to the vigil held in December 1993 for twenty-three-year-old Sophie Filion, who had worked part-time in the sex trade and whose beaten and strangled body was found in a green garbage bag in a parking lot.

After all these vigils, Johnson said, "we were no longer under the illusion that each time we gathered it might be the last" (1998, 8). Minto Park, moreover, had a heritage designation, and there were restrictions around the planting of further trees. The park had become recognized within the community "as a place where women come together to grieve and protest," so when "[t]he idea for a Women's Monument was conceived," it seemed the logical site for such a memorial (Johnson 1999, 315). Women's Urgent Action met with local politicians and women's groups, and in November 1991 they formed the Women's Monument Committee. In collaboration with local community groups, the committee set about raising money to commission "a memorial to all women who have been murdered by their partners and to those women still living in abusive situations," one that would "serve as a rallying point, a reflective place and a catalyst for change … a permanent reminder that violence against women in our society will not be tolerated" (Dewar n.d.).[3] This permanent marker was designed to honour women murdered while encouraging observers to move beyond loss and into action.

There had been some opposition to the original vigils themselves. One police social worker assigned to work with Pamella Behrendt's children, for example, opposed the holding of a vigil on the grounds that it would "make matters worse" for them by focusing on the murder, and the objection led to Pamella Behrendt's name not being mentioned at the service or on the plaque (Johnson 1998, 3). There was also controversy following the establishment of the monument, most notably centred around having Sandra Campbell's name inscribed on one of its stones before the trial of her husband, Robert Campbell, had taken place. As it happened, the murder charge against Campbell was stayed because the judge felt that the six-year wait between his arrest and anticipated trial would be "an excessive and unreasonable delay" (Campbell 2000, D2). Sandra Campbell's name was eventually removed and replaced with "Jane Doe" "to represent the women whose murders have gone undetected, disguised as accidents, suicide, or death from natural causes" (Johnson 2000, A17). But the City of Ottawa, the police and municipal authorities for the most part co-operated with and supported the organizers in the initial stages of planning the monument.[4] The city committed space "in the eastern-most circular garden within Minto Park," but it stipulated that design, construction and installation costs of $10,000, as well as $200 for the dedication ceremony and annual maintenance, were the responsibility of the Women's Monument Committee (Department of Recreation and Culture 1992).[5]

The committee contracted a collaborative team of two feminist artists who had worked together in the past and had earlier engaged "in a continuing discussion about commemorating the Montreal Massacre in a permanent way." c.j. fleury (a visual artist dedicated to work in and with communities) and Mary Faught (a landscape architect) decided to work on the monument under the name of Agents of Gaia, the ancient Amazonian goddess identified with mother earth. As c.j. fleury (2000) explains,

> What was important was the names and the realities of the women whose names were ON the Monument marker stones. For me ... the association of our personal names was not at all important with the monument and i have never really wanted to change this. My belief has always been that the monument design and building could have been Gaian type work, if she was here now, and that if people thought long enough about who Gaia was, they might consider themselves possible candidates for such "agency"... they too could be "Agents of Gaia."

The artists conceived of the site as "a spiralling path leading to a large central boulder, with smaller stone markers to stand for each [local] woman that had been killed. The ground treatment materials would be low growing plants for the area where the small markers would be situated and crushed red brick … for the walk-on part" (fleury 2000). The site was to be wheel-chair accessible, and the last curve of the spiralling path was to culminate into the monument's inner space, or "enclave." Traces of the spiralling path remain in the vortex-like shape of the enclave itself, and in three intersecting spirals engraved on the top of the central stone.

The central boulder, 2 metres (6 feet) high, was conceived of and built as a "woman-stone," the peach-coloured granite taken from a quarry in the Eastern Townships. According to fleury:

> i really didn't want to cut the stone, have it cut and manipulated ... and Mary agreed with this. The importance of finding a stone with hips, letting it stand as it was, not needing to be sawn into some warped standard of beauty ... or gaze of desire and control, and cutting into its natural form [was paramount]. (fleury 2000)

The artists explained the monument's symbolism and projected interactivity and use:

> Agents of Gaia created this monument in the tradition of the massive standing stones. Designed for community participation, the space is welcoming and hopeful. Touch the symbols. Visualize change. Make rubbings. Carry the feeling to a wider circle. This granite marker is set at the hub of a red spiral path, creating a safe space, a rallying point. ENCLAVE is both a place of memory and action. It acknowledges a turning point towards an improved future. The smaller stones honour each of the Ottawa women killed within the past two years. Looking out in their own direction, they stand as guardians of the ENCLAVE. In Spring the mounded spiral garden will blossom, first, with tulips and then be filled with Thyme. (Agents of Gaia n.d.)

They worked "ancient feminine symbols of continuity, renewal, cycles, passage and hope" into the stone, with a spiral at the top representing "childhood, maturity and the elder years ... all stages where abuse may happen ... all stages where action and changes can take place." Changing moons, separating the French and English versions of the monument's inscription, "represent female harmony with the universe and speak of the passage of time." The artists' description of three thickly engraved parallel lines running across the bottom of the stone typifies their joining of mythology and activism:

> The waves represent the cleansing healing properties of waters of the Earth, the waters of the Mother ... the waters in which humanity is formed. They represent the flow of time, the past, the present and the future. Intersected by the large yoni shield shape [on which the monument's dedication is inscribed], HERE AND NOW, we speak out for change. The repeated waves, drawn from a female hand, echo the hope and energy of this sight. Tracing the flowing lines with your own hand, you become part of the voice and action for zero tolerance of abuse and violence. (Agents of Gaia n.d.)

Other images used on the stone include figural representations of women that flank and seem to support the central inscription-bearing shield, and along its top, bottom and sides are the Egyptian signs SA (protection) and Ahnk (life); the Nordic rune meaning "invincible"; the American symbol for the Equal Rights Amendment; a figural representation of the East Indian tree goddess (the spirit of the oak); and a reproduction of a fourth-century BCE Greek head of Athena.

> These signs from Women's heritage are engraved here to represent all women, all ages, and all races. The visual design on the stone and on the Earth focuses on the positive ideas of renewal, and the empowering forces that can grow after intolerable acts are committed towards our sisters, mothers and daughters. The symbols, like the rock, will stand for generations and speak of a time where women and children are respected and thriving. (Agents of Gaia n.d.)

The boulder is a prominent feature within the open, safe and well-lit park, which fills the narrow block bordered by Elgin and Cartier Streets and Lewis and Gilmour. The park's generous branching pathways, benches and picnic tables attract pedestrians from the cafés, stores and restaurants of Elgin Street as well as from the apartments and single-family homes in the economically diverse residential neighbourhood that surrounds it. The boulder sits at the eastern edge of the park in a circle of brick, a light grey against the dark foliage of the surrounding trees. It is unusual and prominent enough to attract curiosity, and designed in such a way as to entice strollers and invite interaction.

The feature of Enclave that is most unusual among memorials, and the one that attracts the most attention, is the cluster of smaller stones, under 1 metre (2 feet) in height, which only separate themselves out as individual memorials within the surrounding circle as the visitor approaches them. This swirl of jagged markers resembles half-buried stones that seem to have emerged as naturally as stalagmites from the red ground. They vary in height and shape, each inscribed with assertive lettering that names one of the murdered women. Each name faces a different direction and slopes at a different angle to encourage active engagement in their reading and to suggest the different directions that their lives may have taken.

The cluster draws many shocked comments for its immediacy, specificity and power, and for those witnessing it over the years, there has been surprise at its capacity to grow as stones bearing the names of new victims have been added. Quite shockingly, its capacity to grow has reached its limit quickly:

the final number is thirty-seven markers. Patricia Allen's name stands out atop a small, slanted, triangular stone on the left-hand side of Enclave's entrance, which is flanked on the right by a squat, sloping stone dedicated to Sharon Mohamed that seems to lean as if for support against the adjacent stone. Huddled next to the central boulder, virtually under the shelter of the left extremity of its etched wave, is a small stone dedicated to Lori Heath, an organizer of community safety meetings and a mother of two teenage girls, whose throat was slashed by her common-law husband in September 1993, at age thirty-four, nine months after the installation of the monument. And so it went, the cluster of stones growing continually to crowd the enclave as new horrors happened and came to light.

If the stones are perhaps the most evocative feature of the monument, they have been made controversial by the monument's bilingual inscription.[6] Powerful in its direct naming of violence, the wording was not explicitly approved by Ottawa's city council or given the artists' full consent. The inscription, composed by Jan Andrews and Donna Johnson of Women's Urgent Action and the monument committee, reads as follows:

À LA MÉMOIRE DE
TOUTES LES FEMMES
QUI ONT SUBI JUSQU'À LA MORT
LA VIOLENCE DES HOMMES

IMAGINONS UN MONDE
OÙ LES FEMMES
LIBÉRÉES DE L'EMPRISE DE LA VIOLENCE
S'ÉPANOUISSENT
DANS LE RESPECT ET LA LIBERTÉ

***

TO HONOUR AND TO GRIEVE
ALL WOMEN
ABUSED AND MURDERED BY MEN

ENVISION A WORLD WITHOUT VIOLENCE
WHERE WOMEN ARE RESPECTED

&

FREE

Like the organizers of the women's monument in Vancouver, the Ottawa committee resisted public pressure for generalization and gender neutrality, and insisted on including the phrase that we have incorporated into the title of this book: "murdered by men." Predictably enough, the local press published letters objecting to the exclusion of male victims of violence and of violence in lesbian relationships, because, according to one correspondent, "abuse knows no gender" (qtd. in Casey 2001, 59). The organizers were attacked for their "agenda of vilifying men." "Some feel such a monument empowers them," wrote Andre Perras in a letter to the *Ottawa Citizen*, "and in some twisted way, educates others. It teaches nothing but hate" (ibid.). Even the artists, who were displeased at not being consulted about the dedication, felt that the wording could be seen to be exclusionary, that it could detract from honouring the women murdered and, through backlash, return the focus to men.

The controversies — whether they concern the wording, or the inclusion of women's names before there is a guilty verdict against the accused spouse or ex-partner or come in the form of vandalism and reactionary rage (the monument was twice splattered with red paint, and Kathleen Kendall reports witnessing a man spitting on the boulder, kicking the individual stone markers and shouting abuse at it) — have not served entirely negative purposes, however. The original controversy over the wording kept the issue of violence against women prominent in the letters section of the *Ottawa Citizen* for some time in 1992. The controversy over the inclusion and later removal of Sandra Campbell's name as a victim of male violence generated similar publicity and served as the occasion for a long and incisive feature article by Donna Johnson in the same paper in March 2000. And the vandalism and backlash, in addition to perhaps deflecting violence from actual women to the monument itself, served as the starting point for Kathleen Kendall's moving address in June 1993 to the Seventh National Roundtable for Women in Prison, later published in *Double Time*.

Not all of the response to the monument, of course, was negative. Indeed, many letters to the editor expressed strong support. More importantly, the monument itself, designed explicitly and effectively to support community action, has served consistently as a site both for individual reflection (Kendall describes visiting the site for inspiration) and for various kinds of women-centred gatherings, from Take Back the Night marches and December 6th vigils to International Women's Day celebrations to public rallies and protests opposing "injustices against women, such as the rape of women in war" (Johnson 1998, 8). Of all the memorials included in this book, Ottawa's has one of the highest profiles across a broad activist community.

In many ways, Enclave's most admirable features are its insistence on the local and on the value of every woman murdered, its energizing and performative inclusiveness and its creation by a group of activist women. As front-line workers in the fight against violence against women, they insisted on the right to name names and maintain control of women's representation. Unfortunately, the monument's ability to expand to accommodate memorial stones for all women murdered is limited, and after only a decade it has reached its capacity. Women's Urgent Action itself, having accomplished so much in ten years, decided to disband in the summer of 2000, passing on their memorializing work to the co-ordinator of the University of Ottawa's Women's Centre, at once institutionalizing it (within however small and underfunded an organization) and rendering it dependent on the shifting commitments of a constantly changing student body.[7] Nevertheless, Enclave in many ways represents the attempt to link memorializing and activist causes. As organizer Donna Johnson writes,

> The space is sacred, evoking deep emotion, inviting all who stand before it into the transformative power of memory. Not just to remember. To remember and be changed.

> There is something going on in this moment in history that we do not want forgotten or erased. The Women's Monument documents in stone the murder of women by men in the latter part of the twentieth century. It provides a permanent record of women's efforts to organize against these murders.

> It will be left to our daughters and granddaughters to carry this work forward. To the extent that we take up space, to the extent that we leave behind solid and permanent documentation of our efforts to eradicate violence, we will make their task that much easier. (Johnson 1999, 316)

Chapter 10

MONTREAL:
LIEUX DE MÉMOIRE

Le site dorénavant un lieu où l'écho répond sans fin.
(The site will be from now on a place where the echo never stops
coming back.)

— ROSE-MARIE GOULET AND MARIE-CLAUDE ROBERT,
DESIGNERS OF THE CITY OF MONTREAL MONUMENT[1]

PIERRE NORA, WHO COINED THE TERM WHICH STANDS AS THE TITLE TO
this chapter, argues that society is losing its collective memory. The very
fabric of continuity, lived experience and group identity is damaged beyond
repair in modern life. That is why we need memory-making places: "*Lieux
de mémoire* exist because there are no longer any *milieux de mémoire*, settings in which memory is a real part of everyday experience" (Nora 1996,
1). And that is why those places — especially those commemorating conditions which many would prefer to forget — stand threatened not only by
hate crimes and vandalism but also by the sheer invisibility that comes with
indifference.

Three memorials in Montreal respond to the pressure of silence in
strikingly different ways. The two memorials to the women murdered on
December 6, 1989, standing as they do in closest proximity to the scene
of the actual violence, are most profoundly enmeshed in the tension between the need to remember and the desire to forget. The monument, Nef
pour quatorze reines (Nave for Fourteen Queens), works this dynamic into

its design, embracing the evanescence of memory and drawing the viewer into the process of recall and reconstruction that is central to active remembrance. Up the hill, at l'École Polytechnique, the memorial retreats into silence in a more troubling way, with a discretion typical of campus memorials across the country. Here, however, the memorial's location at the epicentre of the December 6th violence provokes the viewer to question the blanks, to ask what their presence, in this particular place, might signify. The Montreal Mural Tribute to the Missing Women seizes space much more explicitly and vibrantly than the other two memorials, its size, colour and directness of language all insisting that the city be responsible to women murdered thousands of miles away, as well as to its own citizens. In their very different accents, and with different degrees of intent, all three memorials place "the burden of memory" squarely on the viewer's shoulders (Young 2000, 131).

NEF POUR QUATORZE REINES (NAVE FOR FOURTEEN QUEENS)

The corner of Rue Decelles and Chemin Queen Mary in Outremont is a bustling intersection of cars and pedestrians, the heart of the francophone student quarter. Tucked in at the base of Mont Royal, just down the hill

from Université de Montréal, these two thoroughfares take traffic from La Côte-Des-Neiges on the south, Ste-Catherine on the north, the university on the east, and feed it into mixed blocks of residential apartments and retail buildings, coffee shops, children's playgrounds and subway stations. Streets converge at oblique angles, with multiple traffic lights attempting to control the flow; at busy times traffic gets jammed in tight. On a bleak spring day, negotiating the traffic — in car or on foot — or even sitting in the crowded coffee shop on the corner, it's easy to miss the sign for Place du 6-décembre-1989, hanging high up from a post on Decelles, or to register the monument itself in your peripheral vision. Once discovered, however, the memorial creates a calm centre amidst the bustle, drawing the viewer into a space of reflection and active remembrance.

The site is a grassy rectangle, a city block long by about 18 metres (60 feet) wide, with a path running longways down its centre, flanked on each side by seven, 1-metre (3-foot) high steel stelae (or upright pillars) and, beyond them, parallel rows of mature trees. On closer examination, each of the stela is a raised letter, the initial of the first name of each woman killed on December 6, with the remaining letters of their personal and family names fanning out in an arc of steel against granite, which is embedded in the ground on either side of the path. The design takes some deciphering: first, noticing that the stela is sculpted into a three-dimensional letter, then piecing together the fragmented shapes on the ground. The names are made the more obscure by a covering of dirt and by the objects — white memorial roses, for example, but also pieces of litter — left atop the stelae. Engraved into the granite at the base of each stela are the years of each woman's birth and death. Again, it can take some scrubbing to uncover and decipher these engravings in the paved ground. As the viewer puts these details together, the realization of loss washes over her.

The stated goals of the monument's designers represent several ideals of feminist memorializing. Their aim was to create a kind of "counter-monument" whose horizontal dynamic works against the traditional upright thrust of official war monuments and whose attention to specific names joined in one larger pattern registers both individual loss and a larger systemic wrong. The design features encourage the visitor to participate in the act of memory-making, inculcating an awareness of violence against women as an everyday, systemic threat and attempting to link the individual to the collective in that process. In their published statement, artist Rose-Marie

Goulet and landscape architect Marie-Claude Robert treat the site not as the occasion for a monument to be viewed at a distance but as "lieu de mémoire (a space of memory)" which invites passersby to participate in the "événement commémoratif (commemorative event)." One way in which this spatial participation is designed to work is by shaping the rectangular plot into a passage, both literal and conceptual. The east-west path bounded by the sculptured stones, rows of trees and, at greater distance, apartment blocks leads the visitor physically through the space, with potential stops at the stelae, identified by the designers as "podiums," but also potentially places of rest as armchairs, altars or pedestals.

Also involved in that journey is a passage of understanding, as the viewer pieces together the parts of the names fanning out on either side: "Le promeneur est environné par ces noms. Il ne tourne pas autour de monuments commémoratifs mais traverse plutôt une zone de mémoire. (The walker is surrounded by these names. He/she does not go around commemorative monuments but rather traverses a zone of memory.)" The difficulty of deciphering the names draws the reader into the power of naming, arrested by the puzzle of the one raised letter, then participating in the putting together of letters to trace powerful, evocative family and personal names. Those arcs have an additional resonance. Again in the words of Goulet and Robert:

> Les répercussions et l'impact de l'événement sont comme un écho infini, profondément diffusé dans la société, une onde de choc. C'est ce que cherche à représenter ce site-monument. Les sept arcs de cercle, dont les rayons courent du nord au sud, et qui sont disposés en fréquence de plus en plus distancée, inscrivent la trace de cette onde dans le site, et la symbolisent. (The repercussions and the impact of the event are like an infinite echo, intensely diffused in our society, a shock wave. This is what this site-monument is trying to convey. The seven arcs of the circle, in which the radius runs from north to south, and which are arranged in a frequency of a growing distance, outline the trace of this shock wave in the site and symbolize it.)

There is also religious solemnity suggested in the analogy between the fourteen women's names and the fourteen Stations of the Cross, along with the very specific shock involved in encountering so many different years of birth, each accompanied by the same insistent year of death — 1989 — fourteen times over. Together, these design elements integrate the individual's sense of horror with a collective resistance to violence.[2]

The effect is powerful and profound. The visitor is drawn into the heart of the memorial, first by puzzlement, then a dawning realization and shock, all underscored by a sense of complicity in the implications (as well as in the reconstruction) of the event. There is no text within the sculpture at eye level suggesting how we should think about the murders. Instead, the interactive design draws the visitor into the process of active and collective remembering. The artists' intention is stated explicitly on a modest tablet with informational text under glass, situated at the westernmost edge of the park: "Nous évoquons ainsi, avec force, leur nom et leur prénom de façon que toute personne qui passe par là cherche à les lire, à les répéter et ne les oublie pas (Thus, we are emphatically evoking their family and given names in such a way that all who walk there search to read them, repeat them and don't forget them)."

The monument's materials support the effects of recognition in their symbolic (as well as their enduring) qualities. The granite and steel, which form the fourteen names, were chosen for their associations with, in the first case, funeral monuments and, in the second, the engineering profession towards which the women were working. Setting curving bands of these materials into the grass also evokes, more metaphorically, the rib cage of a body returning to the earth.

As always with memorials to women murdered, however, the process is finely balanced. The passerby might easily miss the densely layered connections and associations, seeing only a set of disconnected shapes marking a path through a small park. She might fail to notice the site at all, lost within the urban congestion and busyness. And, of course, annually the sculpture literally returns to the earth, blanketed under the deep snow of Montreal's arctic winters. This perennial process carries its own power, as each spring the memorial returns to visibility and forgetfulness reawakens into memory, but again the balance between absence and presence is delicate.

The modest location exacerbates the potential for invisibility. One commentator has argued the merits of the site: "The gravel path, which intersects with the monument is a favorite for students; it is easily accessible by public transportation; and the site, lined by trees on both sides, provides a natural frame for the monument" (Casey 2001, 52). Also, as the designers say, the park's position does provide "son ouverture sur la ville (openness to the city)," and reinforces the memorial's intervention into everyday activity and awareness. But the site is not emphatically announced, since its two identifying signs are distinctly obscure. The glass-covered text, quoted above, which contains much suggestive description about the artists' designs and processes, is not prominently positioned. On one of our visits, the face of the tablet was obscured by swastika graffiti; on another, the entire structure had been removed. The signpost on Decelles designates the site — "Place du 6-décembre-1989. En mémoire de l'événement tragique survenue à l'École polytechnique de 6 décembre 1989 afin de promovoir des valeurs de respect et de non-violence (In memory of the tragic event at l'École Polytechnique on 6 December 1989 in order to promote values of respect and non-violence)" — but the plaque shares its post with other municipal notices warning against littering, biking, feeding the birds or letting dogs run in the park and, again, easily gets lost in the jumble. Just southwest, across the street from the Place du 6-décembre-1989, there is an example of a much more elaborately marked city site in the stone pillars, plaque and driveway that sweep into La Cimetière de Notre Dame des Neiges, an architecture that grandly and insistently draws attention from even the most casual or most hurried of passersby.

We read the site's understated features as the imprint of official reluctance, a powerful sculpture played down by its setting. Charles Foran has written about the palpable divisiveness "among officials, both in the

municipal government and at the Université de Montréal" affecting discussions of the memorial project. At the ceremonial announcement of the
finalists in the design competition, held at the proposed site on December
6, 1998, "the one man on the dais, Jean-Paul Gourdeau, president of the
Polytechnique, was visibly unhappy to be there." A year later, around the
time of the unveiling, the local press conducted repeated soul-searching,
reflecting on why it had taken city council such a long time to sponsor a
permanent, public memorial, especially compared to other cities across the
country: "Pourquoi Montréal n'avait pas encore de monument à la mémoire
des victimes alors que Vancouver, Toronto et Moncton ont inauguré le leur
dans les années qui ont suivi la tragédie? (Why did Montreal not yet have
a memorial to the victims when Vancouver, Toronto and Moncton inaugu-
rated theirs in the years after the tragedy?)" (Lachapelle 1999, A1). Several
answers were suggested: Montrealers needed time for their wounds to heal
before they faced the task of memorializing; especially at institutional levels,
a certain avoidance, a wish that the event would recede from public memory had been circulating; and the attempt to move from individual deaths
to their symbolic embodiment was particularly painful and delicate in the
community (see, for example, Lebeuf 1999; Moore 1999; Curran 1999).

Ultimately, the most effective pressure came from those closest to the
murdered women. In 1993, la Fondation des victimes du 6 décembre contre la violence came into being as the organizational face of the families
and friends of the women murdered at l'École Polytechnique. The group
worked with different levels of government to promote anti-violence initiatives, playing a key role, for example, in the intense and effective lobbying
for gun control legislation, which resulted in the passing of Bill C-68 (the
Firearms Control Act) in December 1995. More recently, the foundation involved high-level Quebec ministers and corporate leaders in a public awareness campaign against verbal and physical violence, and it has repeatedly
joined forces with women's groups, victims' groups and the pan-Canadian
men-against-violence White Ribbon Campaign. In 1994, the foundation determined to push for a concrete reminder of the women murdered
and the impact of the massacre on Montrealers. Through Thérèse Daviau
— foundation member, city councillor and mother of Geneviève Bergeron
— they presented a motion for a monument to city council. After consideration by the city's cultural service, the proposal was finally approved
(Curran 1999, A8).

Once the Montreal city council was involved, city politics and proce-dures came into play. The choice of a site took time and negotiation. The park at Rue Decelles was not approved until September 15, 1998, and, although there was no public outrage (such as the Vancouver and London memorial-makers endured), there was a hint of dissension: in the words of one Montreal journalist, "relatives, police and university and city officials, though united in shock and mourning, could not always agree on how or what or where to remember" (Curran 1999, A4). The next step was a design competition, controlled by Le Bureau d'art public du Service de la culture of the City of Montreal, for a piece of public art that would be allotted $240,000 from the city coffers.[3] Each phase of the process was attended by a degree of pomp and circumstance, culminating in the announcement on May 6, 1999, of the winning design by artist Rose-Marie Goulet, as-sisted by landscape architect Marie-Claude Robert and consultant engineers Nicolet Chartrand Knoll Limitée, at city hall in the presence of numerous municipal and provincial dignitaries. Similarly, the unveiling of the monu-ment — now entitled Nef pour quatorze reines (Nave for Fourteen Queens) — attended by nearly 350 people on December 5, 1999, was presided over by the mayor in the presence of several other high-level public officials and Madame Claire Roberge, president of the foundation at the time.

While the site, in its everyday presence, hardly embodies that pomp and circumstance, the foundation has worked to revive the effects of ceremonial dignity and official presence at least once a year. The foundation organizes December 6th gatherings which, typically, involve ceremonial performance quite different from — and in some instances more elaborate than — the huddled gatherings of women at more modest memorial stones across the country. In December 2004, for example, the foundation invited the com-munity to gather at Place du 6-décembre-1989 for a remembrance vigil followed by a torchlight march to St-Joseph Oratory for a choral concert. On other years, women's choral recital has accompanied the laying of roses at the memorial itself. These ceremonies promote public awareness and of-ficial attention in the name of tranquillity and healing. As the notice of the 2001 vigil put it, the annual ritual is held "sous le signe de la simplicité et du recueillement (in the name of simplicity and meditation)"("La commé-moration" 2001).

Clearly, the memorial also brings comfort to family members, embody-ing both their pain and the healing process. Family responses on record echo the designers' emphasis on the ripple-effect of their sculptured arcs: one newspaper account paraphrases the mother of Anne-Marie Lemay, on the pain caused by the massacre spreading "like waves set off by a pebble thrown in a pond," and the father of Maryse Leclair describing the aftereffects "like the shock waves of a bomb" (Ha and Peritz 1999, A20). Claire Roberge appreciates the subtle method by which the names "are fashioned in empty spaces. They are not here. They are absent" (ibid.). And Sylvie Haviernick, sister of Maud Haviernick and a recent foundation president, is quoted as saying the monument "brings serenity"(Moore 1999, A5).

These effects are notably different from the scream of rage orchestrated annually at the Women Won't Forget memorial in Toronto or the searing testimonies of abuse spoken at memorial stones elsewhere. But, in its own ways, the Montreal memorial makes a palpable impact on public memory-making. The first memorial event, on December 6, 1999, the day after the sculpture's unveiling, changed the face of public remembrance locally. Le comité du 6 décembre at l'École Polytechnique called on people to gather at the on-campus memorial plaque, then silently march down the hill to the Place du 6-décembre-1989. The result was the first large-scale show of December 6th solidarity on the Université de Montréal campus, with more university officials and federal, provincial and municipal dignitaries than had ever turned out before. Thérèse Daviau was described in the press as being "happy that the Polytechnique is now taking a more active role in Dec. 6 commemorations and anti-violence campaigns. Until recently, she said, the school had been reluctant to do so because of concern about its image" (Johnston 1999, A5).

Nef pour quatorze reines actively resists the ever-present threat of invisibility and forgetfulness. Its participatory dynamics and its strong resonances for those most intimately touched by the murders qualify it as what Suzanne Lacy (1995) calls "new genre public art": that is, art which engages with its space and its constituencies in politically sensitive, community-oriented ways. For those who find the monument and work out how to read it, this most thoughtful and self-consciously feminist of sculptures promises powerful and provocative remembrance.[4]

L'ÉCOLE POLYTECHNIQUE, UNIVERSITÉ DE MONTRÉAL

Up the hill from the Place de 6-décembre-1989 is the second memorial, both more obscure and more central. Whereas it took ten years to bring the City of Montreal's monument into existence, the commemorative plaque at l'École Polytechnique was dedicated on the first anniversary of the massacre. It is a simple enough plaque, 14 cm (48 inches) square, of dark green granite, with fourteen stainless steel nails — again evoking engineering materials — creating a round design within it. At the top of the circle is the emblem of l'École Polytechnique (a bee), with the words "in memoriam" and two columns of the fourteen women's names, ending in the date "6 DÉCEMBRE 1989." The ground beneath the plaque has been modestly landscaped into a semi-circle of deciduous shrubs bordering some flagstones, creating a small space in which people sometimes leave cut flowers and mementoes. Traditional enough, the memorial derives most of its tremendous charge from its location, flush against the south-west wall of

l'École Polytechnique, between the darkened glass curtain of the student canteen and the walkway to the door of the building. This is as close as the women get to being remembered at the places of their deaths. Rampaging through the building with an assault rifle, Marc Lépine murdered students Anne-Marie Edward, Annie Turcotte and Barbara Klucznik Widajewicz in the canteen; students Geneviève Bergeron, Hélène Colgan, Nathalie Croteau, Barbara Daigneault, Maud Haviernick, Maryse Leclair, Anne-Marie Lemay, Sonia Pelletier, Michèle Richard and Annie St-Arneault in second- and third-floor classrooms; and Maryse Laganière in the corridor outside the budget office where she worked.[5] He also injured thirteen other people throughout the building.

This site is, in several ways, at the heart of the Université de Montréal campus; it is diagonally across from the university's landmark tower, positioned at the top of Mont Royal with expansive views over the city. That placement can be read, simultaneously, as both honouring and containing the memory of the women murdered. In design, the memorial is, explicitly, an institutional production, calculated to fit with the public ethos of the school:

> Le monument commémoratif a été dessiné par M. Louis Courville qui assumait les fonctions de directeur général intérimaire au moment de la tragédie et a été réalisé par les sculpteurs Claude Bernard et André Fournelle. Il répond aux critères que l'École s'était fixés à savoir la permanence, la simplicité, la sobrieété, la qualité des matériaux et du rendu ainsi que l'intégration étroite au bâtiment. (The commemorative monument was designed by M. Louis Courville, who took on the position of interim general director at the time of the tragedy and it was realized by sculptors Claude Bernard and Andre Fournelle. It fulfils the criteria that l'École Polytechnique has set for itself, namely, permanence, simplicity, sobriety, a quality of material that would render it impervious to decay and a tight integration with the building.)[6]

The memorial's design, with its spare shapes and unobtrusive materials, visibly fits the architecture of the building: a huge, square 1960s building with vast expanses of concrete, yellow stone and glass. Indeed, the "tight integration" of the plaque with the building operates to such a degree that the memorial virtually disappears. When the viewer stands to read it, what is reflected back in the polished granite is not one face among many actual and potential victims — as with the evocative women's monument in London, Ontario — but the reader's body dwarfed by the surrounding vertical and phallic shapes of the university's architecture. Adding to this sense of incorporation into the fabric of the university is the fact that, on one of our visits, the memorial was overshadowed by a gigantic fundraising banner stretched across the wall above it.

When the monument was unveiled, there was no press release and the ceremony was treated as a private event. University spokespeople justified the lack of display by citing family sensitivities.[7] Other commentators understood the strategy more as the institution's preoccupation with its own image: "Officials at the Polytechnique, worried that the school's name would be forever linked with a murderous misogynist, refused to authorize any memorial services on campus. Their one concession was a bronze plaque, erected near the entrance to the cafeteria, that listed the names of the 14 women and the date — with no explanation of how or why they died" (Curran 1999, A8). Certainly, Suzanne Laplante-Edward, mother of Anne-Marie Edward, found the university's gesture inadequate, arguing that the city was taking too long to create a monument, "especially given that the very, very modest little monument that is sitting on the wall of École Polytechnique is not public. It is private" (qtd. in Moore 1999, A5).

In this environment, the lack of explanatory text in the memorial has a much more ambiguous effect than in the monument down the hill: the absence feels like silence rather than an invitation to the viewer to make her own meanings. There is no naming of the murder, no connection suggested with wider patterns of violence against women, no recognition even of the lives of the fourteen women. It is their common death not their individual births or lifelines that is recorded. The one counterbalance to this tendency towards invisibility is carried by the viewer herself, in her knowledge that in coming to the place of violence, she has completed the literal journey which is signalled more symbolically in the Nef pour quatorze reines. Contact with the actuality of place can have various effects — when we were there, the site brought some of us closer to the shock of realization, to digesting the reality of murder, to pursuing a process that conjoins political effectivity and personal healing — but none of those possibilities is articulated or enabled in the memorial's concrete form. In the face of the systemic denial of femicide — what Caffyn Kelley analyses as society's "collective amnesia" (1995, 7) — that which is not spoken can too easily become forgotten. In the words of Louise Malette and Marie Chalouh (1991), prefacing a book which they offer as a memorial to the Montreal Massacre: "If, in the weaving of individual existence, there are times when forgetting is therapeutic, for women there are times when remembering is imperative."

MONTREAL MURAL TRIBUTE TO THE MISSING WOMEN

The imperative of remembering operates much more visibly and explicitly in a three-storey-high mural whose splash of colour jumps out among the bustle of downtown Montreal. On the wall of the Native Friendship Centre at the corner of St-Laurent and Ontario Streets, a massive, vibrant red and blue painting depicts and explains a scene of violence and healing. The top third shows boats floating through a starry sky: Ojibway spirit-boats (as the accompanying text explains) carrying souls through the stars, each of which represents one of Vancouver's "missing women." Embedded in each star is a piece of glass from the shore of the Restigouche River that runs along the land of the Listuguj First Nation in Quebec.[8] Below are the silhouettes of the Vancouver and Montreal skylines. The bottom third depicts five figures of various races and genders — a composite of everyone who contributed to the mural — holding a red banner. On the banner, in English, French, Inuit and Mohawk is written "We Honour the More Than 60 Sex Workers Most of Them Indigenous Who Were Killed or Disappeared in Vancouver." Beneath all these Images is the explanation of their meanings and a dedication, again in four languages. The English reads:

WE PAY HOMMAGE TO THESE WOMEN, VICTIMS OF
THE COMFORT AND INDIFFERENCE OF A SOCIETY
THAT WOULD SOMETIMES RATHER SEE THEM AS
SOMETHING TO BE ELIMINATED.

THIS MURAL IS ALSO DEDICATED TO THEIR FRIENDS,
THEIR CHILDREN AND FAMILIES, TO THEIR LOVERS
AND LOVED ONES.

YOU WILL NOT BE FORGOTTEN.

The community which saw this work to completion is a world away from the organizations and institutions responsible for the other two Montreal

memorials. For some years, temporary memorials had been circulating with-in this community. Sheila Swasson — Mi'kmaq supervisor of Haven House, an Aboriginal women's shelter, and an activist in the network of Aboriginal women shelters and the National Aboriginal Circle Against Family Violence — for example, had been mounting a tribute to the missing women, in paper form, at Haven House's annual wellness fair.[9] In summer 2003, the Living Monument Mural Collective, an ad hoc group forged through ac-tivist networks and personal connections, collaborated with the Coalition for the Rights of Sex Workers to craft a more permanent remembrance. Along with individuals from the Native Friendship Centre, and Stella and supporters, they created a more permanent mural, which was officially unveiled on September 18, 2003.[10] Volunteers all, the painters ranged in experience, skill and background, but came together around a commitment to activist remembering.

Like the other two Montreal memorials, this mural carries intimations of healing and dignity, as it pays homage to these women and portrays the survival of their souls. Its difference is that it not only resists societal indifference, it names and protests it. The mural's explicit political analysis challenges passersby — seizing us not so much as individuals, in the way of Nef pour quatorze reines, but as a society — to recognize our own complicity in the indifference that contributed to these murders and to commit to remembering and making change.

Chapter 11

MONCTON AND RIVERVIEW:
COURAGE AND HOPE

With Courage and Hope we will proceed
 One by one, and together
In the knowledge that by reaching down
 To help the one behind
The chain thus formed will carry us all
 To reach our goals.

—Valerie LeBlanc,
"Complementary Equality and Respect"

On the two banks of the Petitcodiac River, in the southeastern corner of New Brunswick, sit two memorials to violence against women. One is in the foyer of Moncton city hall, an elegant new glass-and-concrete building whose heft, architecture and position bespeak considerable municipal authority. The other sits well into a park across from Riverview town hall, a more modest red-brick building within a smaller municipality across the river, which tends to function as Moncton's anglophone suburb. Both works result from women's organizing groups whose membership overlaps; both drew on the local community in their making; and both are crammed with thoughtful language that aims to join memory and change. The defining difference between them is that one is classified as a work of art and the other as a memorial.

We have seen examples of public art all across the country, some by established artists as the result of thousand-dollar design competitions, some by more neophyte artists working on modest commission or for free. Different as they are — from realist to abstract, from metal figures to stone forms — these works tend to cost more and to occupy civic space more declaratively than the conventional boulders and plaques produced without a formal artistic process. The contrast between the Moncton and Riverview memorials points to some consequences of public art's cultural capital: it brings access to resources, prime location and pedagogical reach but also pressure to deliver what James Young calls "art's traditional redemptory function in the face of catastrophe" (2000, 2). In the case of Moncton's sculpture, the pressure is to discover inspiration in the confrontation with violence against women, a pressure redoubled by the corporate decorum of its city hall location.

CASELEY PARK, RIVERVIEW

What is said to be the first December 6th memorial in the Atlantic provinces was unveiled on December 6, 1996, in Caseley Park, Riverview. The location gives the visitor pause, in a couple of ways. The monument sits about a third of the way into the expansive, tidy shrub- and conifer-planted park, flanked on one side by the familiar towering granite obelisk of a war monument and on the other by an armoured tank from the Second World War. Like the London Women's Monument in Victoria Park (discussed in chapter 5), this memorial seems an eruption of women's desire for peace among masculinist homages to what is seen as courage displayed in war. Also, Riverview is an anglophone suburb, not the most central location for political statement. A couple of kilometres across the Petitcodiac River is Moncton, which, as New Brunswick's largest city and with about a third of its population francophone, might seem a more obvious choice.

In fact, it was the first choice of the organizers. In 1993, two Moncton community workers, Helen Partridge (chair of the Women's Committee of the Moncton and District Labour Council) and Jean Claude Basque (Canadian Labour Congress representative), decided that the time was right "for erecting a monument as a permanent memory for all women who have suffered from violence."[1] Support seemed likely in the wake of the 1991 federal declaration of December 6 as a National Day of Remembrance

PLEUREZ—LES AUJOURD'HUI; AGISSEZ DEMAIN
FIRST MOURN: THEN WORK FOR CHANGE

ENVISION A WORLD WITHOUT VIOLENCE
WHERE WOMEN ARE FREE AND RESPECTED
IMAGINEZ UN MONDE SANS VIOLENCE
DANS LEQUEL LES FEMMES SONT
LIBRES ET RESPECTEES.

TO HONOUR AND TO GRIEVE ALL ABUSED WOMEN.
NOUS RENDONS HOMMAGE A TOUTES LES FEMMES
VICTIMES DE VIOLENCE ET DEPLORONS LEUR SORT.

IN REMEMBRANCE OF OUR FOURTEEN SISTERS
WHO WERE KILLED IN MONTREAL ON DEC. 6, 1989.
A LA MEMOIRE DE NOS QUATORZE CONSOEURS
TUEES A MONTREAL LE 6 DECEMBRE 1989.

and Action on Violence Against Women and the decision by the Moncton and District Labour Council to install a monument in memory of all injured workers in Tidal Bore Park (a process that was completed in 1995). Partridge was particularly committed to finding a very visible space that would heighten awareness of the local relevance of December 6th, "to make this day of action very public in … [the] eyes [of the community] because it's happening so many times to a neighbour or a friend, a cousin, but it's kept in the background so many times" (qtd. in Goddu 1996, 1).

For three years, a committee worked to raise funds and find a location. Co-chaired by Helen Partridge and Cathy Murphy, the committee was made up of women already working in other community groups and a student from the Université de Moncton.[2] They raised money piecemeal, from local unions and with fundraising events, eventually commissioning the SMET monument company of St. Stephen to construct the memorial. The real stumbling block was the question of location. Seeking as central a site as possible, the committee approached the City of Moncton, which was in the process of planning its new city hall. The full details of the negotiations have not been made public, but it is on record that the city objected to the form of the memorial. Parks and Recreation told the committee that there were enough monuments and that "maybe if we had a unique sculpture it would be better." Faced with this refusal, the women turned to the town of Riverview across the Petitcodiac. According to Partridge, "They couldn't have been more honoured." With the help of the Riverview mayor and personnel from Parks and Recreation, things went very smoothly from then onwards and a site was agreed on in Caseley Park, next to the town hall.

In coming to that agreement, the committee never entirely surrendered the goal of involving city hall. When they organized the dedication ceremony for the memorial on December 6, 1996, they preceded the unveiling in Caseley Park with a "Public Awareness Forum" earlier in the day in the lobby of the recently completed city hall in Moncton. The two events replayed the different emphases of municipal authority (where officialdom and the rhetoric of "balance" predominated) and the women's organizing committee (with the dedication ceremony explicitly led by and dedicated to women).[3]

The monument, which was unveiled that day before 200 people, is dense with thoughtful images and words. Almost 2 metres (7 feet high), it is a highly polished, circular pink granite form set on a white granite base. Curved around the circle is an exquisitely engraved scroll, unfurled to reveal the words "Pleurez — Les Aujourd'hui; Agissez Demain," "First Mourn: Then Work For Change." Centred beneath this text is a dove that incorporates the woman symbol; below this are words that directly exhort the viewer to reach for a better future:

> ENVISION A WORLD WITHOUT VIOLENCE
> WHERE WOMEN ARE FREE AND RESPECTED.
> IMAGINEZ UN MONDE SANS VIOLENCE
> DANS LEQUEL LES FEMMES SONT
> LIBRES ET RESPECTÉES.

Further down the tablet:

> TO HONOUR AND TO GRIEVE ALL ABUSED WOMEN.
> NOUS RENDONS HOMMAGE À TOUTES LES FEMMES
> VICTIMES DE VIOLENCE ET DEPLORONS LEUR SORT.

Finally, on the base:

> IN REMEMBRANCE OF OUR FOURTEEN SISTERS
> WHO WERE KILLED IN MONTREAL ON DEC. 6, 1989.
> À LA MEMOIRE DE NOS QUATORZE CONSOEURS
> TUÉES À MONTRÉAL LE 6 DÉCEMBRE 1989.

The language and imagery insist on a future of peace while not forgetting the violence of the past. They embrace both the fourteen women in Montreal and "all abused women" in a generic gesture, which (again like the London Women's Monument) does not name individuals. And they repeatedly specify women as the motivating force for this memorial and the effort for change. These emphases shaped reporting by the local press, which linked the new memorial to the need to address the problem of systemic denial and to the release of a 1995 report on family violence, which documented the doubling of reported assaults in New Brunswick in the previous year.[4] The fact that December 6th vigils have continued to take place at the monument is a testament to its ability to speak to local women and exhort them to action.

COURAGE AND HOPE, MONCTON

Two years after the dedication in Riverview, Nancy Hartling, founder and executive director of Support to Single Parents, tried the mayor again, this time proposing that city hall in Moncton house an original piece of art denoting violence against women. The emphasis on art changed the response. The mayor immediately supported the idea, and the resources of officialdom swung into action with a vigour and readiness absent from the earlier memorializing process. The difference is visible in the size of the paper trail, in the agencies that participated in this effort, even in the production qualities of the forms and flyers and invitations circulated to the public.

Hartling pulled together the December 6th Art Project Committee, with representation from public and private agencies, including some

members of the Riverview group.[5] They organized a design competition for local artists, both amateur and professional, with a $5,000 prize. The completed work would be donated to and maintained by the City of Moncton's Collection of Fine Arts. Twenty-eight submissions came in, many of which the committee judged "too violent" or "too gloomy." The organizers wanted something that "would get you moving and recognize the sadness." In other words, they were looking for a balance between remembering the past and changing the future. Ultimately, the committee favoured a design by local artist Valerie LeBlanc. Entitled Courage and Hope, the design's main element was a golden ladder — with "seven rungs to allow us to pass over top of the tragedy that occurred at the École Polytechnique" — tilted against a sheet of glass etched with quotations from local girls and women about their future dreams and plans (LeBlanc 1998a). For LeBlanc, the height of the ladder was particularly symbolic: "'six feet tall' is a recognized descriptive phrase in western society. It speaks of braveness, strength, and achievement" (LeBlanc 1998b). The committee appreciated the work's focus on changing the future for local girls, its communication of hope and encouragement, its ambitious physical dimensions, and the fact that the artist had lived in Montreal at the time of the massacre. The piece also conveyed a degree of productive ambiguity: for the artist, the glass represented the glass ceiling for women; for the organizers, the glass represented the fragility of progress in the women's movement.

LeBlanc planned to visit local schools, gathering the future ambitions of girls and young women of all ethnic backgrounds — Mi'kmaq, French, English, African-Canadian and Jewish (LeBlanc 1998a). During the course of events, the process became a little more bureaucratic, with the committee distributing a form in English and French to administrators of educational institutions, inviting young women to articulate in one sentence their "present dream or plan for the future." The form asked participants to identify their "Cultural Background," and it modelled diversity by including examples of self-identification from mixed backgrounds: Mi'kmaq, English and Scottish; Acadian and Irish; and South Asian. In providing examples of girls' ambitions, the form also encouraged thinking beyond conventional gender roles: "When I grow up, I would like to be a Veterinarian. *or* When I grow up, I would like to be a Mother and a Doctor. I would like to become an athlete. *or* I would like to study science to become an astronaut."[6] It is common to talk of the educational project of public art, especially when it

attempts to shape public or collective memory. The impact here was peculiarly direct. The municipal commission enabled the artist to coach local
girls and young women of the next generation — some of whom would
have been infants at the time of the Montreal murders — to conceptualize
their future in the context of the violence done to those who came before
them.

Throughout the process, the artist and the committee appear to have
worked together amicably. While LeBlanc has commented on the inevitable
"red tape" of city hall, she has praised the organizers for being easy to work
with and for giving her artistic freedom (LeBlanc 2001). She also adapted
her design a little in response to committee suggestions, particularly from
an engineer who proposed that the round base be replaced with a fourteen-
sided design reminiscent of the engineer's ring and that the names of the
Montreal women appear there rather than on the glass between the ladder rungs. Once LeBlanc's proposal was accepted, fundraising was fast and
effective. While it took three years for the Riverview memorial to come
into being, this campaign reached its target of $6,000 (about twice as big a
budget) in three months. Many sponsors may well have found it easier to
support a work of art than a memorial, as the established interest groups of
the area rapidly lined up.[7]

The dedication ceremony for Courage and Hope was as carefully re-
sponsive to municipal and community concerns as all other parts of the
process. The chosen date was December 4, 1998, to accommodate city hall's
hours of operation and to avoid conflicting with the December 6th vigil
at Riverview. At the ceremony, local women murdered were listed by first
name only, after long debates about the appropriateness of naming. The
keynote address was delivered by Marie Robichaud, a sixteen-year-old student from l'École Polyvalante Mathieu-Martin, who addressed both violence — "one in 10 Canadian women is beaten regularly and ... a woman is
raped on average every 17 minutes in this country" — and gender inequity
in the workplace: "The ladder symbolizes that we have to keep striving for
our goals and never settle for the minimum" (Carrol 1998, A3). Female
students, each accompanied by a male student, laid roses on the memorial
for the fourteen women killed in Montreal, and "to emphasize that violence hits close to home, a fifteenth rose was placed in remembrance of ten
women who died violently in Metro Moncton within the past decade"
(ibid.). Close to 200 people attended, and people trickled in for days

afterward to see the sculpture, which was publicized in the local and national media.

The finished piece shows marked poise in its elegance and its balancing of elements. City hall's interior decoration suggests more a work of art in a spacious gallery (or a corporate head office) than a memorial to violence against women in the political arena. The foyer is gleamingly modern, with lots of glass, polished brass, well-tended greenery and uncluttered space for the daily traffic of workers and visitors. Courage and Hope is to date city hall's only permanent memorial installation. Displayed to the right of the main entrance and central to much of the traffic going through this space or up the open-tread stairway, the 2-metre (6-foot) sculpture repeats the building's materials with its angling of a gold-coloured aluminum ladder against a "door-sized" sheet of transparent glass, the ladder's top rung and struts reaching just above its edge. Inscriptions in English and French are sandblasted sideways up the length of the glass. The words rise from the base, some fanning out slightly and curving in and over the top like growing plants, each inscription followed by a female's first name. The support is a metal base with the names of the fourteen women murdered in Montreal on the fourteen edges.

The sculpture walks a fine line politically, as can be seen both in the process of its creation and in its physical details. From the first, the committee's vision balanced commemoration and change, anger and hope, as expressed in its "Call to Artists":

> In Canada an act of male violence against women occurs every 6 minutes. A Statistics Canada survey of 12,300 women stated that more than half of women 18 years and older have suffered physical or sexual abuse at the hands of men. The December 6th Art Project committee believes that even in the midst of despair there is hope. They envision the creation of an original artwork that will generate a greater awareness of the issue of violence against women, evoke reflection on the issue and inspire a desire for change.

LeBlanc (2001) articulated a willingness to compromise with dominant social attitudes so that a better future might be forged out of a violent past: "Although I saw the killer as a monster I've always felt that this is what we have to work with … I have a lot of feminist viewpoints but I live in a public world."

A similar balancing act is evident in one of the sculpture's most distinctive features — the quotations from the next generation — which feels poised between conformity and individuality. For example, the visibility of ethnic and cultural diversity that the artist was so careful to nurture in the solicitation process has been greatly diminished in the finished sculpture. The speakers are represented only by their first names, there is no account of the selection principles and the only languages are French and English, echoing the official languages of the municipal milieu. The admirable reminder of the local cultural specificities so often contained or effaced by generalizing gestures towards "all women" has disappeared. This loss of individuality could have derived from the context in which these quotations came to be submitted, on official-looking forms, administered by teachers and educators, co-signed by parents or guardians if the student was under eighteen. It seems unlikely that they articulate girls' most private hopes and dreams.

In addition, a youthful idealism — sometimes personal, sometimes social — often echoes through all their dreams, in terms which universalize, rather than politicize, their messages:

Mon but, être heureuse dans la vie (My goal is to be happy in life).

—*Madi*

Je rêve que l'être humaine apprécie et respecte toutes choses vivantes et non-vivantes dans l'universe (I dream that human beings will appreciate and respect all animate and inanimate things in the universe).

—*Jessica*

Many bridge traditional and non-traditional roles for women, in a pattern reminiscent of the examples on the response form:

My dream and goal is to be a mother and an orthodontist.

—*Robyn*

To be a veterinarian/marine biologist, and a mother of adopted children.

—*Sarah*

But several take the viewer by surprise with their very specific and experientially grounded sense of social responsibility:

To help take care of premature babies in the hospital.

—*Clarice*

When I finish school I would love to become a detox counsellor
(working with women).

> —*Helene*

The fourteen names on the base are occasionally evoked more directly, through the profession of engineering — "Être appréciée comme une femme, mais être écoutée comme une ingénieure (To be appreciated as a woman, but listened to as an engineer). —Josée" — or the disavowal of violence — "Mon réve est qu'il n'y ait plus de violence dans le monde (My dream is that there will be no more violence in the world). —Sylvie."[8]

The artist's major design change had to do with these inscriptions, and it tipped the rhetorical balance of the sculpture still further towards future prospects. Originally, she planned to inscribe the local girls' quotations horizontally so that they were laid "out in such a manner as to fill the glass surface, in the style of ancient tablets such as the Rosetta Stone, the Ten Commandments, etc.," with the names of the fourteen Montreal women "carved at measured intervals between the rungs of the ladder" (LeBlanc 1998a). This design wrote women — the dead among the living — into official history with some of the feel of Teresa Posyniak's Lest We Forget sculpture in Calgary. When, in response to a committee suggestion, LeBlanc moved the fourteen names to the base and reoriented the quotations into vertical lines, she produced a gentler, more organic effect. Whereas the names of Lest We Forget cascade downwards in a crumbling pillar, these names with the quotations grow upwards from the women murdered in Montreal, the longest and most poetic of them curving around the top of the glass like a frond then curling downwards among the others. It expresses the wish "Que les tristes mélodies des souffrances humaines du 20e siècle inspirent un hymne à la responsabilité de l'autre pour les chants du 21e siècle (A wish that the sad melodies of human suffering in the twentieth century will inspire a hymn of responsibility to others in the songs of the twenty-first century). —Michaëlla." Collectively, with this framing quotation as the capstone, these young voices do indeed redeem a vigorous future from the violence of the past.

A panel on a nearby wall, in a crisp black-on-white and white-on-black design reminiscent of explanatory text in art galleries, makes the redemptory symbolism explicit. In English, it reads:[9]

COURAGE AND HOPE

THE DECEMBER 6TH ART PROJECT COMMITTEE, WHICH REPRESENTS MANY COMMUNITY GROUPS, COMMISSIONED ARTIST VALERIE LEBLANC TO CREATE AN ORIGINAL SCULPTURE, TO COMMEMORATE THE VICTIMS OF THE DECEMBER 6TH MASSACRE AT THE ÉCOLE POLYTECHNIQUE IN MONTRÉAL AND TO PROMOTE AND ENCOURAGE THE DREAMS AND GOALS OF WOMEN IN THE FUTURE.

ENTITLED *COURAGE AND HOPE,* THE UNIQUE DESIGN ACCOMPLISHES THESE GOALS. THE BASE, FORMED TO REPRESENT AN ENGINEER'S IRON RING, IS ENGRAVED WITH THE NAMES OF THE FOURTEEN YOUNG WOMEN WHO WERE MURDERED ON DECEMBER 6TH, 1989. THE DREAMS AND ASPIRATIONS OF LOCAL YOUNG GIRLS AND WOMEN ARE ETCHED INTO THE GLASS AND THE GOLDEN LADDER IS REPRESENTATIVE OF THE BELIEF THAT AS A COMMUNITY WORKS TOGETHER TO ELIMINATE VIOLENCE, THESE GOALS WILL BE ACCOMPLISHED AND SURPASSED.

UNVEILED DECEMBER 4, 1998

A list of donors follows: over two dozen local, provincial and national organizations, community groups, professional associations, commercial businesses, and almost fifty individuals, the majority of whom are women. The total effect speaks again of a kind of professional control or cool officialdom bearing down on delicately balanced meanings.

Valerie LeBlanc had proposed a more poetic text to accompany her sculpture: the verse entitled "Complementary Equality and Respect" that opens this chapter. Like the language on the memorial in Riverview (and others across the country), this text addresses viewers directly, including us in the first-person plural pronoun and exhorting us to act. The proposed dedication does not provide a literal explanation, but instead presents the sculpture as an invocation to act. It puts us as viewers in a more interpretive role, requiring us to work out the meanings of the various features and quotations for ourselves. This more poetic text — like the less angular base and the fluid blending of women's names, living and dead, in the original design — also evokes human connection and mutual support. The replacement text, in contrast, emphasizes the fourteen-sided engineer's ring and stresses the corporate context in which the sculpture sits. In its various rhetorical and material dimensions, then, the upscale civic context focuses attention on hopes for the future growing out of and perhaps overshadowing the violent past and present that the December 6th Art Project Committee set out to remember.

Nonetheless, responses to the Courage and Hope sculpture confirm its inspirational intent. One city hall employee, for example, told the artist, "It's a real joy to see that there everyday" (LeBlanc 2001). The organizers themselves have stressed the positive. Levesque: "It gives me energy not to give up"; Hartling: "It was exciting that the city said yes — that we have a place here, and that I was ensuring a place for my daughter"; and Pilard, who clearly envisions this balance as a process of transformation: "We all have some personal experience of overt and intrinsic violence ... I needed to move it forward." In the final analysis, that delicate balance seems to be what remains: the balance between the less visible, more direct text of the Riverview memorial, which participates annually in the renewal of memory as a spur to activism, and the more centrally located Moncton sculpture, which is part of many workers' daily lives but whose message seems less interventionist. While the Riverview memorial directs us how to think of the past, Courage and Hope directs us to envision faith in the future.

Chapter 12

BEAR RIVER:

IN MEMORY OF ANNIE KEMPTON

It's the evening of December 6, and members of the tiny rural community of Bear River, Nova Scotia, are writing the names of murdered women on paper bags, putting candles into the bags, and floating these lighted memorials down the river. They join in this ritual "to honour the memory of all victims of violence; those who have died as well as giving hope to those victims who still survive"[1]... Some participants write the names of the fourteen women murdered in Montreal, some write the names of more local victims of femicide, and some write names with private, even secret resonances. On one bag, a woman etches a name unfamiliar to most activists: the name of Annie Kempton, murdered in 1896.

THIS QUIET ACT WAS UNDERTAKEN BY THE ORGANIZERS OF THE BEAR RIVER Candle Float. Taking place as it did in a highly picturesque "village-on-stilts" about 5 kilometres inland from Annapolis Basin, just off the French Shore of Nova Scotia, this act of remembrance might not seem as central to the political arena as some efforts recorded in this book. In its way, however, the naming of Annie Kempton in the context of December 6th takes on some central challenges in memorializing women murdered: the great will to contain and control memory-making on the part of established social interests; the depoliticizing which results from that containment; and the need for women to take ownership in the production of memorials if they are to expose systemic violence. Above all, the case of Annie Kempton demonstrates how powerful the eruption of history is. The sustenance of her memory over more than a century reveals just how deeply entrenched the social manipulation of violence against women is and what a crucial role the process of memorializing can play in disrupting it.

There are three permanent memorials to Annie Kempton in Mount Hope Cemetery, which is located high on a steep hillside overlooking the village of Bear River where she lived and died. The small unpolished stone marked "A.K.," sitting obscurely to one side of her burial plot, remembers her privately, as one of the anonymous dead. The much grander column, the

tall white urn sculpture of standard Victorian design, placed at the gravesite by her family, memorializes her as murder victim:

IN
MEMORY OF
ANNIE KEMPTON
WHO FELL BY
THE HAND OF
HER ASSASSIN
ON THE NIGHT
OF JAN. 27 1896
AGED 15 YRS.

Most imposing of all, the four-square polished black granite stone in the cemetery's central area stands as a public monument to virginity:

ERECTED TO THE MEMORY OF
ANNIE KEMPTON
AGED 15 YEARS
WHO LOST HER LIFE JAN. 27, 1896,
IN HER FATHER'S HOUSE, IN A DESPERATE
STRUGGLE TO PRESERVE HER HONOR.

THE SUBSCRIBERS HEREBY EXPRESS
THEIR PROFOUND RESPECT FOR THE DEPARTED
ONE AS A HEROINE IN HER MAINTENANCE
UNTO DEATH OF THE HIGHEST VIRTUE OF
A CHRISTIAN CIVILIZATION — THE SACRED
HONOR OF WOMANHOOD.

The emphasis in this last dedication — on honour, respect, heroism, civilization, virtue and the sacred — suggests a high level of anxiety around the possibility of sexual assault and how that might reflect on the social order of the community at large.

Now a picturesque tourist spot known for its crafts, Bear River in 1896 was still prosperous but on the cusp of decline. Having participated in Nova Scotia's golden age of shipbuilding, the village was seeking new sources of income. The tidal river from which the village takes its name, once thick with lumber for the shipyards, had recently undergone hydro development (it had the first hydraulic power plant in the province), the farmlands remained rich, and the population of about 1,000 was mostly of comfortable means. But the village had failed to secure a railway link and was beginning to feel cut off from the main line of commerce and influence.

Within the close-knit community, class and race lines seem to have been geographically explicit but also in the process of changing. Annie, a schoolgirl and Sunday school teacher whose family were thrifty farmers of the middle class, lived in a comfortable Cape Cod-style house up the hill towards the cemetery. Across the river was Indian Hill, a Mi'kmaq reserve of about 200 inhabitants, while down in the more thickly settled valley of the village was a cluster of single-storey cottages inhabited by labouring families of Acadian, Scots-Irish, Anglo and African-Canadian descent (Hall

1998, 162). Among the villagers and living directly down the hill from the Kemptons was Tillie Comeau, a more unconventional figure than Annie, who had come off the Reserve as a child and now ran her own house, supporting herself and her four children by various means. From time to time she served as companion to Annie when the Kempton parents were absent overnight. She also kept as a lodger one Peter Wheeler, a sometime sailor and odd-job worker, identified as a "Yeoman" on the jury verdict: "It is a term for the lowest class of freeholder and the lowest class of seaman" (Thurston 1987, 106). In the local press attention that came his way, he was very much represented as the outsider — a shadowy figure of mysterious origins in the Mauritius Islands, who had turned up as an odd jobber in Bear River. On June 30, 1896, Peter Wheeler was convicted of murdering Annie, and on September 8, 1896, he was hanged.

The story that came out during the trial was that Wheeler attempted to rape Annie and, when she successfully resisted, he cut her throat. Although Wheeler provided a written confession, his version of events differed from the prosecutor's. The court believed that, having tricked Tillie Comeau into leaving Annie alone at home, Wheeler attacked Annie in the early evening, stunning her with a blow to the head and returning later in the evening to kill her. Wheeler claimed that Annie let him in to the house in the very early hours of January 28, and that, after she resisted his rape, she begged him to murder her. His account was taken as an effort to besmirch Annie's honour by suggesting that, even though unaccompanied, she would allow a man into her home, late at night; it also absolved him of some measure of responsibility by his claiming that she begged for her death. The death date on both inscriptions, January 27, therefore carries some coded significance in the restoration of honour to Annie.

In any event, the murder caused public outrage against the convicted criminal — whose hanging in Digby jail had to be brought forward secretly to avoid a lynching — and public demonstrations of respect for Annie. A floral tribute was sent to her funeral by the Governor General of Canada. Further description comes from a recent publication by Arthur Thurston:

> After the extremely moving service the casket was slowly carried down the church steps by six notable citizens and placed on its hearse. Side by side walked the escort of schoolmates and citizens and it is stated that it was the first time in the history of Bear River that the obsequies of any woman, or girl, however eminent were so honored. (Thurston 1987, vii)

The schools remained closed for the remainder of that week in observation of her death, while a committee of local businesspeople began to raise subscriptions for a monument in her honour.[2] As part of this effort, the local *Bridgetown Monitor* published the following call:

> Are there not one hundred men, yes, and hundreds of women too in these counties who would give a dollar each, or more if required, to place a suitable monument at the grave of Annie Kempton and thus show our appreciation of her valor and commemorate her virtue?
>
> Bear River may very well call Annie Kempton a heroine whose deeds, though they may not appear as history, are worthy of recognition because of their virtuousness.
>
> And is not a person who considers the honor of virtue before life a hero? Is a person less a hero because his or her valor is not spread before the world over a period of years?
>
> There are everyday heroes in our land with heroism unknown, and Annie Kempton was a heroine, we think. (qtd. in Thurston 1987, 115–116)

The call was very successful, attracting over $250 from companies and individuals in the locality. The committee held a competition among local monument makers, selecting what they considered the most imposing design by the Stant Bros. (of Saint John, NB) — a standard 1.5-metre 25-cm (5-foot 10-inch) black granite structure with highly polished and finely chiselled faces.[3] For the inscription, the committee approached "a man well skilled in the use of language," and the letter "K" at the top of the monument was copied from Annie's own script (Thurston 1987, 162; Hopkins n.d.). The committee also decided to place the stone in the cemetery's public square, a more prominent site than the actual gravesite. Mr. and Mrs. Kempton wrote to the local paper, thanking "the public" for contributing to the monument fund (Thurston 1987, 366). All this was done in the months after Annie's death, but the monument was not erected until early October, after Wheeler's execution.

During the same period, the Kempton family ordered a stone for Annie's grave in their family plot. The small surplus remaining from the public-monument fund was donated for this stone, partly because there had been some disagreement over the placing of the public monument. *The Digby Weekly Courier* reported on the morning of Wheeler's execution: "It is proposed to place the monument on the public square in the cemetery, but there is some feeling against this and many side with Mr. and Mrs. Kempton that the monument should be placed over the grave of the young girl" (September 8, 1896). As it was not placed over her grave, the donation meant that the family could buy quite a grand marker. Thurston described it as "a white stone column of the type fashionable in the 1890's bearing the same floral design as evident on Annie's half sovereign love token" (1987, 162, 390). By its colour, shape and conventional associations, this stone speaks more to the feminine than does the heavier design of the public monument. The original grave marker remains in place next to the column, although the small figure of a lamb in white stone, remembered as sitting next to the marker by one of Annie's descendants, has now disappeared (Abriel 2001). Tillie Comeau's grave, in the Gehu family plot of the same cemetery, lies unmarked (Thurston 1987, 379).

In a time and place which seem to have been thick with instances of gendered violence and femicide, these monuments to Annie Kempton are unusual signs of attention paid to a woman murdered. The fact that the community publicly mourned a middle-class white woman murdered prefigures the inequities in memory-making across race and class which have become so stark since 1989. (We have found no mention of violence against women of colour in the annals of Bear River.) To some extent, again in a pattern familiar today, the notoriety is more attached to the male murderer than to the female victim: Peter Wheeler's hanging is remembered as the last at Digby. But Annie remains as a well-known figure locally. Over the years, there have been many poems and songs written in her memory, variously sentimental and sensational, including one from Digby in the 1930s which is a parody of "Sweet Alice Ben Bolt" from the 1931 John Barrymore movie *Svengali*. Town histories consistently include her in their coverage of significant people and events, and there is the 1987 Arthur Thurston book devoted entirely to her story. Her memory also seems to inspire remembrance across race as well as generation: her gravestone appears in a book about the African-Canadian heritage of Bear River because Harry Hill, Black caretaker of the cemetery, has kept up the grave for forty years. Fresh flowers still appear on the two larger memorials to Annie.

Yet the power of the memorial is not yoked in any very explicit nor public way to the struggle against violence against women. Indeed, both contemporaneously and more recently, there seems a will to keep the memory and its associations pure precisely by containing them within a closed community. In 1896, the forces mustered in support of Annie Kempton's memorial speak clearly to a community upholding its own proper image, publicly putting its house in order and reinforcing lines of class and gender. The language of the trial and its press representation, the monuments' inscriptions, the rhetoric and source of the fundraising, all seem to flow from established authority and to reinstate hierarchies of social order. Similarly, the conventional materials and designs of the monuments, along with their positioning in the local cemetery (quintessential spot for "keeping the dead dead") contain the murder within formulas of respectability. The insistent emphasis on Annie's honour and virginity seems as much an insistence on the virtues of the community — "the subscribers" — who are honouring her and an expunging of those who don't belong.

In the "Ballad of Peter Wheeler," composed shortly after these events, this emphasis is made yet more effective by being put in the mouth of the perpetrator who admits to "shedding the blood of one so young, so innocent and good" in a "bold attempt to blighten maidenhood." The moral explicitly presents the events as a cautionary tale about the perils of transgressing class position:

If I had lived as I'd been taught and stayed in my own place

I'd never died this shameful death, my parents to disgrace. (Hall 1998, 87)

The ballad ventriloquizes Peter Wheeler's voice in a complementary way to the public memorial incorporating Annie's voice — the one perspective on the murder we will never know — through her handwritten letter "K." In a community on the cusp of decline, these gestures read like efforts at shoring up the status quo.

In the twentieth and twenty-first centuries, as the economic decline has continued, that sense of containment has mutated into a protectiveness about the past. In Florence Bauld's African-Canadian account of 1995, for example, Mount Hope Cemetery becomes the repository of better times, with Annie Kempton a central presence:

The graveyard is a shrine to the glorious past of the village. Annie Kempton, whose short life spanned a period when Bear River was in flowers, shares this space, with ship builders, merchants, woodworkers, doctors, farmers, the bold enterprising settlers who made this western Nova Scotia community a major industrial and trading centre for almost a century. (Bauld 1995/1997, 24)

For Annie's descendants, the urge to protectiveness turns inward, as a cherishing of the family's privacy. This is a familiar response from more recent murders; clearly, at least in this case, the familial urge does not lessen over time. Even today, the family shies away from media coverage, preferring that it remain a very private, personal family tragedy, and asks that information be circulated in a way that honours and respects the memory of their cherished ancestor. The one attempt that we know of to take Annie's memory out of the cemetery in a more permanent form than the Candle Float — establishing in the village a small museum display of artifacts associated with her — was vetoed by the local historical society. Even after more than a century, the discomfort has not entirely disappeared from this community.

The naming of Annie Kempton at the inaugural Bear River Candle Float, then, is a notable event: the closest her memory has come to the political arena. The connection is also encouraged— again, with quiet suggestiveness — by electronic association. The website "Bear Town Boogie," mounted and maintained by Elizabeth Hopkins who also initiated the Candle Float, features several links, among them one to the Bear River Candle Float and one to Annie Kempton's story.[4] The Bear River Candle Float site is "lovingly dedicated to victims of violence ... and to those who still survive" and is itself connected to local activity and provincial activism, including the Purple Ribbon Campaign launched by the Women's Action Coalition of Nova Scotia in 1990. While there is no explicit commentary accompanying the Annie Kempton link, it does provide the story of her murder, a photographic portrait and images of her memorials. The implication is that by connecting historical femicide with present efforts at memorializing violence against women, a lineage of protest will nurture the contemporary movement.

We hope to contribute to this effort to bring Annie Kempton's memory out of the cemetery and into the political arena by including her story in this book. This is the oldest example of a very public memorializing of femicide in Canada that we have discovered. Although in many ways it couldn't be more different from the post-1989 acts of memory-making, it does evoke utterly familiar issues to do with euphemism, prettification and social control. A century before the massacre of women in Vancouver's Downtown Eastside, Montreal's l'École Polytechnique, and countless sites across the country, the memorializing of a young woman's murder in rural Nova Scotia tells us the same thing: that the meanings that memory takes say at least as much about how a community wants to see itself as about the woman murdered.

Chapter 13

FIRST NATIONS WOMEN REMEMBER

because you are female
because you are Indian
because you are smaller than me
because you inconvenience me
because you're handy

you are in danger
I am your danger

— FROM "MIGRATION," BY JOANNE ARNOTT

(gather[ing] up bones)
I will carry you, I will care for you, I will feed you, and I
will sing you songs of comfort.
I will wash away the dirt, and the ragged flecks of flesh and
skin
And you will be warm
And you will be loved
      And I will build memory

— FROM *The Scrubbing Project*, BY TURTLE GALS

TWO THINGS BECAME APPARENT TO US AS WE UNDERTOOK THE RESEARCH
for this book. The first was that, for reasons that may be both material and
cultural, there are very few conventional memorials to First Nations women

in Canada of the kind on which we have been focusing, in spite of the vast-ly disproportionate number of women murdered who are First Nations,[1] and in spite of the fact that violence against Native women in Canada has served throughout history as a material agent of genocide. As we searched for memorials, we found that there were many personal, impromptu or un-official memorials, such as those to Helen Betty Osborne, often at the sites of women's murders. There are also rituals — such as the traditional heal-ing ceremony held on April 12, 2002, that included the laying of a wreath in Port Coquitlam; the new annual Forget Me Not walk in Vancouver on February 1st; and the long-standing annual Valentine's Day march in the Downtown Eastside — which honour and grieve women murdered there. There are also collective artistic projects. The Living Monument Mural Project in Montreal involved a diverse group of artists, including Aboriginal activists, who painted a three-storey mural on St-Laurent Street in honour of Vancouver's women murdered. The Never Again! Project in Toronto has created the memorial quilt Vanished Voices. According to one of the orga-nizers, Amber O'Hara (Waabnong Kwe):

> This quilt will hold panels honouring missing (cold cases) or murdered women throughout Canada. We hope to have our sisters on this quilt. Once completed, the quilt will travel from community to community rais-ing awareness about society's attitude towards missing women, the lack of investigative procedures being carried out by law enforcement agencies in some cases. We will also provide resource material for services offered in each area the quilt visits. (O'Hara 2003)

There has also been the 2004–05 Sisters in Spirit campaign by the Native Women's Association of Canada. NWAC used the campaign to lob-by the federal government, in the name of "remembering our missing and murdered aboriginal sisters," for a $10-million fund that would be dedi-cated to research and education on violence against Aboriginal women.[2] One prominent publicity tool was a poster listing many of the over 500 Aboriginal women who have gone missing or been found murdered in Canada over the past twenty years.

The second thing that became apparent was that it was not appropri-ate for five non-Native authors simply to include First Nations memori-alizing practices within learned modes of analysis, which have themselves served over history as technologies of colonization and subjection, any more than it was appropriate to leave those practices out of consideration. But in addition to impromptu sites, parades, processions and quilts discovered in our research, we also found poetry, plays and other written rememberings in which First Nations women represent themselves. What follows is a selection of some of these writings, some from previously published sources, some published here for the first time.

HELEN BETTY OSBORNE

Marilyn Dumont

 Betty, if I set out to write this poem about you
it might turn out instead,
to be about me
or any one of
my female relatives
it might turn out to be
about this young native girl
growing up in rural Alberta
in a town with fewer Indians
than ideas about Indians,
in a town just south of the "Aryan Nations"

 it might turn out to be
about Anna Mae Aquash, Donald Marshall, or Richard Cardinal
it might even turn out to be
about our grandmothers,
beasts of burden in the fur trade
skinning, scraping, pounding, packing,
left behind for "British Standards of Womanhood,"
left for white-melting-skinned women,
not bits-of-brown women
left here in this wilderness, this colony.

   Betty if I start to write a poem about you
it might turn out to be
about hunting season instead,
about "open season" on native women
it might turn out to be
about your face   young and hopeful
staring back at me   hollow now
from a black and white page
it might be about the "townsfolk"   (gentle word)
townsfolk who "believed native girls were easy"
and "less likely to complain if a sexual proposition led to violence."

   Betty, if I write this poem

PENUMBRA

Annharte

for Betty

Temporary the shade my straw hat weaves
across my basket face of Caribe pleasure.
The bright sun makes me want to run and jump,
I had been told if I were smart, I'd stay hidden.
On my island, I keep to myself and lie around.
Turtles crawl past me to dig their nests.
Tortuga oil is outlawed and so am I.

Odd, this exposure of my not too recent killing.
Seventeen years it took getting to court
those who mashed my face because of dark skin.
Hating the contrast of each pinky penis
I left The Pas to be a turista and relax.

They understand I stayed away to make sure
I'm not the only witness to their sorry act.
Not even good at it, I might add as insult.

The reserve is a huge donut around the town,
no place to go unless you're Indian like me.
Laughing at the other end of the beach
gets me wondering how it's my turn.

EVERYBIT RACE SHELL

Annharte

to do to want to escape
to slug it out without a shell
shell me dance shell she dance
shell we dance oo wee oo wee
shell fish one buy her product

shell wedge her body in twine
she space shell switch more wine
shell game race shell front score
kick it kick off watch her take off
she must be space shell lady crime
rough husk drops back to earth
lands on the dirt cover shell back
belongs to husky bitch turtle what
dandylion dusky crick neck captivates
where the shell used attached before

never race intended slurry under
pigs trotters slippage on sludge
sea shells sea whore sell shells
race shell mixture not worthy pressure
contents spread dicey wicey on table
purse open an um biblical sow ear
shows sea urchins secret untimely news
plenty pricks great porcupine head
porcine probable shell cases course

rack it up to the racial unknowns
bi-racial multi-racial blown jobs
know what is talk about goes gross
dismember bent meant went vent
hardly an oink was heard above
hard hearing underneath each harley roar
extra space shell why not every
scream might blow out eardrum muff
higher pitch than a siren girl song
held to the ear meat mollusk moans
how space shell again space shell
shell the race begin or end period
bloody biz arterial blood fissure
that huge sow stands to hide behind
block clear view to a tiny piglet
pinch tale caught up in pubic drama
throats not choked combine each grunt

wow find unique condition all shell
except shun shell all face shell
said race shell business shell gain
 brisk sales on ebay won't ever buy it

FOR ANNA MAE PICTOU AQUASH ...
Joy Harjo

*For Anna Mae Pictou Aquash, Whose Spirit is Present Here and
in the Dappled Stars (for we remember the story and must tell it again
so we may all live)*

Beneath a sky blurred with mist and wind,
        I am amazed as I watch the violet
heads of crocuses erupt from the stiff earth
        after dying for a season,
as I have watched my own dark head

appear each morning after entering
the next world
    to come back to this one,
        amazed.
It is the way in the natural world to understand the
place
        the ghost dancers named
after the heart/breaking destruction.
    Anna Mae
        everything and nothing changes.
You are the shimmering young woman
      who found her voice,
when you were warned to be silent, or have your body
cut away
from you like an elegant weed.
    You are the one whose spirit is present in the
dappled stars.
(They prance and lope like coloured horses who stay
with us
through the streets of these steely cities. And I have
seen them
    nuzzling the frozen bodies of tattered drunks
                on the corner.)

This morning when the last star is dimming
        and the buses grind toward
the middle of the city, I know it is ten years since they
buried you
    the second time in Lakota, a language that could
        free you.
I heard about it in Oklahoma, or New Mexico,
    how the wind howled and pulled everything
down
in a righteous anger.
    (It was the women told me) and we
understood wordlessly

the ripe meaning of your murder.

As I understand ten years later after the slow changing
                                    of the seasons
that we have just begun to touch
        the dazzling whirlwind of our anger,
we have just begun to perceive the amazed world the
ghost dancers
        entered
            crazily, beautifully.

In February 1976, the unidentified body of a young woman was found on the Pine Ridge Reservation in South Dakota. The official autopsy attributed the death to exposure. The FBI agent present at the autopsy ordered her hands severed and sent to Washington for fingerprinting. John Trudell rightly called this mutilation an act of war. Her unnamed body was buried. When Anna Mae Aquash, a young Micmac woman who was an active American Indian Movement member, was discovered missing by her friends and relatives, a second autopsy was demanded. It was then discovered she had been killed by a bullet fired at close range to the back of her head. Her killer or killers have yet to be identified.

ABORIGINAL WOMEN REMEMBERING

Jean Becker

This essay is dedicated to all murdered Aboriginal women wherever and whenever they were murdered, whether they are remembered or forgotten. You are our sisters, our mothers, our daughters, our aunties, our grandmothers. I recognize you in me and me in you. When I read your stories the hair on my arms rises as if a cool wind lightly moves across my skin for I know that your life could have been mine. Could have been mine. I honour you, I weep for you, I remember you.

Native Girl Murdered
Faces I have seen
Places I have been.
Is there a song?
"It could have been me."
Shelley Napope- free spirited
"restrictions and discipline of the stuffy classrooms weren't to Shelley's liking"
Disappeared, found murdered, age 16
It could have been me.

Two themes emerge in the literature on murdered Aboriginal women in Canada. The first is the impact on Aboriginal women of the social disruption in Aboriginal communities and the second is the invisibility and marginalization of Aboriginal women in this country — a tribute to the racism and classism that too often continues to define who is important in Canadian society. While Aboriginal women have undoubtedly been murdered in disproportionate numbers throughout the violent history of colonization in Canada it is a subject that has received little attention for most of that history.

Poor social and economic conditions in many Canadian Aboriginal communities are reflected in appallingly high statistics in suicide, accidental death, drug and alcohol use; poor health, including high incidences of tuberculosis, AIDS and diabetes; a high rate of infant mortality, high unemployment and low participation rates in post-secondary education. It is no surprise to learn that the number of murdered Aboriginal women across Canada is also high. Many recent reports suggest that there are 500 Aboriginal women missing in Canada. While there are challenges to this figure, it is clear that the numbers are disproportionately high. In addition, there is a shocking lack of outrage, concern or even interest on the part of the public, the media, government and law enforcement officials about incidents that are often horrific or the numbers of dead women and the degree of brutality used against them.

Murdered Aboriginal women tend to generate little publicity even if they are the victims of a vicious serial killer as in the case of Saskatchewan murderer, John Martin Crawford. Released from prison after serving less than ten years for the 1981 murder of Aboriginal woman Mary Jane Serloin in Lethbridge, Alberta, Crawford was charged in 1992 with raping another Aboriginal woman, Janet Sylvestre. In 1996, he was tried and convicted in the murders of Aboriginal women Shelley Napope, Eva Taysup and Calinda Waterhen — each one murdered in 1992 within months of the Sylvestre rape. In 1994, Janet Sylvestre's body was found in a grove of trees near Saskatoon. During the same period, Shirley Lonethunder also disappeared. In his 2001 book about Crawford, *Just Another Indian: A Serial Killer and Canada's Indifference,* Warren Goulding noted that the Saskatoon police did not need to answer the question of whether these women might have fallen prey to Crawford because "no one was asking" (xiv). Neither the Saskatoon nor any outside media paid much attention to the missing and murdered Aboriginal women of the area. Goulding speculates that this is partly because of the depiction of these women as members of an underworld where people routinely "dropped in and out of sight," and partly because they were women who had no close relationships with immediate family and nobody who cared about them when they were alive. Goulding, however, shows this to be a false picture, as each of these women's families was in frequent contact with the police (xvi). In the cases of Aboriginal women

missing in the Vancouver area, inquiries about many of them were made within days of their disappearance because they had missed a regular call or visit to family or friends.

Reports indicate that as many as 60 percent of the missing women involved in Vancouver's Downtown Eastside investigation may be Aboriginal. When DNA evidence of Aboriginal women was discovered at the Pickton property in Port Coquitlam, memorials and healing ceremonies were held to honour all of Vancouver's missing women. On April 12, 2002, Aboriginal women and elders from across the country gathered for a healing ceremony outside the farm (CBC News British Columbia 2002). On February 15, 2003, the Valentine's Day Women's Memorial March in Vancouver included Aboriginal drums, traditional button-blanketed women and the offering of tobacco and prayers in the Downtown Eastside. Marches were also held in Ottawa and Toronto to coincide with the Vancouver march. In the first months after DNA evidence was discovered, a lot of media attention was paid to the case. As the months have gone by, interest has dwindled and it has become increasingly difficult to get information on an ongoing basis.

As shocking as the Vancouver case is, British Columbia is no stranger to multiple murders of Aboriginal women and girls. In 1994–95 BC's Highway 16 was dubbed the Highway of Tears after four Aboriginal girls between the ages of fifteen and nineteen were murdered along a stretch of that highway, and two others are still missing. Little was widely known about these cases until June 21, 2002, when a non-Native tree planter, twenty-five-year-old Nicole Hoar of Red Deer, Alberta, disappeared while hitchhiking along the same highway. Undoubtedly, she would not have done so had she known of the six missing and murdered women and had she known that the BC Native Women's Society had criticized the police for failing to acknowledge that a serial killer was preying on women who travelled that road (Smith 2002). Police continue to maintain there is no evidence that the cases can be attributed to a serial killer.

Nicole's disappearance generated a lot of media attention in Western Canada, and the biggest ground and air search in northern BC history was undertaken. Sadly, no trace of her has yet been found, despite a $25,000 reward and the thousands of dollars in a trust fund that have been spent to find her. The contrast between the attention paid to Nicole's disappearance and that of the Aboriginal girls is a stark reminder of the invisibility and marginalization of Aboriginal women in Canadian society. Leonie Rivers, executive director of the BC Native Women's Society, made this poignant observation, "Maybe some of the publicity for Nicole might help everyone remember there were six missing women and girls before her" (qtd. in Smith 2002, 29).

One case that has finally received a lot of media coverage is the murder of Nova Scotia born Mi'kmaq activist Anna Mae Pictou Aquash, killed in South Dakota during the conflict between the FBI and the American Indian Movement at Wounded Knee near the Pine Ridge Reservation in 1975. She was killed with a single bullet to the back of her head, "execution style." Almost thirty years later, Arlo Looking Cloud was convicted of her murder and sentenced to life in prison, while another suspect, John Graham, continues to fight extradition from Canada to the U.S. for his trial. The resolution of this case has largely come about through the tireless efforts of Anna Mae's family.

Another case that came to light twenty years after the event, with the release of a book and then a movie, was that of nineteen-year-old Helen Betty Osborne who was murdered in 1971 in The Pas, Manitoba. Helen Betty was killed with a viciousness that is eerily repeated in many of the murders of Aboriginal women. Some are beaten so severely it is as if the murderer sought to obliterate their very identity. The horror of Helen Betty's murder was magnified by the racism that surfaced in the town, which led to speculation that most of the townspeople knew who had killed her and yet protected the identity of the killers for almost twenty years. Of the four men who are known to be involved in her death, only two have been charged and only one has served any prison time. Her case was reviewed in the *Report of the Aboriginal Justice Inquiry of Manitoba* in 1999 and, on December 6, 2000, the Manitoba government introduced the *Helen Betty Osborne Memorial Foundation Act* and created a provincial scholarship fund in her memory (Manitoba Government 2000).

With books, countless articles, Internet sites, a movie and memorials, Anna Mae and Helen Betty Osborne will be remembered. Most other murdered Aboriginal women will be remembered only by the grieving families they have left behind. In an attempt to end the silence surrounding Aboriginal women and violence, the Native Women's Association of Canada (NWAC) launched the Sisters in Spirit Campaign on March 22, 2004. Events were held in various cities across the country to coincide with the national launch in Ottawa. The one-year national campaign intended to raise awareness of the many missing or murdered Aboriginal women in Canada and called on the federal government to establish a $10-million fund to support research and education related to violence against Aboriginal women. The campaign generated a great deal of interest and support across the country and resulted in a number of reports such as one by Amnesty International exposing the magnitude and severity of the issue. (See www.sistersinspirit.ca.) The federal government has rejected NWAC's request for funding for research and education around the issue of violence against Aboriginal women.

*

I REMEMBER

Jean Becker

Helen Betty dreamed of becoming a teacher.
Shelley's grandmother called her "Owl" in honour of her hugh, dark eyes. She loved berry picking, swimming, music, art, and phys ed.
Ramona's family gathers every year on her birthday for a memorial at the site where her body was found — they will continue until the case is solved.
Calinda's Cree name was Dancing Leaves Woman.
Jaime was a 3rd year psychology student.
Maxine had a Tasmanian Devil tattooed on her stomach.
Pamela was the mother of two.
Edna was the mother of six, the youngest of which was a newborn.
Jennifer loved to sit cross-legged on the couch and read a book.
Cherish was a good student in Grade 11.
Georgina treasured her native heritage, made regalia for powwows, danced, and loved to make bannock.
Maria had pain in her legs.
Cassandra was a popular student who was a positive influence in her school.
Cheryl was a fine mom who loved her children unconditionally.
Tania was an enthusiastic soccer player.
Jennifer was a special student — bright, with high marks, and a natural leader.

Elena believed in the good of all people.

Jocelyn, at age seven, was the youngest person to ever receive Canada's Star of Courage for her rescue of her five-year old cousin from an abductor.

(All of these are Native Women missing and/or murdered in Canada.)

THIS WOMAN THAT I AM BECOMING ...

Marcie Rendon

this woman that i am becoming
is a combination of the woman that i am
and was
this journey backward will help me to walk forward

sister
the rape of a woman
is the rape of the earth
the rape of a child
the rape of the universe

as i voice these words
i watch you turn your well-kept
sunday morning presence
from this body that is heavy
with emotion
surviving
i have violated
your myths of motherhood
knowing full well
some silent summer night
my daughter's screams
will invade your
peaceful sleep
as they echo off the stars
some dew-covered morning
you will walk outside
to gather strawberries

and find instead
a gaping cavern
the ultimate rape
having finally been committed

sister
hear me now
let us take this journey
together

I AM SAD STILL

Monique Mojica

     I wake up —
suffocating   my mouth and nose filled with dirt
Was I dreaming again of drowning?
of being crushed against the ceiling of
     a room suddenly shrinking?
It's hard to breathe so I breathe as little as possible.
My legs are cramped and I have to pee.

     I wake up —
I am in Canada chunks of earth in my nostrils
     roots poking into my side
I taste dirt   and something else ...
     I wake up —
I see the man's face — impassive calm
He looks into the camera
     releases a breath

     I wake up —
I am in Canada gasping to breathe against
     the dust and smell of blood
     "Bueno," he tells the cameraman,
     "I will show you where I hid."

An arroyo   flies still buzzing around the sticky drying blood
      buzzing thick
where the bullets swarmed thick around the people of the bees
      Las Abejas.

The camera moves to ...   women's shoes two pairs
      carefully set side by side.
There is a small cave in the bank of the arroyo
      crumbling earth dark
"Aquí señores," he says, "here I hid as if I were dead
          saved
    two   of my children.
    I am sad still
My wife was killed with another child. My sister, two brothers in
    law, three nephews."

    I wake up —
I am in Canada   we lie very still   chunks of earth in our
      nostrils and mouths
      not breathing — not moving
         I have to pee.
         Ten hours
In this hole   three of us lie.

Outside   screams
      outside hack hack CHUN of the machetes
      bullets buzzing swarms of bullets
         swarms of flies
Bullets made in Canada
      M-16's assembled in Canada
         bullets swarm like flies

    I wake up —
I am suffocating   my mouth and nose filled with dirt.
My legs are cramped and I have to pee.

I wake up —
>I am in Canada
>I wake up —
>>on a pile of dead

I wake up —
>in the snow at Wounded Knee/hiding along the riverbank at
>Batoche/being crushed in a boxcar to Treblinka

I wake up —
>I am in Acteal
>December 22, 1997
>>and I am sad still.

PACO AND THE SHOES

Monique Mojica

from *The Scrubbing Project*
Turtle Gals Performance Ensemble
(Jani Lauzon, Monique Mojica, Michelle St. John)

ESPERANZA: Mi amado. Beloved.

>*ESPERANZA takes ribbons to altar, "smudges" them, almost
>lays them down then puts them in her pocket*

BRANDA: How many babies are born out of this hate?

>*Silence*
>### **Paco**

>*(Ophelia hands Esperanza a burlap bag)*

ESPERANZA: Some babies died. Some survived beneath the bodies of
>their mothers.

(Esperanza upends the bag and dumps a pile of shoes and a rope onto the stage She begins to smudge shoes and tie them onto the rope as if making tobacco ties)

He said,

ALL: (he said, he said, he said, he said, he said)

ESPERANZA: "The first time I saw a dead body —
               I was six years old."

Memory as gaping wound.
What sutures will bring the jagged edges
     of torn flesh together?
Will it scab over? Only to leave a firey,
     raised and angry scar?
     Or —
will the skin never renew itself —
but remain a thin blue membrane
     fragile
and prone to bursting open
     to reveal
the boiling blood just beneath the surface —
     unable to contain
     the memory
     a moment longer?

He told me,

ALL: (he said, he said, he said, he said, he said)

ESPERANZA: "I always knew when there'd been a
               massacre
               by the shoes ..."

I see the scattering of forlorn shoes
     abandoned in the plaza
          orphaned
left to lie on their sides/upside-down

empty of feet that gave them life
and movement.

A man's oxford here, a sneaker there
    but mostly women's shoes
        tacones
pink, turquoise, white and black high heels
        debris
left behind to litter the square
        the only evidence of
the hungry, vicious teeth of
        automatic weapon fire.
A boot here, a *caite* there.

OPH: Did they jump straight up out of those shoes?

ESP: I wonder.

BRANDA: Did they have time to bend to untie them?

ESP: Did they struggle to squirm a foot out
            over the back of the shoe with a
            desperate heel?

OP: Did they step on glass as they ran?

ALL: as they fell

ESP: as they

ALL: heard
           breath

ESP: expelled around them?

OPH: Did they run blindly

BRANDA: on unprotected feet

OP: along

OP & BRANDA: asphalt and cobblestone?

ESP: Did they know their lonely shoes had relations
          in the piles of detritus
          from the Death Camps
          now

ALL: catalogued, acquisitioned and museumed?

ESP: Or, did they simply lie there

ALL: choking

ESP: on their own entrails
    while

ALL: their shoes —

ESP: mouths yawning death masks/

ALL: their shoes

BRANDA: called out to
     their lost owners and
schoolchildren counted the dead from
     beneath half-closed eyelids
     as their books were searched
     on their way home from school?

     He said,

ALL: (he said, he said, he said, he said, he said)

OPHELIA: "I always knew when there'd been a
     massacre
     by the shoes ..."

BRANDA picks up the "tobacco tie" shoes, and smudges the sacred bundle in a deliberate gesture. It is offered up to the spirits.

RESISTANCE
Connie Fife

resistance is a woman
whose land is all on fire
perseverance and determination
are her daughters
she is a Palestinian mother who
hands her children a legacy of
war together with the
weapons to fight in it
she is a black woman draped
in purple satin who strolls
down a runway allowing only
the clothes she wears to be sold
resistance is the absent native woman
who died at the hands of
a white artist
who lives inside herself
while thriving inside of me
resistance is a girl child who
witnesses her mother's death and
swears to survive no matter
where the hiding place
she is a woman beaten with hate
by the man she loves who
decides to escape to a world
where touch is sacred
resistance is the woman who defies
the male definition of love
and loves another woman
then heals an entire nation in doing so
she is a woman torn apart by
the barbed wire surrounding her home
who plots a way out
despite the consequences

resistance is every woman who
has ever considered taking up
arms writing a story leaving the abuse
saving her chidren or saving herself
she is every woman who dares
to stage a revolution complete a novel
be loved or change the world
resistance walks across a landscape
of fire accompanied by her daughters
perserverance and determination

RESPECTFULLY

Amber O'Hara (Waabnong Kwe)

There appears to be a war against First Nations women in this country, and little is being done about it by those sworn in to protect *all* Canadian citizens. Family members of missing women in our communities report that visits to their local RCMP, months and even years after their loved ones have disappeared, reveal that the files remain untouched. Investigations, at times, are at best shabby and appear to be undertaken grudgingly. Much more could and should be done to expose these cases in order to enlighten the general public and possibly lead to a speedy resolution. Racism continues within law enforcement agencies and it results in society's lack of understanding and unspoken approval of a situation in which it is acceptable to harm or even murder a First Nations woman. There must be ongoing, mandatory sensitivity training for *all* law enforcement agencies and for *all* police officers and investigators. The RCMP and other investigative law enforcement agencies within this country dismiss these cases much earlier than they do those cases involving non-Native women.

The Aboriginal Justice Inquiry of Manitoba was created in response to two specific incidents in late 1987 and early 1988. The 1987 incident involved the rape and murder of Helen Betty Osborne of The Pas, Manitoba, and the investigation and trial that followed. The "Conclusions" of the Inquiry read in part:

It is clear that Betty Osborne would not have been killed if she had not been Aboriginal. The four men who took her to her death from the streets of The Pas that night had gone looking for an Aboriginal girl with whom to "party." They found Betty Osborne. When she refused to party she was driven out of town and murdered. Those who abducted her showed a total lack of regard for her person or her rights as an individual. Those who stood by while the physical assault took place, while sexual advances were made and while she was being beaten to death showed their own racism, sexism and indifference. Those who knew the story and remained silent must share their guilt.

(For the complete report see www.ajic.mb.ca/volume.html.)

Little if anything has been done to implement the recommendations of the Inquiry. The mass numbers of unresolved cases of missing or murdered First Nations women in Canada is testimony to the validity of this statement. There have been an estimated 500 such cases in Canada since Helen Betty Osborne was murdered, most of which remain unsolved. These cases are often filed in the "cold case files" much earlier than in cases involving non-Native women. We disagree with the report's claim that "much has changed in the years since Betty Osborne's life was taken in 1971."

My website (www.missingnativewomen.ca) is the result of ten years of research into these cases. It is updated daily with newer cases, and sadly, with other much older "cold cases." The purpose of the site is to bring to the public's attention the fact that the promises made in the Aboriginal Justice Implementation Commission, November 1999, are not being honoured. I continue to research our missing women and will add them to my site on a regular basis. *Please read and sign the petition to the Canadian government located at www.petitionOnline/tsalagi/petition.html.* We cannot allow our sisters to disappear, to die in vain. We must remember them in a good way, in hopes that this history will not continue to be repeated.

ACKNOWLEDGEMENTS

We would like to thank the following authors for allowing us to publish their work in this chapter.

Monique Mojica and Turtle Gals Performance Ensemble for permission to publish "*(gather[ing] up the bones)*"and "Paco and the Shoes" from their unpublished play *The Scrubbing Project*. A version of "Paco and the Shoes" was previously published in Yvette Nolan, ed., *Beyond the Pale: Dramatic Writing from First Nations Writers and Writers of Colour* (Toronto, ON: Playwrights Canada, 2004).

Monique Mojica for permission to publish "I Am Sad Still," a version of which was previously published in Judith Thompson, ed., *She Speaks: Monologues for Women* (Toronto, ON: Playwrights Canada, 2004).

Joanne Arnott for permission to use the excerpt from her poem "Migration," reprinted from Jeannette C. Armstrong and Lally Grauer, eds., *Native Poetry in Canada: A Contemporary Anthology* (Peterborough, ON: Broadview, 2001).

Marilyn Dumont and Brick Books for permission to reprint "Helen Betty Osborne," first published in *A Really Good Brown Girl* (London, ON: Brick Books, 1996), and reprinted here from Jeannette C. Armstrong and Lally Grauer, eds., *Native Poetry in Canada: A Contemporary Anthology* (Peterborough, ON: Broadview, 2001).

Marie Baker (Annharte) for permission to reprint "Penumbra," first published in *Being on the Moon* (Winlaw, BC: Polestar, 1990), and reprinted here from Jeannette C. Armstrong and Lally Grauer, eds., *Native Poetry in Canada: A Contemporary Anthology* (Peterborough, ON: Broadview, 2001); and for permission to print "every-bit race shell" here for the first time.

Joy Harjo and Wesleyan University Press for permission to reprint "For Anna Mae Pictou Aquash…," originally published in *In Mad Love and War* (Middletown, CT: Wesleyan University Press, 1990), and reprinted here from Connie Fife, ed., *The Colour of Resistance: A Contemporary Collection of Writing by Aboriginal Women* (Toronto, ON: Sister Vision, 1993).

Jean Becker for permission to publish "Aboriginal Women Remembering" here for the first time.

Marcie Rendon for permission to reprint "this woman that I am becoming…," first published in Beth Brant, ed., *A Gathering of Spirit: A Collection by North American Indian Women* (Toronto, ON: Women's Press, 1988), and reprinted here from Connie Fife, ed., *The Colour of Resistance: A Contemporary Collection of Writing by Aboriginal Women* (Toronto, ON: Sister Vision, 1993).

Connie Fife for permission to reprint "Resistance," first published in *Beneath the Naked Sun* (Toronto, ON: Sister Vision, 1992), and reprinted here from Connie Fife, ed., *The Colour of Resistance: A Contemporary Collection of Writing by Aboriginal Women* (Toronto, ON: Sister Vision, 1993).

Amber O'Hara (Waabnong Kwe) for permission to publish "Respectfully" here for the first time.

Conclusion

AGAINST ALL ODDS

It just seemed like of course *there should be a monument and* of course *it should be in town and it should be visible and everybody should have access to it and why wouldn't there be something like that?*

— Member, London Women's Monument Committee, 2000

This is the voice of a feminist organizer, describing her group's confidence in its plans for a monument in London to women murdered the moment before one of the biggest backlash controversies on record hit the project. What this book has shown is that every project to create a visible and explicit memorial against violence against women has had to fight for its existence. Struggles have erupted over location, language, resources, design and public sponsorship. Women have had to rely on their own networks—often feminist or lesbian feminist activists — to fight the odds, drawing on their political acumen, social connections, and well-placed women administrators and funders. Sometimes those odds simply overwhelmed memorial-makers' efforts. In spite of the over three dozen successes this book records, to the extent that there are hundreds of women murdered annually for whom there are no public memorials, the memorializing project as a whole remains under-realized. And of course, insofar as the ultimate goal of memorializing is to stop violence against women, it remains unrealized by the larger society. Violence against women has continued to escalate, to the point at which in the year leading up to the tenth anniversary of the Montreal Massacre a coroner's jury reported that "domestic abuse was reaching epic proportions in Canada" (Honey 1998, S11).

Thinking about the odds that face feminist memorializers might well give theorists pause. When James Young addresses the challenges which face memorializers of the Holocaust in Germany, he focuses on conceptual and ethical impediments, not funding. The resources available to artists on whom the Bundestag, municipal committees or private donors smile are enormous. Geoffrey Hartman and Andreas Huyssen worry about a flood of memorializing in the postmodern age, as an *ersatz* "memorial culture" in inverse proportion to the real remembering going on (Huyssen 1993, 253). Feminist memorializing remains so contingent, so scattered and so poorly resourced that it cannot afford this kind of anxiety. We have tried to include a sense of the more mundane obstacles that threaten to defeat those who undertake oppositional remembering in public, because such impediments set the bar for feminist memorial-makers over and over again. One of our most disturbing discoveries was the memorial to Annie Kempton in 1896. Its presence brought home to us the historical entrenchment of violence against women, its social manipulation and both the tenuousness and the persistence of memory. More than one hundred years have brought us to all the women and girls named and unnamed by the public monuments discussed in this book: Wendy Poole, Helen Betty Osborne, Theresa Vince, Lynda Shaw, Marianne Goulden, Marlene Moore and Nina de Villiers; Sharon Mohamed and the thirty-six local women named on Enclave; the fourteen women students and staff massacred at l'École Polytechnique; the sixty-nine or more "missing women" of Downtown Eastside; the 135 women and children named on Lest We Forget; the latest report of a woman murdered in our newspapers and on our television screens (the one last week and this, and the next). How do we measure the successes and theorize the meanings of memorializing against a violence that is so endemic and systemic?

FACING THE OBSTACLES

One place to start is by computing the obstacles in realistic, grounded terms, for they are the benchmark against which we assess accomplishment. One major challenge is resources. "You have no idea how much work, and how much it costs, paying bills; it's a lot, a lot, a lot of work," laments one organizer (Buist et al 2000). While some groups, such as the women responsible for the Marker of Change in Vancouver and the Women's Monument in London, have registered signal successes in fundraising, there are many projects that have stalled or been compromised by a lack of money. In Simcoe, Ontario, for example, the 2.5-metre (8-foot) metal sculpture with fifteen candle holders created by artist Charlotte Boerkamp for the Haldimand Norfolk Women's Centre's vigil in 1994, which toured the province accompanied by an explanation of the link between the Montreal Massacre and systemic violence against women, remains in storage. According to Regina Homeniuk at the Women's Centre, they "don't have a community, or a common focus or a spot just right now." The logistics of moving and storing the sculpture became too complicated, resources ran out for touring and the sculpture is now brought out only once a year for December 6th ceremonies.

In some cases, unanticipated last-minute costs around installation threaten the successful completion of a memorial project. The London Women's Monument organizers, confronted with the threat that their memorial might at some point be removed from its prime downtown location, faced a huge additional expense with their decision to ground it in seven feet of concrete. Less obviously controversial is the case of Teresa Posyniak's sculpture in the University of Calgary Law Building, where the cost of the glass case designed to protect the sculpture was considerably more than that of the sculpture itself; in fact it was the main expense faced by those fundraising to bring the artwork into a public building.

Even when memorials have been successfully established, lack of maintenance can seriously erode their prominence and effectiveness. The organizers of the London Women's Monument report the difficulties urging the local parks department to so much as replace the light bulbs that illuminate the monument at night. In Ottawa, Vancouver, Montreal, Alberta and elsewhere, deeply disturbing graffiti defacing memorial sculptures can remain for weeks without removal. Poor maintenance was the reason given for removing the memorial by University of Alberta students altogether. Perhaps learning from other undertakings, the organizing committee for the Women's Grove Memorial in Winnipeg included in its $65,000 fundraising goal "an endowment for any vandalism that could occur in the future" (Money 1995,10).

There are other reasons for which memorials remain unfinished or are under-realized, ranging from bureaucratic entanglement through lack of commitment to active hostility. For example, a proposed project at the University of New Brunswick in Fredericton, as far as we can determine, remains completely unrealized since a committed female engineering faculty member left the university. Even more dramatically, Yukon College in Whitehorse removed an installation of fourteen 20 cm x 27 cm (8 inch x 11 inch) plaques honouring the women murdered in Montreal and changed its mission statement after "a lot of people remarked in the hallways . . . that we were inappropriately honing in on violence against women. What about violence against men and children?" (Wright 2001).

These obstacles clearly expose an uneven distribution of social power between women and men and among women. Take, for example, the disproportionate representations of class and race in memorials to women murdered in Canada. While statistics tell us that the vast majority of femicide victims are societally marginalized, public memorials with civic or mainstream institutional sanction tell a different story, most often representing white, middle-class women whose friends and families are best positioned, socially and economically, to enter them into the public record. Three researchers for this book — Cawo Abdi, Sabina Chatterjee and Christine Lenze — with histories of social justice service in their communities specifically searched for memorials to First Nations women and women of colour.[1] They reported minimal success, noting that "visible minority" women remain virtually *in*visible as victims of male violence — apart from the many "unofficial," personal and impromptu memorials left by friends and family of murdered women, often at murder sites. Community protectionism can exacerbate such invisibility, as members of threatened communities resist public associations with violence, but the greatest causes are lack of resources and, as one anonymous interviewee said, "lack of real interest [on the part of] mainstream women's groups."

Thus, for example, women from the India Mahila Association in Vancouver held a vigil for a time on the anniversary of the murder of a woman from the Southeast Asian community, killed by her estranged husband in Vancouver in the 1980s. Due to a lack of funding and increased demands on the organization, they discontinued the annual vigil. Similarly, friends and members of women's organizations attempted to hold a vigil on the anniversary of the murder of a Hispanic woman in Ottawa, but the protestations of her family halted their plans. The woman remains un-named here, at the request of the family. Similar reports have emerged from Montreal. The most notable exception to this rule, in addition to the memorials to First Nations women that we have discussed, are the memorials to Ottawa's

Sharon Mohamed, whose name is included on one of the stones clustered around Enclave in Minto Park, and whose mother, Shadikan Mohamed, has started the Sharon Nasin Mohamed foundation in her daughter's memory. In addition, Shadikan donated the money which she had saved for Sharon's education to building a mosque in the village of Zelughy in her native country of Guyana, and in 2001 a blood drive was organized for the Red Cross in Ottawa in Sharon's name.

Even when memorials come to fruition, their potential often remains under-realized. Conscious or unconscious compromise regularly accompanies memorial-making, as private traumas enter the public realm, as families and feminists enter into negotiation with one another and with the mechanisms of social control, and as memorializing shares public space with activism. Such compromises are an inevitable and necessary part of effecting change in society and in public consciousness. They include negotiations with institutional sponsors, families and women's groups over site, design, language, local specificities and general or symbolic gestures.

We see, for example, how municipal or institutional standards can contain a memorial's impact. Guidelines for the design of gardens or monuments in public parks can produce conformity, even invisibility, and can serve to contain any disruptive intent that might rupture complacency around systemic violence against women. In extreme cases, such as the Lynda Shaw tree at the University of Western Ontario, horticultural details almost completely overwhelm the memorial intent. In many cases institutional practices can also constrain use, as at Marianne's Park in Guelph, where the routine procedures of parks department landscaping inadvertently limit the site's capacity to host December 6th vigils or Take Back the Night gatherings. Even common-sense choices made quickly in the wake of traumatic events can lead organizers unconsciously towards conventionalized and socially dominant forms of hegemonic memorializing — plaques, trees, gardens, boulders, benches or public art — that may not best serve their own more resistant purposes. A case in point is the general conformity of many memorials to the Montreal murders mounted by engineering schools — often unobtrusive plaques signalling more institutional and professional solidarity than outrage, and often mentioning neither gender nor murder in their remembering of "colleagues."

The location of memorials in peaceful or reclusive settings, parks or gardens, often invoking the comforts of nature, can lead to their failure to insert themselves more directly into public consciousness (and public policy). More promising in terms of policy impact are locations at legislative assemblies (as in Winnipeg) or city halls (as in Moncton and Hamilton), where, however, institutional protocols can be at their most stringent. An alternative tactic, in attempting to create impact, is to move memorials away from institutional public space to the very local space of daily living. In O'Leary, PEI, for example, the West Prince Family Violence Prevention Committee installed a cedar park bench and planter dedicated to "the eradication of violence and poverty against women in the 21st century," in a popular gathering place, in front of the post office.

Many questions and tensions surface around the issue of language, where compromises and negotiations are often legible in the wording of plaques and dedications. Chief among these issues is that of naming — naming the women murdered, naming the fact of murder and naming the murderers. The naming of the women who have been murdered is often part of the initial impetus for, and lasting effect of, a memorial project: the insistence that this woman (or these women) not be forgotten. There is, of course, a tension here, as individual women, named and recognized as having lived valuable lives, come to represent "all women," their memorials serving as symbols of a systemic problem. On the one hand, to the extent that named women are honoured as unique, as individuals, there is a danger that their murders will also be seen as unique, isolated events rather than part of a larger pattern of gendered violence on which a patriarchal capitalist society rests. On the other hand, to the extent that memorials, often dedicated to women of relative privilege, become symbolic of violence against all women, they risk effacing differences in culture, class and race that make some women more likely to be subject to male violence than others.

"MURDERED BY MEN"

The title of our book declares solidarity with those who insist on naming the fact of murder and naming the murderers. We deliberately echo the phrase — "murdered by men" — for which the organizers of Vancouver's Marker of Change fought with such determination and against such powerful opposition. Part of the impetus for that monument was rage that the name of the perpetrator of the Montreal Massacre was widely known, while those of the women he killed was not. Indeed, Mary Billy reports that, when she wanted to print a list of the fourteen women murdered one year later, on the front cover of her magazine *Herspectives*, she was shocked at how long it took her to track down the information. These experiences account for the prominent citation of the fourteen names on so many of the memorials we have looked at across the country. But while that injustice has frequently been addressed in plaques and dedications that celebrate women's lives while refusing to contribute to the notoriety of their killers, many of the memorials we have looked at also shy away, in varying degrees, from naming with the directness of Vancouver's Marker of Change or Ottawa's Enclave the perpetrators of daily violence against women.

Many prefer to refer to women "killed" or "slain" (an antiquated word that perhaps evokes a romantic reverence for the dead and the decorum of funeral services and cemeteries), and often do so in the passive voice, as though the deaths were agentless. Many are still less direct, referring to women who "died" or "lost their lives" (as if they were themselves the agents), or citing "all acts of violence, especially against women and children." Many invoke a distancing rhetoric of "tragedy" or "loss," avoiding direct confrontation with the often brutal and horrific circumstances of their murders, not to mention the systemic nature of the violence inflicted on them. Others, aimed at creating contemplative, healing spaces focus on "courage and hope" or "peace" to the point that, for example, the "Peace Gardens" at the Trafalgar and Davis campuses of Ontario's Sheridan College were initially installed without plaques or other explicit acknowledgement of their role as December 6th memorials. The wording on Michèle Mitchell's sculpture, A Vision of Hope, on the other hand, at Edmonton's Mary Burlie Park — "killed because they were women"–is clear and exemplary. The plaque also includes a "recognition of all women hurt by men" and a dedication to "all women abused, raped and killed by men," stirring considerable controversy from the local right. But even there, the original reference to "the war on women" was removed by the organizers at the request of a sponsor who felt it was too strong.

Controversies and compromises over wording, of course, express unease in the larger society about how (or even whether) to name violence against women. The circumlocutions common in memorializing reflect similar ones in common usage elsewhere, such as the ubiquitous and ungendered phrase "domestic violence" (in contradistinction to the less common "intimate femicide"), or the continuing use of "missing women" in reference to the women murdered in Vancouver's Downtown Eastside.

All these odds and obstacles demonstrate that women who memorialize other women murdered, especially when they do so in explicitly feminist terms, do not work from a position of privilege. The objections that they encounter over language, location, design and resources, and the impediments that are thrown up by municipal protocols and what Donna Johnson calls "the tangled web of bureaucracy," all amount to one thing: the attempt to deny the pervasive and horrendous fact of femicide which statistics (local, national and international) have proven over and over again. While some memorials to the Montreal massacre located at some remove from that city provoked relatively little opposition, the more local the women on whom the memorials focus, the more ferocious the attempts to obstruct and silence their memory-makers.

Such denial was never clearer than in the story of Sudbury, Ontario. A decade-long struggle to establish a high-profile memorial to local women murdered hit one roadblock after another. Controversy flared around naming, design and location, as community members shied away from publicly acknowledging the violence in their midst. While city officials dragged their heels and flexed their political muscles, the Coalition to End Violence Against Women gradually splintered. The stand-off ended in an unhappy compromise. Over the protests of local women's groups, city council put a "tombstone size marker" in the Civic Memorial Cemetery, a location that denies both public visibility and a space for solidarity building to the struggle against femicide (Pusiak 2002, 5). Sick at the refusal to publicly honour women murdered and women struggling against abuse, Barb Garon of the Sudbury Women's Centre — a leading advocate for a visible, explicit memorial — asked rhetorically, "By placing the monument in the cemetery, wouldn't you think the issue is 'out of sight, out of mind'?" (Garon 2002, A7). Another bitterly disappointed activist declared, "This is what abused women have to look forward to ... their graves."

BUILDING MEMORY

We offer these accounts of under-realized sites not as a depressing litany of failure but as a tribute to all the unseen and unheralded memorial efforts across the country. If those with political and financial power had supported these efforts to the point of fruition, this book would have documented twice as many as the three dozen captured here. More unstinting support would also have issued in fewer compromises, silences and euphemisms in those monuments that made it to completion. Any measurement of a memorial's larger social impact or consciousness-raising success needs to start from the simple fact that dominant social conditions make it much easier not even to *think* of embarking on a memorial to women murdered than to create one — not even to begin the necessary, if sometimes regrettable and always exhausting, process of negotiation and ideological compromise. Any theorizing of feminist "counter-monuments" needs to start from the symbiosis between memorializing and analysis. Those who offer the most powerful systemic analysis are often those who do the uphill job of resistant memorializing and vice versa. The inscription on A Vision of Hope speaks to systemic analysis when it declaims "killed because they were women." This analysis is what drove Winnipeg's December 6th Memorial Committee, according to Keith Louise Fulton: "So when a man with a gun walked into École Polytechnique on the night of December 6th, 1989, and began shooting women for being where he thought they did not belong, women and men across the country were horrified — but not surprised. The values, beliefs and attitudes he acted on were those which we meet everyday. Is it so different for 14 women to die in one evening instead of one year? To die in one place instead of 14 separate places? To die together in terror instead of alone in terror?" (1999, 320). And Manitoba's Aboriginal Justice Inquiry acknowledged systemic violence based on race as well as gender: "It is clear that Betty Osborne would not have been killed if she had not been Aboriginal."

These stories tell us that the making of counter-monuments is risky, arduous and labour intensive in the extreme. Feminist memorial-makers also tell us that achieving such counter-monuments brings power to survivors and organizers and dignity to women murdered. Facing down bomb threats and personal vilification, memorial makers in Vancouver and London relish the triumph of planting memorial stones so deeply in the ground that they can never be moved. Donna Johnson (1998) is proud to declare of Enclave in Ottawa: "Our monument will stand as testament to future generations of the efforts of women in this century to create a safe society for women." Teresa Posyniak feels equally positive about Lest We Forget in Calgary: "It made me feel very happy to do because there was some kind of vehicle so these women were finally commemorated in a dignified way" (qtd. in Scott

1994, 5A). The mother of a woman who worked in the sex trade when she was murdered and who is named on Lest We Forget agrees: "It gives her a place in society she would never have had otherwise" (ibid.). Part of the power comes from reversing the dominant pattern by which society remembers the murderer and not the murdered: "They are the first forgotten, the last remembered, as society focuses its fascination on the killers, not the killed" (Ford 1994, A5).

Mary Billy (2000), who recorded femicides for ten years, passed on the task to others in 2000 with the list at 1,850: "I think working so intimately with so many gruesome deaths of women breaks my heart … It is called *Facing the Horror: The Femicide List,* and that is what I urge everyone to do — *face the horror.* Don't turn away from these women. Make their deaths count for something." Esparanza from The Scrubbing Project says it differently: "And you will be loved/And I will build memory." This is why women organize, calculate, negotiate, compromise, rally together and face down controversy — to build memory, to ensure that the lives and deaths of women murdered in Canada are not forgotten, to confirm that they count. So many of the stories we have told throughout this book represent just how tremendous an achievement it is that, particularly since the deaths of fourteen women at l'École Polytechnique on December 6, 1989, memorials to women murdered have accumulated exponentially across the landscape of the country, carving the lives of women murdered into the public record and public space, raising awareness of what throughout history has been a dirty secret. It is our hope that this book contributes to that work, honouring both the women who have been murdered in this country and those who have worked so hard against the odds to make sure that their names and stories are permanently etched in our landscapes and our memories.

Appendix

Memorials to Women Murdered across Canada

The list below includes the monuments, sculptures and annual rituals we have documented in the course of our project, travelling west to east across the country. We do not list all the December 6th vigils, Take Back the Night marches and similar activities, and we know that many more sites exist than we have found. Please send information about additional memorials to www.globalwomensmemorial.org.

* Montreal Massacre plaque installation, Yukon College (Whitehorse, YK) — removed

* December 6th memorial, Malaspina University College (Nanaimo, BC)

* Marker of Change/À l'aube du changement, Thornton Park (Vancouver, BC)

* Memorial boulder and bench, CRAB Park (Vancouver, BC)

* Wendy Poole memorial, Wendy Poole Park (Vancouver, BC)

* Annual Valentine's Day March, Downtown Eastside (Vancouver, BC)

* Women's Memorial Garden, Strathcona Community Gardens (Vancouver, BC)

* Memorial Pole, Oppenheimer Park (Vancouver, BC)

* Annual Forget Me Not Walk (Vancouver, BC)

* The Lasting Memorial (Vancouver, BC) — in progress

* Lest We Forget, Law Building, University of Calgary (Calgary, AB)

* December 6th Commemorative Worktable, Engineering Building, University of Calgary (Calgary, AB)

* December 6th Commemorative Bench, Quad, University of Alberta (Edmonton, AB) — boulder removed

* December 6th Commemorative Boulder, University Administration Building, University of Alberta (Edmonton, AB)

* December 6th Memorial plaque, Engineering Teaching and Learning Centre, University of Alberta (Edmonton, AB)

* Trinity Sculpture, Faculté St. Jean, University of Alberta (Edmonton, AB)

* A Vision of Hope, Mary Burlie Park (Edmonton, AB)

* Memorial Cross (Edmonton, AB) — in progress

* The Missing Sisters Walk (Saskatoon, SK)

* Helen Betty Osborne Memorial, Guy Hill Park (The Pas, MN)

* Women's Grove Memorial, Manitoba Legislature (Winnipeg, MN)

* Forever, Lin Gibson's fourteen-plaque installation, 1990–91 (Winnipeg, MN — part of Gibson's series Murdered by Misogyny, which appeared in Toronto and Halifax and published in C Magazine)

* Fourteen Not Forgotten Memorial Garden, University of Windsor (Windsor, ON)

* Memorial Rose Garden for Theresa Vince (Chatham, ON)

* Annual Demonstration at Sears in Memory of Theresa Vince (Chatham, ON)

* London Women's Monument, Victoria Park (London, ON)

* 14 Dancing Women, Femmes Dansantes, Brescia College (London, ON)

* Montreal Memorial Garden, University of Western Ontario (London, ON)

* Tulip Tree in Memory of Lynda Shaw, University of Western Ontario (London, ON)

* Women's Monument, Civic Memorial Cemetery (Sudbury, ON)

* December 6th Memorial Rose Garden, Conestoga College (Kitchener, ON)

* Annual December 6th showing of Charlotte Boerkamp sculpture, Haldimand Norfolk Women's Centre (Simcoe, ON)

* Marianne's Park (Guelph, ON)

* Reflection Garden (Guelph, ON)

* December 6th Cactus Garden, Thornbrough Building, University of Guelph (Guelph, ON)

* Memorial to Helen, Ludvik, Christopher, Suzy, and Nancy Kirec, Family Transition Place (Orangeville, ON)

* Stepping Stone in Memory of Shirley Snow, Family Transition Place (Orangeville, ON)

* Marlene Moore Memorial Tree, Royal Botanical Gardens (Hamilton, ON)

* Nina de Villiers Memorial Rose Garden, McMaster University (Hamilton, ON)

* Joan Heimbecker Memorial Rock, Plaque and Tree, Bates Residence, McMaster University (Hamilton, ON)

*End the Violence Memorial, City Hall (Hamilton, ON)

* December 6th Memorial Stone, John Hodgins Engineering Building, McMaster University (Hamilton, ON)

* Peace Gardens, Davis and Trafalgar Campuses, Sheridan College (Brampton and Oakville, ON)

* Pathway of Peace by Yellow Brick House, Aurora Park (Woodbridge, ON)

* Women Won't Forget Memorial, Philosopher's Walk, University of Toronto (Toronto, ON)

* Tree of Hope, Ryerson University (Toronto, ON)

* December 6th Memorial Boulder, Bowmanville Visual Arts Centre (Bowmanville, ON) — removed

* Enclave, Minto Park (Ottawa, ON)

* December 6th plaque, Faculty of Engineering, University of Ottawa (Ottawa, ON)

* Nef pour quatorze reines (Nave for Fourteen Queens) (Montreal, PQ)

* December 6th plaque, l'École Polytechnique (Montreal, PQ)

* Montreal Mural Tribute (Montreal, PQ)

* Memorial Table, Université Laval (Quebec City, PQ)

* Silent Witness Project, Travelling Exhibit (New Brunswick)

* December 6th Women's Monument, Caseley Park (Riverview, NB)

* Courage and Hope sculpture, City Hall (Moncton, NB)

* Memorial Bench and Planter, West Prince Family Violence Prevention Committee (O'Leary, PEI)

* Annual December 6th ritual with plaque, PEI Legislature (Charlottetown, PEI)

* Annie Kempton Memorials, Town Cemetery (Bear River, NS)

* December 6th Bear River Candle Float (Bear River, NS)

* Monument for Marlene Moore (1992) by Lori Clermont (Halifax, NS)

* December 6th plaque, Engineering School, Memorial University (St. John's, NF)

NOTES

INTRODUCTION

1. There are numerous ways of statistically documenting violence against women, all of them shocking. The Sisters in Spirit Campaign website estimates that the numbers of Aboriginal women missing and/or murdered in Canada may be as high as 1,000 (www.sistersinspirit.ca). Lauren Carter reports: "Over the last year, 50 or 60 names have been added to the previous estimate of 500 women who have gone missing or been murdered in the last 20 years" (2005, 21). As of February 2005, the website dedicated to the missing Vancouver women noted that sixty-nine women from the Downtown Eastside are listed as missing by the RCMP/VPD Task Force (www. missingpeople.net). Quebec Men Against Sexism/Collectif masculine contre le sexisme has assembled a detailed database that indicates, in the fifteen years since the Montreal massacre, at least 768 women and children have been murdered by men in Quebec, "and these are only the cases where bodies have been found and identified and victim names made public, an acknowledgement often denied to children and to immigrant, Native or senior women" (Dufresne 2004). According to a national survey on violence against women, "one-half of all Canadian women have experienced at least one incident of physical or sexual assault since the age of 16" (CCJS 1994, 4). On the international front, Irene Khan, secretary general of Amnesty International, noted in 2002: "According to the World Bank figures, at least one in five women and girls have been beaten or sexually abused in her life time." A memorial pole in Oppenheimer Park, commemorating all those who have died in the Downtown Eastside, also serves as a gathering place for protests against and vigils for women murdered in this area.

2. The named authors are white. At different times, our group has included researchers from various cultural, racial and ethnic locations. Cawo Abdi, Sabina Chatterjee, and Christine Lenze played crucial roles in exploring memorials to women of colour and First Nations women. For a preliminary discussion of the vexed questions surrounding memorializing violence against women, particularly women of colour, within minoritized communities, see the conclusion to this volume.

3. The Sisters in Spirit Campaign (launched by the Native Women's Association of Canada) secured $5 million from the federal government to launch a national registry of missing and murdered Aboriginal women, engage in public education, undertake research and policy analysis, and make comprehensive recommendations

for changes (www.sistersinspirit.ca).

4. As of December 6, 2005, the Global Women's Memorial website project by Christine McDowell is in development with the National Film Board of Canada, and is being co-produced by Cari Green and Karen Middleton. It is the intention of the project to provide websites to all the women's memorials in Canada, and perhaps someday to those created beyond our borders. See www.globalwomensmemorial.org.

5. Notable use of these terms is made by Kelley (1995), Huyssen (1993) and Young (1992, 1993, 1997, 2000).

6. Among the feminist and other socially conscious scholars who have worked to bridge the divide between activism and scholarship are Benmayor (1991), Gordon (1993), Gottfried (1996), Harvey (1995), Maguire (1987), Naples (1998) and Whyte (1991).

7. For further analysis of the Cultural Memory Project's workings, see Bold, Knowles and Leach (2003).

8. For an account of one of those trips and the analysis which followed from it, see Cultural Memory Group (2005).

CHAPTER 1: VANCOUVER

1. Meanwhile, Bert and Anna Draayer developed a memorial garden "In memory of Vancouver's eastside women" at their home in Vancouver. In February 2005, with the Draayers putting their home up for sale, the women's memorial garden was moved to the Strathcona Community Gardens (Leng 2005a, 2005b). A memorial pole in Oppenheimer Park, commemorating all those who have died in the Downtown Eastside, also serves as a gathering place for protests against and vigils for women murdered in this area.

2. All quotations concerning the Marker of Change are taken from Simpson's video (1998) unless otherwise indicated.

3. McDowell (1999a) called this first phase of the committee's work "the dreamer phase," as the group developed the proposal, giving it greater meaning and depth, but also, almost inevitably, making it more difficult to accomplish. The committee hired a fundraising co-ordinator, began drafting guidelines for a national design competition, evaluated possible sites for the monument and approached the city for a particular site (the then nascent, but already prime waterside location, Science World Park) (McDowell 1999b). This approach met with significant opposition from planners, investors and neighbourhood groups, but finally Thornton Park was suggested to them. City council and its powerful elected park board authorized the choice, with the support of the park board engineer who felt that the monument would enhance what had been a neglected park, but full approval was delayed pending details of the monument's making as set forth in the design competition guidelines. The guidelines were careful and thorough, outlining information about eligibility (individual women or groups of women), the application process, the

purpose and concept for the project, its location, funding, projected use and plans for maintenance.

4. Slightly different versions of the original dedication are reported by various sources; this one appears in Simpson (1998).

5. The final wording on the monument's main dedicatory plaque is as follows:

Geneviève Bergeron, Hélène Colgan, Nathalie Croteau, Barbara Daigneault, Anne-Marie Edward, Maud Haviernick, Barbara Klucznick Maryse Laganière, Maryse Leclair, Anne-Marie Lemay, Sonia Pelletier, Michèle Richard, Annie St-Arneault, Annie Turcotte

Murdered December 6, 1989, University of Montreal. We, their sisters and brothers, remember, and work for a better world. In memory and in grief for all women who have been murdered by men. For women of all countries, all classes, all ages, all colours.	Assassinées le 6 décembre 1989, à l'Université de Montréal. Nous, leurs soeurs et leurs frères, nous souvenons àelles, et nous travaillons à bâtir un monde meilleur. À la mémoire de toutes les femmes assassinées par des hommes, femmes de tous les pays, de toutes les classes sociales, de tous les ages et de toutes les races.

6. There are, however, two postscripts to this success story. The first involves maintenance. In 1999, McDowell wrote that the monument "really needs a power washing and a new coat of anti-graffiti sealant. We paid a $12,500 maintenance fee but the money was taken and given to the City of Vancouver not the Van Park Board — meanwhile the Van Park board is responsible for the actual maintenance and are reluctant to do maintenance because they are resentful they were not given the money. However, they will send people out to clean off the graffiti. Sigh" (1999c). The other postscript has to do with park-board policy: less than a year after the installation of the women's monument, the board ushered in a new policy that would have made the production of the Marker of Change impossible. According to Douglas Todd in the *National Post* (who again named the murderer and not the women murdered): "The new guidelines aim to head off the kind of bitter debate provoked by Vancouver's proposed memorial to people who died of AIDS, and an existing monument to 14 women in Montreal murdered by Marc Lépine. 'We don't really want to have any controversy' when approving new memorials for Vancouver's public parks, commissioner Gabriel Young said yesterday. The parks board's stricter guidelines, introduced in late November, oppose memorials that commissioners believe have been designed to antagonize the public."

7. According to committee member Lianne Payne, the average donation, including corporate and governmental contributions, was between $25 and $35, what people could give.

8. McDowell, herself a former rape crisis worker, responds to this criticism by saying that "the whole concept of doing an art piece was a step back from direct service. It's a conceptual approach to changing society." "The monument's a gamble," she says. "It's a gamble on the powers of art" (Simpson 1998).

9. The CRAB Water for Life Society is a primarily environmental group which has worked since 1982 to seize and maintain public parkland for that neighbourhood. The www.missingpeople.net website has attempted, since 1998, to keep the missing women's cases in the public eye. Other relevant websites include the following: www. orcagirl.com/missingwomen; www.missingwomenslegacy.ca; www.vanished-voices.com; groups.yahoo.com/group/vancouvermissing; www.findfran.com; groups. yahoo.com/group/coldcases; www.doenetwork.org; www.lookoutmagazine.ca; www. outpostforhope.org.

10. The bench was intended for installation opposite the boulder, but is now positioned a short stroll away across a gravel path several metres to the west.

11. After a long, losing legal battle against the Crown corporation that owned and planned to develop what Larson says was the richest undeveloped land in western Canada at that time, the society was able to win the land for the neighbourhood residents to use as a park and site of social activism by staging a seventy-five day camp-in. He feels that media attention to the camp-in ultimately swayed public opinion in his group's favour: "All those colourful tents and weird transient people" Larson relates, "the journalists were thanking us" (2000). The park was officially opened on July 29, 1987.

12. The full text of the Story Stone reads as follows:

URBAN INDIAN
FRED ARRANCE, FEBRUARY 2000

WE AS INDIAN PEOPLE SOMETIMES FORGET
WHERE WE CAME FROM.
OUR CUSTOMS, SONGS, TRADITIONAL METHODS
LOST ALONG THE WAY
CAUGHT WITHIN THE WALLS OF THIS CEMENT JUNGLE

INDIAN PEOPLE ARE DYING
TRYING TO FIND THE WAY.
SOUP LINES REPLACE TRAP LINES.
MIGHTY WARRIORS NOW HUNT IN SAFEWAY.
WARRIORS WHO ONCE FOUGHT FOR MOTHER EARTH
NOW FIGHT TO STAY SOBER AND OUT OF JAIL.

OUR ELECTED INDIAN LEADERS
DEAF AND DUMB TO OUR CAUSE.

HOW CAN THEY WORK FOR THE MARGINALIZED
IF THEY ARE DYSFUNCTIONAL THEMSELVES?
DO NOT LET THE SMELL OF MONEY FOOL YOU.
INDIAN WAYS ARE NOT FOR SALE.

13. For further discussion of the CRAB Park memorial — particularly its relationship to Aboriginal naming practices and to local activism — see Burk (2003), 324–27, 330. For some of the chronology of the criminal investigation and of growing attention from the mainstream media, see Greene (2001, 1–10).

14. Lobbying efforts involved gathering support from other social justice organizations; talking at length with individual council members; council receiving supportive phone calls and faxes from the more affluent and enfranchised voting community of Vancouver's westside; piquing the interest of the media, some of whom brought cameras to council meetings; and a phone call in support of the dedication.

CHAPTER 2: CALGARY AND EDMONTON

1. In 1989, in response to the Montreal massacre, the Canadian Council of Professional Engineers created the Canadian Engineering Memorial Foundation (CEMF) to increase the number and level of participation of women in the engineering profession, partly by offering "scholarships and awards that encourage young women to choose engineering as a career" (www.ccpc.ca). Ten years later, the foundation launched the Dean's Millennium Award Competition with "the goal of establishing a unique venue for communication and discussion of the implications of the 1989 École Polytechnique tragedy," a discussion clearly needed in a field in which more than one student confessed to not previously knowing of the killings (CEMF 1999).

2. The student members were Tanya Brusse-Gendre, Roch DeMaer, Janice Miller, Brian McGough, Ramy Mohamed, Sarah Saleh; faculty advisors were Dr. Elizabeth Cannon, Dr. Cathy Laureshen, Dr. Janet Ronsky; technical advisor was Rob Scorey; external advisor was architect Lynn Webster. A few years earlier, the school had developed a Women in Science and Engineering Committee and received a CEMF award for Most Improved Women-Friendly Engineering Faculty.

3. Professor Elizabeth Cannon (2001), NSERC/Petro-Canada Chair for Women in Science and Engineering at the University of Calgary, confirms that the "'table and seats' that we developed is used daily by our engineering students and we are very proud to have it as a key symbol in our engineering foyer."

4. The members of the volunteer team were Roberta Bathory-Frota, Nicole DesRochers, Eileen Dempster, Carl Loeffelmann, Ronald Kwan, Brent Schmitt, Mark Teasdale and James Brown. Pragmatic considerations — "ease of gathering materials, construction feasibility, and weather"— influenced their design choices ("Dean's Millennium Award Project" n.d.). Although it took some time to pull the volunteers together and secure the necessary permissions, once the group had chosen a location and site design and assigned responsibilities, they purchased all the materials and

built the memorial within a week. The group won second place in the competition, earning their school the $5,000 to be used according to the CEMF's mandate at the dean's discretion (Dempster 2001; Worrad 1999).

5. Pembina Hall, built in 1914, winner of a Heritage Canada Award for its painstaking renovation in 1977, is now a mature students' residence. The vertical mural on the Civil/Electrical Engineering Building was by Professor Norman Yates, "representing human progress through technology — a fitting concept for a University" ("Building Directory").

6. The plaque was badly dented in an apparent attempt to pry it off the boulder (J. Smith 2005; Buckle 2005).

7. The sculpture commemorates "the occasion of the official hand-over, by Chief Walter P. Twinn of Sawridge Enterprises Ltd., of the Universiade '83 Flame Tower, to the University of Alberta."

8. All of the violence-against-women memorials on the two campuses owe their exis-tence to supportive administrations. Sheilah Martin, Dean of Law at the time of the installation of Lest We Forget, worked strenuously to secure the necessary funds with the awareness that "we're not just training lawyers, we're educating people"(Martin 2001). The engineering student team at the University of Calgary was nurtured by several women faculty and staff people, including Dr. Elizabeth Cannon, NSERC/ Petro-Canada Chair for Women in Science and Engineering (Prairie Region). Although some conflict developed between the University of Alberta administration and the students who created the bench there regarding who was responsible for the site's maintenance, the engineering faculty supported their students through congratulatory letters, assistance with access to resources and the extension of awards to undergraduates involved in the project. Of course, it is institutional reality that each university wanted something in return for its support. While avoiding making overtly political statements about male violence — avoiding, that is, the violent, anti-feminist circumstances of the Montreal massacre — the institutions could claim the memorials as evidence of their faculties' social conscience. The University of Alberta houses another December 6th memorial sculpture — an abstract metal work by Patrick Jacob — in the main building on the Faculté Saint-Jean campus (Schoeck 2005).

9. Ringma explains that the sub-committee consisted of Del Marlow and Debbie Felder. The monument selection committee included Del Marlow, Sexual Assault Centre; Laurie Blakeman, MLA Edmonton Centre; Dina Floreancig, Edmonton Women's Shelter; Carol Hutchings, Status of Women Canada; Elaine Micklos, Edmonton art-ist; Heidi Veluw, community member; Felice Young, Alberta Federation of Labour.

10. Mike Kroening (2001), parks and recreation branch manager, also notes that "there was considerable community support, including some prominent political people" behind the monument committee's proposal.

11. The group announced a demonstration outside city hall, and sent letters and peti-tions to donors, the city and the press, arguing that it was entirely inappropriate

to privilege female victims of male violence through public remembrance. One of MERGE's pamphlets, under the signatures of self-identified "members of 'visible minorities,'" argued that accusing innocent men of violence is equivalent to accusing racial minorities for high rates of crime ("Message Of Protest" n.d.).

12. MERGE criticizes feminists for being unable to support their gender inequality claims statistically. In 1998 alone, 82.6 percent of victims in reported cases of sexual assault were women; 98 percent of the accused were men (Juristat: Canadian Crime Statistics 19, no. 9 [1998]). It is true that men are also murdered, but they are not murdered by women en masse because they are men, nor has their gender resigned them to socially subordinate roles systemically constructing their vulnerability such that they have served as scapegoats for all of recorded history.

13. Vigils for women murdered have proliferated around Edmonton as the murders of local women working in the sex trade — many of them of Aboriginal descent — have escalated. As of late 2005, the number is variously cited as twelve in the past sixteen years and seven since 2002. Carter talks of the "haunting echoes" from Vancouver's Downtown Eastside (2005, 23).

CHAPTER 3: WINNIPEG AND THE PAS

1. This chapter uses the term "Aboriginal," which appears to be the preferred term of media such as *The Drum* and *Windspeaker*, as well as official usage of the Manitoba Legislative Assembly, to indicate First Nations, Métis and Inuit peoples. The Foundation's first board of trustees, appointed in July 2001, included Cecilia Osborne (Helen Betty Osborne's sister), Rebecca Ross (director of the Cross Lake Education Authority), Wendy Whitecloud (co-commissioner of the Aboriginal Justice Implementation Commission), Gerry Friesen (author and history professor at the University of Manitoba), Marcy Richard (Aboriginal consultant, Community Learning and Youth Programs for Manitoba Education, Training and Youth) and, as chair of the Foundation, Sgt. Bob Urbanoski.

2. The December 6th Women's Memorial Committee, 1989–95, included Debra Blair, Bonnie Dickie, Janice Freeman, Babs Friesen, Keith Louise Fulton, Pat Hrabok, Judith Kearns, Audrhea Lande, Diane McGifford, Sally Papso and Vicki Verville.

3. The display sites were Winnipeg City Hall, University of Winnipeg, Winnipeg Art Gallery, West End Cultural Centre, Centre Culturel Franco-Manitobain, University of Manitoba's Faculty of Engineering, Women's Health Clinic, Manitoba Museum of Man and Nature, Augustine United Church, Klinic Community Health Centre, Manitoba Union Centre, Artspace, Plug-In Inc. and the Manitoba Legislative Building. For further discussion of Lin Gibson's work, see Rosenberg (1997, 188–191) and Yeo (1991).

4. Funds were raised from private individuals, the Winnipeg Foundation, the United Way and through concerts and sales. The provincial government of the time did not commit any public funds, but it did provide the lighting, engineering and services of legislative grounds gardener and greenhouse staff. Fulton also credits Roger Brown,

Stu Ursel and Cy Howard, the legislative grounds gardener, government representatives and Gillis Quarries, which donated some of the stone, and Scouts Canada for donating and planting the blue spruce.

5. For these and other details on the Women's Grove Memorial Garden, we are grateful to Jane Mcbee (2003).

6. This emphasis was underscored in the legislative assembly of December 6, 1995: Rosemary Vodrey announced the evening's candlelight vigil in the Women's Grove Memorial Garden; Diane McGifford, former president of the December 6th Memorial Women's Committee and at that moment critic for the Status of Women, read into the record the names of the fourteen women murdered in Montreal and "the two Manitoba women who were murdered as a result of domestic violence this year: Rhonda Michelle Lavoie and Dawn Brunsel"; and the Task Force Report on Violence Against Women was released ("Proceedings" 1995).

7. Johnston was released on parole in 1997.

8. The official name was the Public Inquiry into the Administration of Justice and Aboriginal People.

9. Including Best Mini-Series, Best Screenplay, Best Actor, Best Supporting Actress and Best Director. Appearing in the production were Kuna/Rappahannock playwright-actor Monique Mojica, Cree/Métis actor-singer Jani Lauzon and Pequot/Carib performer Michelle St. John who subsequently formed The Turtle Gals Performance Ensemble; their work is featured in chapter 13.

10. Elected MLA for Rupertsland in 1993, Robinson became Aboriginal and Northern Affairs Minister in 1999, then Minister of Culture, Heritage and Tourism in 2002.

11. The petition was created by the "Vanished Voices — NEVER AGAIN! Project" and written by Amber O'Hara (Waabnong Kwe). See www.petitiononline.com/tsalagi1/petition.html.

12. "After the unveiling, some 25 vehicles and two full sized school buses travelled into The Pas for the Feast of Life at the KCC [Keewatin Community College] cafeteria in honour of Helen's memory, where beef stew and bannock was served. Northern Buffalo Cree Singers performed an honorary song for Helen and her family, while Hector Menow played a beautiful melody dedicated to Ms. Osborne on his classical guitar" (Cooper 2000). There was also a traditional give away of gifts collected by the students after the unveiling (Lenze 2001).

13. Some of the research for this chapter was conducted by Ojibway scholar Christine Lenze.

14. Histories of residential schools differ somewhat in their details. The earliest school seems to date from the 1840s; the last federally run school closed in 1996. About 130 residential schools operated over that time, about 100 of which have been or expect to be named in abuse cases (see Grant 1996; "Indian Residential Schools" n.d.). According to Sto:lo scholars Suzanne Fournier and Ernie Crey, by the 1930s

almost 75 percent of all Native children in Canada between the ages of seven and fifteen were attending residential schools (1998, 61). As Cree/Métis scholar Kim Anderson writes, these schools were frequently the sites of "rape, sexual assault, induced abortion, and sexual/psychological abuse" (2000, 93; see also Chrisjohn, Young and Maraun 1997; and Assembly of First Nations 1994).

15. On sexual violence as an agent of genocide when enacted upon the bodies of First Nations women, see also Knowles (2003, 248).

16. Against a backdrop of continuing Aboriginal protest and anger across the country, in 1991 the federal government appointed four Aboriginal and three non-Aboriginal commissioners as a Royal Commission on Aboriginal People. Their 400-page report, released in November 1996, recommended that an additional $1.5 to $2 billion annually be spent over the next twenty years on Aboriginal people. In 1998, the federal government issued a document, "Gathering Strength — Canada's Aboriginal Action Plan," which included a statement by Jane Stewart, Minister of Indian Affairs and Northern Development, on residential schools: "The Government of Canada acknowledges the role it played in the development and administration of these schools. Particularly to those individuals who experienced the tragedy of sexual and physical abuse at residential schools, and who have carried this burden believing that in some way they must be responsible, we wish to emphasize that what you experienced was not your fault and should never have happened. To those of you who suffered this tragedy at residential schools, we are deeply sorry" ("Notes" 1998).

   In 2001, the federal department, Indian Residential Schools Resolution Canada, was "dedicated to strengthening partnerships within government and with Aboriginal people, religious denominations, and other citizens to address and resolve issues arising from the legacy of Indian residential schools" ("Indian Residential Schools" n.d.). In 2005, the federal government, insisting on a shockingly slow dispute resolution process, appeared to be reneging on some of these promises.

17. "In the beginning was thought, and her name was Woman. The Mother, the Grandmother, recognized from earliest times to the present ... To her we owe our lives, and from her comes our ability to endure, regardless of the concerted assaults on our, on Her, being, for the past five hundred years of colonization. She is the Old Woman who tends the fires of life. She is the Old Spiderwoman who weaves us together in a fabric of interconnection. She is the Eldest God, the one who Remembers and Re-members ... and we endure into the present, alive, certain of our significance, certain of her centrality, her identity as the Sacred Hoop of Be-ing" (Allen 1986, 11).

18. Christine Lenze witnessed some of the personal memorials at Clearwater Lake. However, out of respect, she chose not to record the details of these private acts of homage. She also pointed out to us that there are many "unofficial" memorials to many First Nations women whose stories are similar to that of Helen Betty Osborne.

19. The reparative work of memorial-making also brought the language of healing into Manitoba's legislative assembly. At the hearings for the Helen Betty Osborne

Memorial Fund Act, Robinson, Cree witnesses, members of the Osborne family and Attorney General Gord Macintosh all spoke the language of healing; in Macintosh's words, "It is hoped that the work of the foundation can be part of the healing process" (Simard 2001).

20. Big Joey's line is actually "Because I hate them! I hate them fuckin' bitches. Because they — our own women — took the fuckin' power away faster than the FBI ever did" (Highway 1989, 120).

Chapter 4: Chatham

1. There is a resting place with chairs and a table with dried or fresh roses, a candle and a photograph of Theresa Vince at the Chatham-Kent Sexual Assault Centre. The Chatham-Kent Women's Shelter has a meeting room dedicated to Theresa Vince's memory, with a wall plaque and photograph. The women's community in London, Ontario, also holds memorials for Theresa Vince, most often at the London Women's Monument.

2. The population of Chatham was 43,000 at the time of Theresa Vince's murder in 1996. Since then it has been amalgamated with Kent, and the combined population of Chatham-Kent is 110,000.

3. The Vince family and supporters also urged the Ontario government to proclaim a province-wide Sexual Harassment Awareness Week. The Progressive Conservative government of the day, under the leadership of Mike Harris, declined to do so (Crouch 1998). In June 2005, Pat Hoy introduced a private member's bill in memory of Theresa Vince that would make the first week of June Sexual Harassment Awareness Week in Ontario (Barlow 2005).

4. Writing in 2000, McCrindle also reports that "sexual harassment in the workplace is estimated to affect 40 to 70 percent of workers ... yet less than 0.3 percent of complaints launched with the Ontario Human Rights Commission are heard." The inquest into Vince's death produced a range of recommendations (Verdict 1997), many of which have yet to be acted upon, but continued pressure that has emerged out of Chatham and spread across the province seems to be having a direct and positive impact on changing attitudes towards harassment in the workplace.

Chapter 5: London

1. Quoted in the memorial vigil program, Women Won't Forget, Toronto, December 6th 1991.

2. The organizers included Margaret Buist, Lorraine Greaves, Louise Karch, Leslie Reaume, Gail Hutchinson and Constance Backhouse (see Money 1995; W.A.A.A.V.E. 1994; Buist et al. 2000).

3. Unless otherwise indicated, the information and quotations in this and subsequent paragraphs on the establishment of the London Women's Monument derive from an

interview by the book's authors with Margaret Buist, Gail Hutchinson, Louise Karch and Leslie Reaume, in London, Ontario, 9 June 2000.

4. *The Goddess Is Crying* came to have pride of place in law offices of the firm of Margaret Buist and Leslie Reaume.

5. Art committee members were Carol Brooks (manager of The Circle and prime mover in fundraising efforts), Sister Patricia McLean, Karen Wells and Shelley Siskind.

Chapter 6: Guelph

1. Timothy Weldon was found guilty of first-degree murder and was sentenced to twenty-five years. His conviction was appealed and, in 1995, the Ontario Court of Appeal quashed the conviction and found him not guilty by reason of mental disorder. He is currently at a maximum security mental health facility.

2. Information about the park comes largely from knowledge within our authorial group, as well as from Justine Howarth, Linda Reith and Joan Kotarski.

3. The tree is part of a memorial plot kept up by a local funeral parlour and is not individually identified.

4. Crucial to the victory was the intervention of a well-connected local lawyer whose father had been the dedicatee of a city park and who himself had been a member of the WIC board.

5. This information was confirmed by Janice Olbina, parks planner at the time that Marianne's Park was purchased and designed. Olbina also spoke of how the plans for the formal garden incorporated plants which Marianne's family identified as her favourites.

6. WIC continues to lobby for accessible electrical outlets for microphones; there is nothing to serve as a speaker's podium and no natural arena for group activity.

7. A second plaque, at the opposite end of the oval from the dedication, acknowledges the list of local companies who were donors, while the dedication pamphlet lists another 150 individual donors, overwhelmingly women.

8. It seems significant that the decision by the Canadian Federation of University Women not to locate their memorial in Marianne's Park was articulated in aesthetic terms (the organization did not want to spoil the "symmetry" of Marianne's Park), which did not take into account the fracturing of activist efforts which might result (Colter 2001).

9. Indeed, Guelph's Engineering Faculty was the first recipient of the Canadian Engineering Memorial Foundation's award for the most Women-Friendly Engineering School, in 1999. In 2003, Professor Valerie Davidson, long-time member of this school, became holder of the distinguished NSERC/HP (Canada) Chair for Women in Science and Engineering.

CHAPTER 7: HAMILTON

1. Quoted in Johnson (1998).

2. The quotation comes from an in-process website dedicated to Marlene "Shaggie" Moore, at http://www.tropicevader.com/shaggie.htm. Retreived 1 May 2003.

3. Kershaw and Lasovich raise some doubts about the suicide verdict.

4. The Canadian Association of Elizabeth Fry Societies' "Mission Statement" reads: "CAEFS is a federation of autonomous societies which works with, and on behalf of, women involved with the justice system, particularly women in conflict with the law. Elizabeth Fry Societies are community based agencies dedicated to offering services and programs to marginalized women, advocating for legislative and administrative reform and offering fora within which the public may be informed about, and participate in, aspects of the justice system which affect women." (http://www. elizabethfry.ca)

5. The toll continues: "In February 1996, another woman committed suicide at P4W after being advised that she would no longer have visits with her children. In November 1998, two women killed themselves at the Joliette Institution. In 2000, an Aboriginal women committed suicide in the segregated maximum security unit for women in the Saskatchewan Penitentiary (a men's prison) despite being under 'suicide watch'" (Elizabeth Fry Society).

6. The resources included both materials–crushed-brick walkways, select cultivares, wrought-iron fencing, a large decorative rock, an irrigation system–and expertise: the director of the Royal Botanical Gardens, the University's President's Committee on Horticulture, the University gardener, various University bodies, managers, supervisors, superintendents, the City of Hamilton, and private sponsors (see, for example, *The McMaster Courier* of 15 September 1992).

7. CAVEAT was a victims' rights group, headed by Priscilla DeVilliers, that lobbied for legal reform. It disbanded in 2001, after ten years of operation.

8. Elsewhere on campus another institutionally contained memorial is explicitly dedicated to December 6th. In front of the John Hodgins Engineering Building — a familiar 1970s structure, massively rectangular with a great deal of glass and stone-coloured brick — is an open brick square surrounded by grass, young trees and ranks of benches and garbage cans. Looming, quite startlingly, from between and slightly behind two of these benches is a large grey stone, approximately 2 ft x 3 ft. The effect is exactly that of a large headstone, and its size, location and colour contrast shout for attention in a way that the decorous, fenced-in rose garden does not. Beyond that initial shock of presence, however, there is little to connect the memorial to activism for change. The inscription again avoids naming the act of murder which has provoked the call to community and memory:

THE ENGINEERING COMMUNITY
AT MCMASTER UNIVERSITY

REMEMBERS THE FOLLOWING:

GENEVIEVE BERGERON

HELENE COLGAN

NATHALIE CROTEAU

BARBARA DAIGNEAULT

ANNE-MARIE EDWARD

MAUD HAVIERNICK

BARBARA MARIE KLUEZNICK

MARYSE LAGANIERE

MARYSE LECLAIR

ANNE-MARIE LEMAY

SONIA PELLETIER

MICHELLE RICHARD

ANNIE ST-ARNEAULT

ANNIE TURCOTTE

WHO LOST THEIR LIVES ON DECEMBER 6TH, 1989
AT ECOLE POLYTECHNIQUE, MONTREAL

The positioning of the stone also mitigates against the mobilization of anger or activism: its location makes it difficult to get close to and impossible to gather around. The memorial seems to have been the lone initiative of a woman engineering student–Eloise Harvey–with minimal institutional support or publicity. We have been unable to retrieve any information about the precise timing, resourcing or intention of the stone's placement.

9. Unless otherwise indicated, information and quotations come from Donelle de Vlaming and Renate Manthei interview.

10. Compare the impact of this resonant contraction with the committee's original wording: "END THE VIOLENCE AGAINST WOMEN."

CHAPTER 8: TORONTO

1. Sharon Rosenberg (1997) discusses temporary exhibits in Toronto by Lin Gibson, Pati Beaudoin and Katherine Zsolt (83–115) and lists additional feminist memorial responses in Toronto and across the country in her Resource Bibliography (184–204).

2. All quotations concerning the Ryerson memorial that are not otherwise attributed derive from Cara Scott-McCron's e-mail to Lisa Schincariol (2001).

3. According to George Hume, a member of the committee, "to ensure that it was done, and done right."

4. A masonry school, for example, offered at one point early on to donate thousands of dollars in material and labour to place a flagstone at the base of each tree, each with the name of one of the fourteen women engraved on it, but the proposal was vetoed by the university as "too depressing" (Lewis 2001). The university then proposed placing benches between the trees, but the group felt that this would too closely resemble the design of Vancouver's Marker of Change.

5. In December 2003, an apparently marginalized group within the university, "The Centre Formerly Known as The Women's Centre at U of T" — co-sponsored the vigil with Women Won't Forget. The Status of Women Office at the university organized a separate ceremony in Hart House on campus.

6. All of these quotations are taken from programs from the annual December 6th vigils organized by Women Won't Forget and held at Philosopher's Walk, supplied courtesy of Janet Lewis.

CHAPTER 9: OTTAWA

1. The plaque at the engineering faculty at the University of Ottawa, installed at the expense of the engineering faculty itself, is similar to many others at engineering schools across the country. It names, "In Memoriam," the fourteen women killed at l'École Polytechnique, but includes no other tribute or information beyond the naming of l'École Polytechnique and the University of Ottawa. The 60-by-75 cm (2-by-2½ foot) brass framed plaque, with brass lettering on a brown, leather-textured surface, is mounted adjacent to a smaller plaque dedicated to a murdered male student on a prominent and well-lit wall at the edge of the main stairway opposite the entrance to the Engineering Building. Neither the plaque nor the foyer of the building serves as a privileged site for memorial vigils, however, which happen, when they do, in an ad hoc fashion at various sites and with programs that vary according to the interests of the student organizers. On some occasions, remembrance services have coincided with the awarding of Engineering Memorial scholarships for female engineering students with top grades, also funded from the faculty budget, but the occasion, formerly held on the resonant date of December 6th, has in recent years been moved forward to accommodate fall semester examination schedules.

2. The information in these paragraphs is taken from Johnson (1998, 4–6).

3. The proposal drafted by the Women's Monument Fund asserted: "Violence of any form is horrific and unacceptable. The tragic, untimely ending of young women's lives at the hand of their partners undermines an essential cornerstone in the structure of society. The death of Patricia Allen, caused by the violent murder by her husband, has brought to the forefront of our consciousness that all abusive and violent acts must stop now. It instigated the beginning of collective efforts by women to establish a marker, a place wherein all women lost through violence could be commemorated. More importantly, it marks a response to move beyond the losses

and remind us to initiate action to end ALL violence. With this monument, The Women's Monument Committee hopes to become the flicker of light that will dispel the darkness of violence so peace and harmony will prevail" ("Women's Monument Proposal" n.d.).

4. In September 1992, city council approved the department of recreation and culture's endorsement of the Women's Monument Committee request to install "a significant memorial for those women who have died (at the hands of men) and to express support for those women who are still living with abuse, at risk and in crisis." "By approving this request," the proposal indicates, "the City will be recognizing and supporting community efforts to raise awareness of the issue of women's safety, violence against women and for promoting zero tolerance of violence" (Department of Recreation and Culture 1992).

5. Although it is not mentioned in the City of Ottawa documents, the $300 cost of each of the stones subsequently added to commemorate women murdered was also the responsibility of the Women's Monument Committee fundraising and private donations. Nevertheless, and unusually, the police themselves contributed to the fundraising, collecting $1,500 through a series of barbeques in the Summer of 1992, and the city eventually waived the required maintenance deposit from the Women's Monument Committee, absorbing ongoing maintenance costs within its own budget, on the motion of a supportive female councillor, when it became apparent that the committee was having difficulty living up to its initial financial commitment (City of Ottawa 1994).

6. Note that the English and French are not precise equivalents, the French version inviting the reader to imagine a world where women, freed from the grip of violence "brighten" or "bloom" in respect and freedom.

7. As of July 2005, ownership rests with the women's community, the University of Ottawa Women's Centre having lost much of its funding. Events at the moment (including December 6th vigils, International Women's Day rallies and Take Back The Night marches) are organized by the Women Events Network (www.geocities. com/wenottawa).

CHAPTER 10: MONTREAL

1. This and subsequent quotations by the designers, except where noted, are excerpted from "Communiqué, Ville de Montréal, le 6 mai 1999," forwarded by Rose-Marie Goulet to Cawo Abdi, in French and English, 11 January 2002.

2. "La conscience collective face à la violence n'a-t-elle pas d'abord une assise indivi-duelle? C'est le plus souvent seul que nous y faisons face et que nours y sommes exposés. Et ne sommes-nous pas d'ailleurs tous individuellement sujets à y céder? (Does not the collective conscience confronting violence first have an individual basis? It is often alone that we face it and that we are exposed to it. And aren't we all moreover subject to give in to it?)"

3. The jury consisted of one member of La Fondation des victimes du 6 décembre 1989, a Quebec artist, an architect, a landscape architect and a representative from the municipal city public art commission (Casey 2001, 53).

4. Nef pour quatorze reines won National Citations in 2001 from the Canadian and American Societies of Landscape Architects.

5. These details are taken from "The List," kept in the University of Calgary Law Library as a descriptive record of the names on Teresa Posyniak's sculpture Lest We Forget. The list appears to amalgamate Mary Billy's femicide list with Posyniak's records.

6. This and subsequent quotations are extracted from an undated press release, forwarded by Constance Forest, Service des communications, École Polytechnique Montréal, 22 August 2000 (translated by Cawo Abdi).

7. "André Bazergui, executive director of École Polytechnique, said the ceremony is kept low-key so the families can mourn in their own way, and know the school is there for them" (Hanes 1997, A4).

8. Sheila Swasson, director of Haven House and Mi'kmaq from the Listuguj First Nation in Quebec, provided this information to Wayne Leng. Retrieved 12 March 2005 from www.missingpeople.net/montreal.

9. Retrieved 12 March 2005 from National Aboriginal Circle Against Family Violence Board Member Biography, www.nacafv.ca/board.

10. Retrieved 12 March 2005 from www.cybersolidaires.org.

CHAPTER 11: MONCTON AND RIVERVIEW

1. Unless otherwise indicated, information and quotations concerning the Riverview memorial come from an undated, handwritten statement by Helen Partridge, sent to Lisa Schincariol in August 2001.

2. At first a Regional Women's Committee, later expanded and renamed the December 6th Committee, the group was made up of women working for Public Service Alliance of Canada, Support to Single Parents and Coalition Against Abusive Relationships, Crossroads for Women transition house and Victim Services RCMP. The first group included Helen Partridge, Cathy Murphy (PSAC representative), Ellen Lewis (Support to Single Parents and Coalition Against Abusive Relationships), Monique LaPlante (PSAC), Beth McLaughlin (Teacher and Crossroads for Women), Nicole LeBlanc (Université de Moncton student) and Danielle Godin (PSAC). New members in 1995 included Nancy Hartling (Support to Single Parents), Ginette Petitipas (Victim Services RCMP), Yolande Sonier (Crossroads for Women), Diane Fiske, Nicole Leger, Angela Rizell and Brigitte Donovan (all from Support to Single Parents).

3. At city hall, Education Minister Jim Lockyer introduced the speakers who included Marcelle Mersereau, minister responsible for the status of women. The quoted language is heavy with the euphemism of physical health, a common trope among

public officials addressing systemic injustice. Of violence against women, Lockyer said, "We must do all we can to cure this social illness"; Mersereau echoed him: "A community that is faced with violence can never reach its potential as a healthy, vibrant society." The men in attendance were asked to sign a petition, sponsored by the Muriel McQueen Fergusson Foundation, stating "their commitment to do all that they can to eradicate male violence against women" (Goddu 1996, 1). Later that day, about 200 people gathered for the unveiling of the stone at Caseley Park. Danielle Godin, PSAC worker and member of the original organizing committee, hosted the ceremonies; the guest speakers included Elizabeth Weir, leader of the NDP for New Brunswick. Solange sang in the background as fifteen female students from various schools, colleges and universities laid roses — fourteen in memory of the women massacred in Montreal in 1989 and one in memory of all victims of violence. A candle light vigil and a reception in Riverview town hall followed.

4. The press quoted Brenda Sansom, chair of the New Brunswick Advisory Council on the Status of Women: "'What I think is perplexing at times is the feeling that there is still denial, that there is still a problem of violence against women' ... 'It is important to continue raising public awareness about the problem of violence against women and children,' she said" (Goddu 1996, 1).

5. Representatives came from the City of Moncton, Support to Single Parents, Crossroads for Women, Muriel McQueen Fergusson Foundation, Université de Moncton, Aberdeen Cultural Centre, Enerplan Consultants Ltd., Coalition Against Abusive Relationships, Public Service Alliance of Canada and Moncton District Labour Council Women's Committee. The committee spent some time arriving at a common vision, agreeing to emphasize local, current conditions and to focus on "healing" and "moving on," by which they meant achieving "progress in the fight against violence against women and improved conditions for women." They wanted to make "a link between Montreal and Moncton." Unless otherwise indicated, information and quotations concerning the Courage and Hope sculpture come from an interview by Lisa Schincariol with Nancy J. Hartling, Gisèle Levesque, and Christine Pilard, Moncton, NB, 22 August 2001.

6. The form also explained the selection process: "All dreams and plans for the future have equal importance, therefore in the event of receiving too many names for the glass, Valerie LeBlanc and the December 6th Art Project Committee will draw the names by chance. To ensure equal representation, the names will be drawn according to grouping them by cultural background."

7. The chair of the Greater Moncton Chamber of Commerce chaired the fundraising campaign; a city councillor helped secure a $2,500 donation from the Police Association; well-connected businessmen in the community drew on their financial networks for support; and a broad-based approach was made to business people, the general public, unions and non-profits.

8. The other quotations on the sculpture are: "To find a cure for cancer and to help others. — Kippy"; "J'amerais être une chanteuse ou une enseignante, ou une actrice. — Mellissa"; "I want to be a professional snowboarder. — Jill"; "To become an

architect. — Missy"; "Mon rêve est de m'exprimer librement. — Marie-elaine"; "My dream is to someday be a good mother, a journalist, and to do work in the social area. — April; "To become a lawyer that makes a difference in our world. — Katie"; "Mon rêve est d'aider tout le monde qui sont pauvres. — Chanelle"; "Mon rêve est que l'avenir nous réserve l'égalité et le respect. — Josée."

9. The French text reads:

Courage et espoir

Le Comité du 6 décembre, qui représente de nombreux organismes communautaires, a demandé à l'artiste Valerie LeBlanc de créer une sculpture originale dans le but de commémorer les victimes du massacre qui a eu lieu le 6 décembre 1989 à l'École Polytechnique de Montréal ainsi que d'encourager les femmes à se fixer des rêves et des buts pour l'avenir.

Intitulée *Courage et Espoir*, cette oeuvre de conception unique atteint l'objectif visé. L'oeuvre repose sur un socle, dont la forme représente la bague de l'ingénieur et sur lequel est gravé le nom des quatorze jeunes femmes qui ont été tuées le 6 décembre 1989. De plus, les rêves et les aspirations de jeunes filles et de jeunes femmes de la région sont gravés sur une plaque de verre sur laquelle repose une échelle dorée, qui symbolise la croyance que si les membres de la communauté travaillent ensemble pour enrayer la violence, ces filles et ces femmes pourront réaliser leurs buts, voire les dépasser.

Dévoilement: le 4 décembre 1998

Chapter 12: Bear River

1. Retrieved 1 May 2002 from the Bear River Candle Float site at the "Bear Town Boogie" website: http://members.tripod.com/Beartown/special/ float.html.

2. Secretary was Frank B. Miller, clerk of the Digby court; other members were Cereno H. Purdy, chairman, VT Hardwick, WW Clarke (Thurston 1987, 57–58, 159).

3. The wording of the contract suggests that the monument came from a series of designs: it was identified as "'design Number 456 Series 13' of Spoon Island Granite. It is sarcophagus style, with two bases: the first roughly finished, 5ft 6ins long, 3ft 4ins wide, 1 ft 4ins high; the next base, slightly smaller — 4'8" x 2'6" x 1'2" — and of polished granite. With the top, the overall height is 5ft 10 ins." (Thurston 1987, 160–161).

4. See "Bear Town Boogie " website at http://members.tripod.com/Beartown/special/ float.html, and follow the links to the Candle Float and Annie Kempton.

Chapter 13: First Nations Women

1. According to Sherry Lewis, executive director of the Native Women's Association of Canada, citing Government of Canada statistics, "Aboriginal women with status under the Indian Act, and who are between the ages of 24 and 44, are five times

more likely to experience a violent death than other Canadian women in the same age category." Retrieved 28 March 2005 from turtleisland . org / discussion / viewtopic.php?t=2131. See also Amnesty International's October 2004 report, *Stolen Sisters: A Human Rights Response to Discrimination and Violence Against Indigenous Women in Canada.*

2. Retrieved 28 March 2005 from www.sistersinspirit.ca/engremember.htm (posted 11 February 2005). In May 2005, the federal government announced $5 million in funding for the Sisters in Spirit campaign. Retrieved 26 November 2005 from www. sistersinspirit.ca/enghome.htm.

CONCLUSION

1. For information and statistics about "The Color of Violence Against Women" in the United States, see the special issue under that title of *Colorlines* (Winter 2000–01).

PHOTO CREDITS

Every effort has been made to track down and credit photographers, but this has not always been possible. We would be grateful for any information that could be sent to us.

REFERENCES

PRIMARY MATERIALS

Abriel, Gilda (Kempton). 2001. "Annie Kempton Memorial." Unpublished manuscript. 20 August.

Agents of Gaia (c.j. fleury and Mary Faught). n.d. "Enclave: Statement about Design and Symbols of Women's Monument." In possession of c.j. fleury.

Allen, Judy. 2001. Telephone interview with Lisa Schincariol, 6 April.

Billy, Mary. 2000. "Facing the Horror — The Femicide List." Announcement and Letter, 1 December.

Bowerbank, Sylvia, Michelle Corneau, and Cynthia Hill. 2000. "Towards the Greening of Undergraduate Research: A Pilot Project in the Humanities." Unpublished manuscript in possession of authors.

Buckle, Trevor. 2005. Telephone interview with Lisa Schincariol, 16 February.

Buist, Margaret, Gail Hutchinson, Louise Karch, and Leslie Reaume. 2000. Interview with Cultural Memory Group, London, ON, 9 June.

"Call to Artists." 1998. December 6th Art Project Committee. Moncton, NB.

Cannon, Elizabeth. 2001. E-mail to Sherry Kinsella, 25 January.

Carr, Elaine M. n.d. "Artist's Words of Description: Memorial to the 14 Women Killed in the Montreal Massacre." Installation at Brescia College, London, ON.

———. 1994. Artist's Statement in Commemoration Ceremony Pamphlet for the Installation of "14 Women Dancing, Femmes Dansantes." Brescia College, London, ON, 6 December.

———. 2001. Telephone interview with Lisa Schincariol, 1 August.

Carr, Jacquie. 2001. E-mail to Lisa Schincariol, 12 March.

Casey, Annik. 2001. "Commemorating the Montreal Massacre: *Marker for Change* and Other Monuments Dedicated to Victims of Violence Against Women." MA Research Paper, Carleton University.

City of Ottawa. 1994. Response to Request of a Council Member. Diane Holmes Motion, 30 May.

Colter, Barbara. 2001. "The Planning and Realization of the Reflection Garden in Guelph." Unpublished manuscript, March.

Colter, Barbara, Nancy Coates, and Wendy Schearer. 1999. Memorandum to Mayor Joe Young and City Council Members [Guelph], 20 December.

"Communiqué, Ville de Montréal, le 6 mai 1999." Forwarded by Rose-Marie Goulet to Cawo Abdi, in French and English, 11 January 2002.

Davidson, Valerie. 2003. E-mail to Christine Bold, 20 May.

"The Dean's Millen[n]ium Award Project." n.d. [University of Alberta Project Description.]

Dempster, Eileen. 2001. E-mail to Lisa Schincariol, 30 April.

Department of Recreation and Culture, City of Ottawa. 1992. Administrative Action: The Women's Monument — Minto Park, 30 September.

de Vlaming, Donelle, and Renate Manthei. 2001. Interview with Lisa Schincariol and Sly Castaldi, London, ON, 25 June.

DeVries, Pat. 2001. Telephone interview with Lisa Schincariol, fall.

Dewar, Marion. n.d. "Women's Monument Fund: Fundraising Campaign Drive." Letter. In possession of authors.

Dufresne, Martin. 2004. Press Release, Quebec Men Against Sexism, 24 November.

Elizabeth Fry Society. n.d. "The Tree Ceremony — History." Unpublished manuscript, EFS, Hamilton, ON.

fleury, c.j. 2000. Email to Lisa Schincariol. 13 October.

Goulet, Sara. 2002. Letter to the Trustees of the Helen Betty Osborne Foundation, 14 August. Retrieved 8 May 2003 from www.helenbettyosbornefdtn.ca.

Hartling, Nancy J., Gisèle Levesque, and Christine Pilard. 2001. Interview with Lisa Schincariol, Moncton, NB, 22 August.

Hopkins, Elizabeth. n.d. Personal note sent to Lisa Schincariol, June.

Howarth, Justine. 2000. Interview with Sly Castaldi and Belinda Leach, London, ON, 17 May.

Hoy, Pat. 2001. "Sexual Harassment." Ontario Hansard. Session 37:2, 7 June.

James, William. 2001. E-mails to Lisa Schincariol, 6 February.

Khan, Irene. 2002. "Acceptance Speech, Women of the Year Lunch and Assembly." London, ON, 14 October. Retrieved 22 April 2005 from http://web.amnesty.org.

King, Marylin. 2000. "Women's Memorial Society of Ontario." Paper presented at

Feminist Memorializing: Remembering Women Murdered/Demanding an End to Violence Against Women, Victoria College, University of Toronto, Toronto, ON, 23 March.

Kroening, Mike. 2001. Telephone interview with Lisa Schincariol, 5 June.

LaRocque Emma. 1990. Written presentation to Aboriginal Justice Inquiry, 5 February. Retrieved 13 May 2003 from www.ajic.mb.ca/volume.html.

Larson, Don. 2000. Telephone interview with Lisa Schincariol, 7 November.

———. 2001. Letter to Lisa Schincariol, 16 February.

———. 2001. Interview with Lisa Schincariol, 6 May.

———. 2005. Telephone interview with Lisa Schincariol, 2 March.

"Law School to Receive Memorial Sculpture in Tribute to Murdered Women." n.d. Information Sheet from The Lest We Forget Fund.

LeBlanc, Valerie. 1998a. "Description." Proposal Form, 22 March.

———. 1998b. Letter to Christine Connor, 5 May.

———. 2001. Interview with Lisa Schincariol, 13 August.

Leng, Wayne. 2005a. E-mail to Lisa Schincariol, 18 February.

———. 2005b. E-mail to Lisa Schincariol, 28 February.

Lenze, Christine. 2001. E-mails to Ric Knowles et al., 1, 9 March.

Lewis, Janet. 2001. Telephone interview with Lisa Schincariol, 19 June.

Lindsay, Alyssa. 2003. E-mail to Christine Bold, 16 May.

Maheux, Pauline. 2001. Telephone interview with Lisa Schincariol, 18 April.

Manthei, Renate. 2001. Telephone interview with Lisa Schincariol, 25 April.

Marlow, Dell. 2001. Telephone interview with Lisa Schincariol, 26 February.

Martin, Sheilah. 2001. Telephone interview with Lisa Schincariol, 29 May.

Mcbee, Jane. 2003. E-mail to Christine Bold, 11 June.

McDowell, Christine. 1999a. E-mail to Mary Newberry, 17 June.

———. 1999b. E-mail to Mary Newberry, 30 June.

———. 1999c. E-mail to Mary Newberry, 2 October.

McLean, Sister Patricia. 1994. Dedication Speech, Installation of "14 Dancing Women." Brescia College, University of Western Ontario, London, ON, 6 December.

———. 2001. Telephone interview with Lisa Schincariol, 5 June.

"A Message of Protest, and of Hope." n.d. Tom George, Abdulahi Mahamad, Kristine

Acielo, Hope Neale, and Peter Aran. MERGE pamphlet.

O'Hara, Amber (Waabnong Kwe). 2003. E-mail to multiple recipients, 3 May.

Olbina, Janice. 2000. Interview with Ric Knowles and Lisa Schincariol, Guelph, 8 June.

Peacock, W. Hugh. 2001. Telephone inteview with Lisa Schincariol, 22 April.

Posyniak, Teresa. n.d. "The Building of 'Lest We Forget': A Monument Dedicated to Murdered Women." Faculty of Law Library, University of Calgary.

——. 2001. Telephone interview with Lisa Schincariol, 23 May.

Reith, Linda. 2000. Interview with Sly Castaldi and Belinda Leach, London, ON, 5 June.

Schoeck, Ellen A. 2005. E-mail to Lisa Schincariol, 7 March.

Schryer, Michelle. 2000. Interview with Lisa Schincariol, London, ON, 20 February.

——. 2005. Letter to Ric Knowles, 23 March.

Scott-McCron, Cara. 2001. E-mail to Lisa Schincariol, 29 May.

Smith, Janet. 2005. Telephone interview with Lisa Schincariol, 16 February.

"Submission to the Canadian Engineering Memorial Foundation (CEMF) for the Dean's Millennium Award." 1999. Faculty of Engineering, University of Calgary, 15 November.

Tarasuck, John. 2001. Telephone interview with Lisa Schincariol, 24 May.

"Uniting for Change/S'unir pour faire changement." 1999. Memorial and Candlelight Ceremony Program. University of Alberta, 6 December.

Vancouver Board of Parks and Recreation, Public Affairs Department. 2000. "Parks Naming Report," 13 September.

Verdict of Coroner's Jury into the Deaths of Theresa Vince and Russell Davis. 1997. Ministry of the Solicitor General for Ontario, Chatham, ON, 2 December.

W.A.A.A.V.E. (Women for Action, Accountability and Against Violence Everywhere). 1994. Program for the annual vigil and the dedication of The Women's Monument, 6 December.

Webb, Nicole. 2003. E-mail to Christine Bold, 26 May.

Wilkinson, Jeff. 2001. E-mail to Lisa Schincariol, 24 May.

"Women's Monument Proposal." n.d. Ottawa. In possession of authors.

Women Won't Forget. n.d. "We Hereby Reclaim the Right of All Women to Live in Hope and Not Fear: Herstory of Women Won't Forget." Provided by Janet Lewis from Women Won't Forget Files (March 2000).

Worrad, Deborah. 1999. Letter to Dr. D.T. Lynch (Dean, Faculty of Engineering, University of Alberta) 29 November.

Wright, Esther. 2001. Telephone interview with Lisa Schincariol, 28 February.

PUBLISHED WORKS

Aboriginal Justice Inquiry of Manitoba. 1991. "Report of the Aboriginal Justice Inquiry of Manitoba." Retrieved 13 May 2003 from www.ajic.mb.ca/volume.html.

Abraham, Carolyn. 1992. "Monument Will Honour Women Killed by Men." *Ottawa Citizen*, 18 April: D1.

Allen, Paula Gunn. 1986. *The Sacred Hoop: Recovering the Feminine in American Indian Traditions*. Boston, MA: Beacon.

Amnesty International. 2004. *Stolen Sisters: A Human Rights Response to Discrimination and Violence against Indigenous Women in Canada*. Retrieved March 2005 from www. amnesty.ca/stolensisters.

Anderson, Kim. 2000. *A Recognition of Being: Reconstructing Native Womanhood*. Toronto, ON: Sumach Press.

Armstrong, Jane. 2002. "O Brothers, What Art Thou?" *The Globe and Mail*, 25 May: F4.

Arnott, Joan. 2001. "Migration." In Jeanette C. Armstrong and Lally Grauer, eds., *Native Poetry in Canada: A Contemporary Anthology*, 294–296. Peterborough, ON: Broadview Press.

Assembly of First Nations. 1994. *Breaking the Silence: An Interpretive Study of Residential School Impact and Healing as Illustrated by the Stories of First Nations Individuals*. Ottawa, ON: Assembly of First Nations.

Barlow, Larissa. 2005. "Vince Family Still Waiting for Government Response." *Chatham This Week*, 8 June. Retrieved 1 July 2005 from www.chathamthisweek.com.

Bauld, Florence L. 1995/1997. *Bear River, Untapped Roots: Moving Upward*. N.p.: Minuteman Press.

Beacom, Chris. 1994. "Victims Remembered." *The Calgary Sun*, 1 December: 5.

Benmayor, Rina. 1991. "Testimony, Action, Research, and Empowerment: Puerto Rican Women and Popular Education." In E. Sherna Berger Gluck and Daphne Patai, eds., *Women's Words: The Feminist Practice of Oral History*, 159–174. New York: Routledge.

Bold, Christine, Ric Knowles, and Belinda Leach. 2002. "Feminist Memorializing and Cultural Countermemory: The Case of Marianne's Park." In Marianne Hirsch and Valerie Smith, eds., *Gender and Cultural Memory*. Special Issue. *Signs: Journal of Women in Culture and Society* 28: 125–148.

———. 2003. "How Might a Women's Monument Be Different?" In Roxanne Rimstead, ed., *Cultural Memory and Social Identity.* Special Issue. *Essays on Canadian Writing* (Fall): 17–35.

Boose, Lynda E. 2002. "Crossing the River Drina: Bosnian Rape Camps, Turkish Impalement, and Serb Cultural Memory." In Marianne Hirsch and Valerie Smith, eds., *Gender and Cultural Memory.* Special Issue. *Signs: Journal of Women in Culture and Society* 28: 71–96.

Brant, Beth. 1989/2001. "Telling." In Jeanette C. Armstrong and Lally Grauer, eds., *Native Poetry in Canada: A Contemporary Anthology*, 51–56. Peterborough, ON: Broadview Press. The poem was first published in 1989.

Burk, A.L. 2003. "Private Griefs, Public Places." *Political Geography* 22: 317–333.

Burrows, Matthew. 2005. "Missing Women Must Not Be Forgotten to Time, Say Locals." *MissingPeople.Net*, May 19. Retrieved 15 November 2005 from www.missingpeople.net.

Campbell, Jennifer. 2000. "Man Wants Wife's Name Off Murder Memorial." *Ottawa Citizen*, 8 February: D1–D2.

Canadian Centre for Justice Statistics (CCJS). 1994. *Family Violence in Canada.* Catalogue 89-5410XPE. Ottawa, ON: Statistics Canada.

Carr, Jacquie, Audrey Huntley, Barbara MacQuarrie, and Sandy Welch. 2004. "Workplace Harrassment and Violence Report." Centre for Research on Violence Against Women and Children. Retrieved 4 February 2005 from www.crvawc.ca/research_ crvawcpubs.htm.

Carrol, Frank. 1998. "Hope Springs from Tragedy." *Times & Transcript* (Moncton), 5 December: A3 – A4.

Carter, Lauren. 2005. "Where Are Canada's Disappeared Women?" *Herizons* (Fall): 20–21, 23, 45–46.

CBC News British Columbia. April 12, 2002. Retrieved 23 June 2003 from http://vancouver. cbc.ca.

CEMF (Canadian Engineering Memorial Foundation). 1999. "Press Release." December 3. Retrieved 1 May 2003 from http://www.cemf.ca

Chrisjohn, Roland, Sherri Young, and Michael Maraun. 1997. *The Circle Game: Shadows and Substance in the Indian Residential School Experience in Canada.* Penticton, BC: Theytus.

Clermont, Lori. 1992. "Monument for Marlene Moore." Retrieved 8 May 2003 from www. global serve.net/~artnet/artnetarchives.htm.

Coad, Steve. 1994. "We Asked You: What Do You Think about a Sculpture to Victims of Violence Against Women?" *The London Free Press*, 28 November: B1.

Connerton, Paul. 1989. *How Societies Remember*. Cambridge, UK: Cambridge University Press.

Cooper, Melissa. 2000. "Plaque Unveiled in Memory of Helen Betty Osborne." *The Drum: Manitoba's Source for Aboriginal News*, 21 August. Retrieved 8 May 2003 from http://collection.nlc-bnc.ca.

Crouch, Simon. 1998. "Vince Garden Opens." *The London Free Press*, 3 June: A6.

Cultural Memory Group. 2005. "'In Memory of Theresa Vince': Research, Activism, and Feminist Memorializing." In Tracy Kulba, Mary Elizabeth Leighton, and Cheryl Suzack, eds., *Concrete Matters: Feminist Cultural Materialism*. Special Issue. *Topia: Canadian Journal of Cultural Studies* 13 (Spring): 121–134.

Curran, Peggy. 1999. "10 Years after the Massacre, a Memorial." *The Gazette* (Montreal), 4 December: A1, A8.

Dault, Gary Michael. 1998. "Towards a Public Narrative." *Canadian Architect* 43, no. 4 (April): 20–23.

"Dedication and Renewal." 1994. *McMaster Courier* 27 September: 3

De Vries, Maggie. 2003. *Missing Sarah: A Vancouver Woman Remembers Her Vanished Sister*. Toronto, ON: Penguin.

Dey, Phoebe. 1999. "Remembering December 6." *Folio*, 10 December. Retrieved 4 March 2001 from www.ualberta.ca/folio.

Doe, Jane. 2003. *The Story of Jane Doe: A Book about Rape*. Toronto, ON: Random House Canada.

Elizabeth Fry Society. 2003. "Human and Fiscal Costs of Prison." Fact Sheet. Retrieved 22 May 2003 from www.elizabethfry.ca/eweek03/factsht.htm.

Faulder, Liane. 1999. "Memories of Massacre Fade as New Memorial to be Erected." *The Edmonton Journal*, 23 October: B3.

Ferguson, Rosanna. 1998. "'Gathering Strength': Canada's Aboriginal Action Plan." January. Retrieved 15 May 2003 from www. abinfohwy.ca/Weetamah/news1.htm.

Feschuk, Scott. 1991. "Body identified as missing teen-ager." *Globe and Mail* , 19 August.

Fontaine, Phil. 1993. "We Are All Born Innocent." In Linda Jaine, ed., *Residential Schools: The Stolen Years*, 43–60. Saskatoon, SK: University Extension Press, University of Saskatchewan.

Foran, Charles. 1999. "1989 Revisited: Ten Years after Tiananmen Square and the Montreal Massacre." *Saturday Night* 114 (June): 74–79.

Ford, Catherine. 1994. "Quit Whining and Do Something to End Violence." *Calgary Herald*, 2 December: A5.

Fournier, Suzanne. 2002a. "Rites for Women." *The Province* (Vancouver), 12 April: A20.

———. 2002b. "Stars to Sing of Fury over Missing Women." *The Province* (Vancouver), 2 May: A4.

———. 2002c. "Families of Missing Women Divided over Tribute." *The Province* (Vancouver), 30 May: A6.

———. 2002d. "Women Lived in 'Desperate Circumstances.'" *The Province* (Vancouver), 3 October: A6.

Fournier, Suzanne, and Ernie Crey. 1998. *Stolen from Our Embrace: The Abduction of First Nations Children and the Restoration of Aboriginal Communities.* Vancouver, BC: Douglas and McIntyre.

Fulton, Keith Louise. 1999. "A Living Commitment: The December 6th Women's Grove Memorial." In Joan Turner and Carol Rose, eds., *Spider Women: A Tapestry of Creativity and Healing*, 318–322. Winnipeg, MB: J. Gordon Shillingford.

Garon, Barb. 2002. "No Peace: Monument to Slain Women Not Getting the Respect It Deserves." Interview with Laura Stradiotto. *The Sudbury Star* 14 July: A7.

Goddu, Jenn. 1996. "Violence Against Women Doubles in N.B." *Times & Transcript* (Moncton), 5 December:1.

———. 1998. "Emotions Rekindled at Massacre Remembrance." *Times & Transcript* (Moncton): 1.

Gordon, Deborah A. 1993. "Worlds of Consequences: Feminist Ethnography as Social Action." *Critique of Anthropology* 13, no. 4: 429–443.

Gottfried, Heidi, ed. 1996. *Feminism and Social Change: Bridging Theory and Practice.* Urbana, IL: University of Illinois Press.

Goulding, Warren. 2001. *Just Another Indian: A Serial Killer and Canada's Indifference.* Calgary, AB: Fifth House.

Grant, Agnes. 1996. *No End of Grief: Indian Residential Schools in Canada.* Winnipeg, MB: Pemmican Publications.

Greene, Trevor. 2001. *Bad Date: The Lost Girls of Vancouver's Low Track.* Toronto, ON: ECW Press.

Ha, Tu Thanh, and Ingrid Peritz. 1999. "Slaying of 14 Women Students Took Minutes, but Effects Lingered." *The Globe and Mail*, 4 December: A20.

Halbwachs, Maurice. 1992. *On Collective Memory.* Edited and translated by Lewis A. Coser. Chicago, IL: University of Chicago Press.

Hall, E. Foster, ed. 1998. *Heritage Remembered: The Story of Bear River.* Presented by the members of the Bear River New Horizons' Centre, under the editorship of E. Foster Hall. 2d ed. New Minas, NS: Kentville Publishing.

Hanes, Allison. 1997. "Remembering the Massacre." *The Gazette* (Montreal), 6 December: A4.

Harvey, David. 1995. "Militant Particuralism and Global Ambition: The Conceptual Politics of Space, Place, and Environment in the Work of Raymond Williams." *Social Text* 42 (Spring): 69–98.

Heakes, Greg. 1999. "Prayer Service Held for Missing Prostitutes." 13 May. Retrieved 6 November 1999 from APBNews.com.

"Helen Betty Osborne Memorial Foundation." 2002–2003. Retrieved 13 May 2003 from www.helenbettyosbornefdtn.ca.

Highway, Tomson. 1989. *Dry Lips Oughta Move to Kapuskasing*. Saskatoon, SK: Fifth House.

——. 1998. *The Kiss of the Fur Queen*. Toronto, ON: Doubleday Canada.

Hill, Valerie. 1993. "Park Honors Slain Woman." *Guelph Mercury*, 7 December: 1.

Hirsch, Marianne, and Valerie Smith. 2002. "Feminism and Cultural Memory: An Introduction." In Marianne Hirsch and Valerie Smith, eds., *Gender and Cultural Memory*. Special Issue. *Signs: Journal of Women in Culture and Society* 28: 1–19.

Honey, Kim. 1998. "Home Violence Called Epidemic." *The Globe and Mail* 3 July: S11.

Hooper, Roxanne. 2002. "Missing Women: Sister Leads Vigil, Hoping for Word." *Maple Ridge–Pitt Meadows News*, 29 June. Retrieved 29 June 2002 from www.missingpeople.net.

Huyssen, Andreas. 1993. "Monument and Memory in a Postmodern Age." *The Yale Journal of Criticism* 6: 249–261.

"Indian Residential Schools Resolution Canada." Retrieved 30 May 2003 from www.irsr-rqpi.gc.ca/english/index.html.

Irwin-Zarecka, Iwona. 1994. *Frames of Remembrance: The Dynamics of Collective Memory*. New Brunswick, NJ: Transaction Publishers.

Johnson, Donna F. 1998. "How One Canadian Community is Responding to the Murder of Women." Paper presented at the International Conference on Family Violence. Singapore, Malaysia, 10 September.

——. 1999. "The Women's Monument: In Memory of *Our* Fallen Comrades." In Joan Turner and Carol Rose, eds., *Spider Women: A Tapestry of Creativity and Healing*, 314–316. Winnipeg, MB: J. Gordon Shillingford.

——. 2000. "Sisters of Slaughter." *Ottawa Citizen*, 3 March: A17.

Johnston, David. 1999. "Solemn Day of Remembering." *The Gazette* (Montreal), 7 December: A5.

Kaplan, Temma. 2002. "Reversing the Shame and Gendering the Memory." In Marianne Hirsch and Valerie Smith, eds., *Gender and Cultural Memory*. Special Issue. *Signs: Journal of Women in Culture and Society* 28: 179–199.

Keewatin Community College Board of Governors. 2000. *Communiqué* 10, no. 1 (January/February).

Kelley, Caffyn. 1995. "Creating Memory, Contesting History." *Matriart* 5, no. 3: 6–11.

Kendall, Kathleen. 1993. "Creating Safe Places Reclaiming Sacred Spaces." *Double Time* (December): 8 – 9.

Kershaw, Anne, and Mary Lasovich. 1991. *Rock-A-Bye Baby: A Death Behind Bars.* Toronto, ON: McClelland and Stewart.

Kimmelman, Michael. 2002. "Out of Minimalism, Monuments to Memory." *New York Times*, 13 January: A1, A37.

King, Thomas, ed. 1990. *All My Relations: An Anthology of Contemporary Canadian Native Fiction.* Toronto, ON: McClelland and Stewart.

Knowles, Ric. 2003. "The Hearts of Its Women: Rape, Residential Schools, and Re-membering." In Sherrill Grace and Albert-Reiner Glaap, eds., *Performing National Identities: International Perspectives on Contemporary Canadian Theatre*, 245–264. Vancouver, BC: Talon Books.

Lachapelle, Judith. 1999. "Retenir son nom." *Le Devoir* (Montreal), 6 December: A1.

"La commémoration du 6 décembre 2001." Retrieved 25 September 2002 from www.fondationsixdecembre.com.

Lacy, Suzanne, ed. 1995. *Mapping the Terrain: New Genre Public Art.* Seattle, WA: Bay Press.

Le Moal, Dan. 2000. "Province Apologizes to Helen Betty Osborne Family." *The First Perspective: News of Indigenous Peoples of Canada*, 14 August. Retrieved 18 May 2003 from http://collection.nlc-bnc.ca.

Lebeuf, Sophie-Hélène. 1999. "J'ai compris que la vie n'était pas logique." *Le Devoir* (Montreal), 6 December: A4.

Lees, Nick. 1999. "A Sculpture for 14 Slain Women." *The Edmonton Journal*, 3 December: B4.

Le Sueur, Meridel. *The Girl.* [1936] 2000. Albuquerque, NM: West End Press, 2000.

Lowery, Bob. 1995. "Former Students Wrestle with Past." *Winnipeg Free Press*, 8 August: B2.

Lupu, Noam. 2003. "Memory Vanished, Absent, and Confined: The Countermemorial Project in1980s and 1990s Germany." *History & Memory* 15, no.2: 130–164.

Maguire, Patricia. 1987. *Doing Participatory Research: A Feminist Approach.* Amherst, MA: Center for International Education, School of Education, University of Massachusetts.

Malette, Louise, and Marie Chalouh, eds. 1991. *The Montreal Massacre.* Translated by Marlene Wildeman. Charlottetown, PEI: Gynergy Books.

Manitoba Government. 2000. News Release, 6 December. Retrieved 4 June 2003 from www.gov.mb.ca/chc/press.

"Manitoba Sorry." 2000. *Canadian Chronicle,* 15 July.

McCrindle, Kate. 2000. "Harassment May Be Health & Safety Issue." *The Chatham Daily News,* 3 June: 3.

——. 2001. "Theresa Vince Not Forgotten." *The Chatham Daily News,* 4 June: 1, 3.

McMaster, Geoff. "Montreal Massacre Remembered in Silence." 2004. *Express News* (University of Alberta), 6 December. Retrieved 28 February 2005 from www.uofaweb.ualberta.ca/expressnews.

"Memorial Rose Garden Being Established." 1992. *McMaster Courier,* 15 September: 3.

Mills, Josephine. 1998. "Beth Alber." *Parachute* 90 (April/May/June): 51–52.

"Missing Women Investigation Tops $10 Million." 2002. Canadian Press. Retrieved 6 August 2002 from www.missingpeople.net.

Mojica, Monique. 1991. *Princess Pocahontas and the Blue Spots: Two Plays.* Toronto, ON: Women's Press.

Money, Janet. 1995. "Monuments Stand as a Tribute to Women's Spirit." *Herizons* (Spring): 10–11.

Moore, Lynn. 1999. "A Place for Healing." *The Gazette* (Montreal), 29 October: A5.

Moynagh, Maureen. 2002. "'This History's Only Good for Anger': Gender and Cultural Memory in *Beatrice Chancy*." In Marianne Hirsch and Valerie Smith, eds., *Gender and Cultural Memory.* Special Issue. *Signs: Journal of Women in Culture and Society* 28: 97–124.

Naples, Nancy, ed. 1998. *Community Activism and Feminist Politics: Organizing Across Race, Class, and Gender.* New York: Routledge.

"New War Memorial to be Built in Toronto." 2003. *The Globe and Mail,* 3 June: A6.

Newton, Michael. 2002. "Robert Pickton: The Vancouver Missing Women." Retrieved 17 June 2002 from www.missingpeople.net.

Nora, Pierre, ed. 1996. *Realms of Memory: Rethinking the French Past.* Vol. 1, *Conflicts and Divisions.* Edited by Lawrence D. Kritzman. Translated by Arthur Goldhammer. New York: Columbia University Press.

"Notes for an Address by the Honourable Jane Stewart Minister of Indian Affairs and Northern Development on the Occasion of the Unveiling of Gathering Strength — Canada's Aboriginal Action Plan Ottawa, Ontario." 1998 (January 7). Retrieved 30 May 2003 from www.ainc-inac.gc.ca/nr/spch/1998/98j7_e.html.

Priest, Lisa. 1989. *Conspiracy of Silence.* Toronto, ON: McClelland and Stewart.

"Proceedings of the Legislative Assembly of Manitoba,1995 (December 6)." Retrieved 30 May 2003 from www.gov.mb.ca/leg-asmb/hansard/2nd-36th/vo12/ h002_ 1.html.

Pusiak, Rick. 2002. "City Approves Monument; Critics Unhappy about Location." *Northern Life* 12 July: 1, 5.

Ramsey, Kathy. 1999. "Mourning the Montreal Massacre a Decade Later." *The Manitoban* (University of Manitoba), 1 December. Retrieved 13 May 2003 from www.umanitoba.ca/toban/archives/dec/dec1/articles/news/massacre.html.

Razack, Sherene H. 2002. "Gendered Racial Violence and Spatialized Justice: The Murder of Pamela George." In Sherene H. Razack, ed., *Race, Space, and the Law: Unmapping a White Settler Society*, 121–156. Toronto, ON: Between the Lines.

Richer, Shawna. 1994. "Brescia College Monument 'Reflective.'" *The London Free Press*, 5 December: A3.

Ringma, Miranda. 2000. *Concrete Change, Constructed by Many*. Edmonton, AB: December 6th Planning Committee.

Rosenberg, Sharon Michelle. 1997 "Rupturing the 'Skin of Memory': Bearing Witness to the 1989 Massacre of Women in Montreal." PhD diss. Ontario Institute for Studies in Education of the University of Toronto.

———. 2000. "Standing in a Circle of Stone: Rupturing the Binds of Emblematic Memory." In Roger Simon, Sharon Rosenberg, and Claudia Eppert, eds., *Between Hope and Despair: Pedagogy and the Remembrance of Historical Trauma*, 75–89. New York: Rowan and Littlefield.

Schirmer, Jennifer. 1994. "The Claiming of Space and the Body Politic within National-Security States: The Plazo de Mayo Madres and the Greenham Common Women." In Johathan Boyarin, ed., *Remapping Memory: The Politics of TimeSpace*, 185–220. Minneapolis, MN: University of Minnesota Press.

Schmidt, Susannah. 1998. Interview with Tomson Highway, May. Retrieved 29 May 2003 from www.playwrightsworkshop.org/tomsonint2.html.

Scott, Susan. 1994. "Lest We Forget the Victims." *Calgary Herald*, 5 July: 5A.

Severson, Anne. 1994. "Sculpture in Law Will Recall Murdered Women." *The University of Calgary Gazette*, 13 June: 3.

Shuttleworth, Joanne. 2000. "A Slight Chill Teases Garden Opening." *Guelph Mercury*, 17 August: A5.

Sillars, Les. 1994. "Feminist's 'Grotesque Celebration': U of C Sculpture Implicates All Males in the Marc Lépine Massacre." *Alberta Report*, 19 December: 46.

Simard, Colleen. 2001. "Remembering Helen Betty Osborne." *The Drum: Manitoba's Source for Aboriginal News*, 16 July. Retrieved 8 May 2003 from http://collection. nlc-bnc.ca.

Simon, Roger I. 2005. *The Touch of the Past: Remembrance, Learning, and Ethics*. New York: Palgrave Macmillan.

Simpson, Moira, dir. 1998. *Marker of Change: The Story of the Women's Monument*. Vancouver, BC: Moving Images.

Smith, Peter. 2002. "Vanished: Somewhere Along the Highway of Tears Nicole Hoar Simply Disappeared." *The Calgary Sun*, 14 July: 28 – 29.

Sturken, Marita. 1999. "Narratives of Recovery: Repressed Memory as Cultural Memory." In Mieke Bal, Jonathan Crewe, and Leo Spitzer, eds., *Acts of Memory: Cultural Recall in the Present*, 231–248. Hanover, NH: University Press of New England.

Taillon, Joan. "Manitoba Government Apologizes to Osbornes." 2000. *Windspeaker News*. Retrieved 8 May 2003 from www.ammsa.com/windspeaker/ WINDNEWSSEPT2000.html.

Thurston, Arthur. 1987. *Poor Annie Kempton ... She's in Heaven Above*. Yarmouth, NS: Arthur Thurston Publications.

Todd, Douglas. 1998. "Parks Rule Out Controversial Monuments: Vancouver Decision: Women's, AIDS Memorials Opposed." *National Post*, 11 December: A11.

Tracey, Scott. 2002. "City Woman Seeks Answers, Not Memorial." *Guelph Mercury*, 25 April: A1–A2.

"Tradition Influences Aboriginal Woman's Learning." 2002. *About Women* (Manitoba Women's Directorate) (Fall): 6.

Turtle Gals Performance Ensemble. 2002. *The Scrubbing Project*. Unpublished manuscript.

"Two Suits Filed in Missing Women Case." 2002. Canadian Press. Retrieved 23 April 2002 from www. missingpeople.net.

Whyte, William Foote, ed. 1991. *Participatory Action Research*. Newberry Park, CA: Sage.

Wirasinghe, Dean S.C. 1999. "Remarks." 11 December. Retrieved 1 May 2003 from www.eng. ucalgary.ca/CEMF.

Yeo, Marian. 1991. "Murdered by Misogyny: Lin Gibson's Response to the Montreal Massacre." *Canadian Woman Studies/les Cahiers de la Femme* 12, no. 1 (Fall): 8–11.

Young, James E. 1992. "The Counter-Monument: Memory against Itself in Germany Today." *Critical Inquiry* 18: 267–296.

——. 1993. *The Texture of Memory: Holocaust Memorials and Meaning*. New Haven, CT: Yale University Press.

——. 1997. "Germany's Memorial Question: Memory, Counter-Memory, and the End of the Monument." *South Atlantic Quarterly* 96, no. 4: 853–880.

———. 2000. *At Memory's Edge: After-Images of the Holocaust in Contemporary Art and Architecture*. New Haven, CT: Yale University Press.